In pursuit of politics

Manchester University Press

Studies in
Modern French History

Edited by
David Hopkin and Máire Cross

This series is published in collaboration with the UK Society for the Study of French History. It aims to showcase innovative short monographs relating to the history of the French, in France and in the world since c.1750. Each volume speaks to a theme in the history of France with broader resonances to other discourses about the past. Authors demonstrate how the sources and interpretations of modern French history are being opened to historical investigation in new and interesting ways, and how unfamiliar subjects have the capacity to tell us more about the role of France within the European continent. The series is particularly open to interdisciplinary studies that break down the traditional boundaries and conventional disciplinary divisions.

Titles already published in this series

Emile and Isaac Pereire: Bankers, Socialists and Sephardic Jews in nineteenth-century France   Helen Davies

From empire to exile: History and memory within the pied-noir and harki communities, 1962–2012   Claire Eldridge

Catholicism and children's literature in France: The comtesse de Ségur (1799–1874)   Sophie Heywood

Aristocratic families in republican France, 1870–1940   Elizabeth C. Macknight

The republican line: Caricature and French republican identity, 1830–52   Laura O'Brien

Robespierre and the Festival of the Supreme Being: The search for a republican morality   Jonathan Smyth

The routes to exile: France and the Spanish Civil War refugees, 1939–2009   Scott Soo

The Society for the
Study of French History

In pursuit of politics

Education and revolution in eighteenth-century France

ADRIAN O'CONNOR

Manchester University Press

Copyright © Adrian O'Connor 2017

The right of Adrian O'Connor to be identified as the author of this work has been asserted
by him in accordance with the Copyright, Designs and Patents Act 1988.

Published by Manchester University Press
Altrincham Street, Manchester M1 7JA, UK
www.manchesteruniversitypress.co.uk

British Library Cataloguing-in-Publication Data is available

ISBN 978 1 5261 2056 4 *hardback*
ISBN 978 1 5261 4303 7 *paperback*

First published by Manchester University Press in hardback 2017

This edition published 2019

The publisher has no responsibility for the persistence or accuracy of URLs for any external or third-party internet websites referred to in this book, and does not guarantee that any content on such websites is, or will remain, accurate or appropriate.

Typeset by Servis Filmsetting Ltd, Stockport, Cheshire

Contents

Acknowledgments — page vi

Introduction: Politics: a revolutionary idea and a practical problem — 1

Prologue: the educational "system" of eighteenth-century France — 18

1. Education and an ambivalent Enlightenment — 26
2. National education: promise and paralysis — 48
3. Public instruction: a new pedagogy for a new politics — 70
4. Constitutional principles and concrete proposals: reconsidering Talleyrand and Condorcet on public instruction — 97
5. Revolutionary politics *à la plume*: the public on education and politics — 126
6. New wine in old bottles? Ancien Régime schools imagine the future — 160
7. Republican instruction: an elusive ideal — 199

Conclusion: Politics: real, pursued, and promised — 231

Bibliography — 240

Index — 257

Acknowledgments

In the research and writing of this book, I have been aided, inspired, and supported by many individuals and institutions. It is a great pleasure to thank them here.

From genesis to publication, this project has benefited from the support of Warren Breckman, who was and remains an excellent advisor and mentor. I am similarly indebted to Lynn Hollen Lees and Roger Chartier, whose advice and counsel helped this work to take shape and to develop across many years and iterations, and to David Bell, whose suggestions and support have been invaluable. I have also benefited from the assistance and example of Rita Copeland, Ronald Granieri, Alan Charles Kors, Edward Peters, Thomas Safley, and Jonathan Steinberg, and from the friends, classmates, and colleagues who offered me their encouragement and attention as this work progressed.

This manuscript has been immeasurably improved by the insightful questions, criticisms, and commentary of participants at a host of scholarly conferences and symposia, including meetings of the Society for French Historical Studies, the Society for the Study of French History, and the American Historical Association. I am especially grateful for the astute commentary, generous feedback, and helpful suggestions I have received from Micah Alpaugh, Keith Michael Baker, Robert Blackman, Claire Cage, Jeremy Caradonna, Stephen Clay, Jennifer Heuer, Hugh LaFollette, Brian Newsome, Pernille Røge, Sophia Rosenfeld, Jennifer Sessions, Rebecca Spang, David Troyansky, Kent Wright, and many others to whom I must now owe apologies as well as acknowledgment.

ACKNOWLEDGMENTS

Research for this project was supported and made possible by a number of institutions. I would like to thank the University of Pennsylvania for the generous support it offered me while I was there, first as an undergraduate and then as a doctoral student. Also the Institut Français de Washington, the University of South Florida system, and the University of South Florida St Petersburg. The research for this project would have been impossible without the assistance of archivists and staff at the Archives nationales (especially Pascal Riviale, Jean-Marc Roger, and Michel Thibault), the Bibliothèque nationale, and the Bibliothèque de la Sorbonne, as well as the Centre de Recherche et de Ressources of the Institut national de recherché pédagogique in Mont Saint-Aignan (especially Emilie Terrieux), the Bibliothèque de l'Arsenal at l'Université Toulouse 1 Sciences Sociales, the Archives Municipales de Toulouse, and the Archives départementales de la Haute-Garonne. In the United States, the assistance of research librarians and staff at the University of Pennsylvania's Van Pelt Library, at New York University's Elmer Holmes Bobst Library, at the New York Public Library, and at the University of South Florida St Petersburg's Nelson Poynter Memorial Library has been invaluable.

Earlier versions of some parts of this book were published as articles. Part of Chapter 1 appeared as "Nature, nurture, and the social order: imagining lessons and lives for women in Ancien Régime France" in *French Politics, Culture & Society*, 30:1 (2012); part of Chapter 2 was published as "From the classroom out: educational reform and the state in France, 1762–1771" in *French Historical Studies*, 39:3 (2016); and an earlier version of arguments presented in Chapter 3 appeared as "'Source de lumières & de vertus': rethinking education, instruction, and the political pedagogy of the French Revolution" in *Historical Reflections/Réflexions Historiques*, 40:3 (2014). Those materials are reproduced here with the publishers' permission.

I would like also to thank the editors of the Studies in Modern French History series, Máire Cross and David Hopkin, the editors and staff at Manchester University Press, and the anonymous readers who offered such helpful and constructive feedback on the manuscript. Working with Manchester University Press has been a tremendous pleasure.

More personally, I would like to thank my father, David O'Connor, and my mother, Carolyn O'Connor, as well as my brother, Jeremy, and my sister, Sarah. I have relied upon their love, interest, and patience more than I can express. Veronika Sikorski and Drew Youngren have sustained me and my family with generosity, interest, antics, and affection for which I am constantly grateful.

To Larissa Kopytoff I am grateful for everything, day in, day out, and always.

My son, Felix, makes everything more interesting, more exciting, and more important. I dedicate this book to him.

Introduction
Politics: a revolutionary idea and a practical problem

Quel serait le meilleur plan d'éducation pour le peuple?
Académie des Sciences, Arts et Belles-
Lettres de Châlons-sur-Marne, 1777[1]

When the Académie des Sciences, Arts et Belles-Lettres in Châlons-sur-Marne announced the topic for its 1779 essay contest – the seemingly straightforward "What is the best plan of education for the people?" – it raised issues that extended well beyond matters of curriculum, institutional organization, and pedagogy. After all, which people? And by whom should they be educated? What sorts of knowledge and skills was it important – or desirable – for these people to have? For what purpose were they to be educated, and for what sort of future were they being prepared by this education? To invite plans for the education of the people was to raise all of these questions and more and, in so doing, to invite debate and dispute over the nature and foundations of French society, culture, and politics.

Writing fourteen years after the contest in Châlons-sur-Marne was announced, the author of a 1791 pamphlet entitled *Appel à l'opinion publique sur l'éducation nationale* offers us insight into what had become of such questions in the French Revolution, declaring that "for every individual living under a representative government ... the art [of reading and writing] should be considered the fundamental source of his moral existence, and so truly indispensable."[2] Enshrined in the constitution of 1791 as a right of the citizen and an obligation of the state, education had been recognized as indispensable to the legitimacy and sustainability of representative government. But it remained the subject of intense debate and disagreement. If anything, the debates had become more contentious as the limits and strains of participatory politics were revealed and as the pursuit of pedagogical and political futures complicated one another. Attempts to redesign the institutions of political administration, to imagine new forms of civic life, and to "regenerate" French society had practically forced the academicians' inquiry onto the revolutionaries' agenda.

The early years of the Revolution witnessed a series of amazingly ambitious efforts to reform and reinvent the nation's political institutions, cultural politics, and social order. These efforts took shape in summer 1789 as the Estates-General gave way to the National Assembly and as the deputies clarified the project before them: to draft and ratify a constitution for France, one that would establish a system of representative government legitimized by the consent and participation of the nation. This was as much a social and cultural undertaking as it was an exercise in constitutional or institutional design, and so the deputies found themselves trying to simultaneously establish a new political order, invent a new model of national citizenship, and engender new modes of political association.[3] For their efforts to succeed, it seemed that French citizens had to possess particular skills and habits, embrace new forms of civic sociability, and develop new ways of thinking about themselves and their place in the national community. The revolutionary project relied, at least in part, on a system of "public instruction."

Deputies, political commentators, and private citizens alike recognized that reinventing French politics and transforming French society would require rethinking the principles and practices of education. The Assembly embraced this idea in July 1789, when its constitutional committee listed the organization of "national and public instruction" among its priorities, and again when it included the promise of "public instruction" in the constitution of 1791. This promise reflected what had become a near-consensus view: that education represented a uniquely powerful instrument of social and political change and that meaningful social and political changes were unlikely to take root if they were not accompanied by changes in how people were educated. But recognizing the need for educational reform was a far cry from knowing how to reform education, and the emergence of revolutionary politics reignited a decades-old debate over the role of schools in shaping French society and France's future.

The revolutionary debates over education were remarkable, as deputies and citizens across France came to see the schools as microcosms of the new social and political regime. Schools became a canvas onto which people could project hopes for, and anxieties about, the Revolution, and the reform of education served as a conceptual bridge across the now-and-then of revolution, an institutional representation of how the tumultuous revolutionary present might give way to a stable post-revolutionary future. Because of this, the debates over education attracted participants from a wide range of political, social, and ideological camps, including future regicides and radicals, royalists and émigrés, the devout and the anti-clerical, the young and the old, the learned and the almost illiterate. To each of these groups, the schools – existing or anticipated – offered an opportunity to indict or defend the Ancien Régime, to express views of the Revolution unfolding around them, and to imagine futures that resembled neither past nor present. This can make the revolutionary debates over education seem like exercises in political fantasy rather than attempts to solve institutional and social problems, and in some cases this is probably right. It has also allowed historians to find the "origins" of a great many political and pedagogical traditions in the Revolution, to see 1789 (or 1792) as a launching pad for the competing ambitions associated with political "modernity." Most plausibly, the debates of these years have been described as having established an initially unfulfilled promise of "modern" education as national, secular, democratic, and (at least in principle) universal.[4]

To those who participated in the pre-revolutionary and revolutionary debates, however, each of these apparently paradigmatic attributes was a source of uncertainty – and often ambivalence – and it was not at all clear that any of them represented a plausible or desirable future for French education or French society. As Vincenzo Ferrone reminds us, this period – what he calls the "late Enlightenment" – did not share in the "historical construct we now identify as *modernity*, using the term to confer a sense of something completed and definitive. It was, rather, the *laboratory of modernity*."[5] Those working in the part of that laboratory devoted to education agreed that certain problems should be priorities, and there were particular points on which they thought concrete progress might be made, but these did not necessarily cohere, nor did they point towards a general program or suggest a particular educational model. This was true across the range of issues that had been central to the "education question" since the 1760s: how to best recruit, train, and certify instructors, how to balance, prioritize, or reconcile the interests of the Church and the State, how to fund and oversee new institutions, whether and how to increase popular access to education, and how to anticipate the consequences that changes in education might have for society at large. None of these questions had clear answers when the deputies convened in Versailles, and if these appear to be the origins of modern approaches to education, this tells us as much about Third Republic historiography and more recent attempts to historicize political and pedagogical liberalism as it does about the Enlightenment or revolutionary debates over education.[6]

That the outcome of these debates was uncertain does not diminish their centrality to the intellectual and cultural politics of eighteenth-century France or dilute their role in shaping the nature and ambitions of the Enlightenment; if anything, this uncertainty highlights how much they mattered and why. Inspired by the works of François Fénelon and John Locke, the writers, thinkers, and political authorities of the eighteenth century emphasized education's role in shaping the lives and character of individuals, societies, and states. The "education question," as it has come to be known, both contributed to and reflected concerns over nationalism and the nation, the sources of political legitimacy and role of the public in political affairs, the stability or fluidity of the social order, the relationship between the sexes and the gendered assignment of roles in public, private, and political arenas, and the power of human agents to collectively influence human affairs. Education emerged in the eighteenth century as perhaps the single greatest instrument with which one might seek to "plan the social future."[7]

The debates over education were thus central both to the Enlightenment and to the idea that new ways of thinking might be translated into new ways of living. To be something more than a new Scholasticism or an addendum to the Republic of Letters, Enlightenment thinkers had to reckon with their place in the early modern world and imagine what their ideas might mean beyond the walls of academies and salons.[8] Debates over education offered them a chance to imagine the transmission and translation of proposals into practice, providing the *philosophes* and their interlocutors with a set of institutional and social parameters within which to conceptualize the spread and influence of ideas, a body of inherited practices and expectations against which to compare innovations, a purposeful language with which to promote, attack, or defend proposed reforms, and a promise that the Enlightenment might represent a turning point in human history.[9]

As a result, the debates over education were shaped not only by disputes about what sort of education was best, but also for whom such an education was appropriate and what it ought to offer them. Many members of even "enlightened" circles worried that expanding access to education was likely to have "pernicious" effects; as Harvey Chisick noted, "the *philosophes* and other educated men of the time were aware of the social utility of ignorance and illusion, and they were less concerned with enlightening the lower classes than with occupational training, economic utility and social control."[10] Some – like Voltaire – argued against offering education to "the people," while others proposed expanding access to the schools only insofar as doing so might benefit the economy or help to maintain social and political order; but there were others still who came to see popular education as a means by which to transform those orders and to reimagine France and its future. Similar tensions shaped debates regarding female education, where claims about the "natural" attributes and necessary responsibilities of each sex were increasingly challenged by arguments about the powers of "nurture" to shape each person's character and capacities and, with that, the possibility that new approaches to education might transform the social, sexual, and familial hierarchies of French life. In cases such as these, to disagree about education was to disagree about much more besides, and the Enlightenment debates over education emerged as a sort of ante-politics, a political debate about the prospect and purpose of politics.

The intensity of these debates stemmed in large part from the influence attributed to education in sensationist philosophy – a theory of mind, knowledge, and psychology most often associated with Locke, disseminated in France during the first third of the eighteenth century, and celebrated in Voltaire's *Lettres philosophiques*. Rejecting original sin, the existence of innate ideas and, in some of its more radical iterations (like those of Condillac and Helvétius), innate characteristics and capacities as well, sensationism imagined the infant child as a tabula rasa to be marked by experience. This seemed to obliterate the necessity or immutability of a person's character and to entail the possibility that people and, with them, societies could be purposefully reimagined and redesigned.[11] The consequences for how people thought about education were tremendous.

Sensationist philosophies of mind and of the self quickly became intertwined with debates about the character and composition of the French nation and about the foundation and legitimacy of the social order. Jan Goldstein notes that sensationist views of imagination "had a … pronounced tendency to become involved in social, political, and economic discourse."[12] This tendency was all the more pronounced, and the resulting discourse all the more important, because ideas about society and the nation were themselves undergoing significant changes in the eighteenth century. Unmoored from notions of divine will or providence, the social order and the social good emerged as barometers by which to judge the suitability of institutions and behaviors and, at the same time, as the result of human choices and actions.[13] Society and the nation came to be seen as "products of human will," as entities that were "actively constructed through political action."[14] Schools promised to be at the center of any such action, and they were increasingly imagined as capable of "shap[ing] the character, tastes, and mores of a people."[15] Perhaps unsurprisingly, then, writers from the mid-eighteenth century on stressed the need for political and pedagogical regimes to complement one another.

The entanglement of political, social, material, and institutional concerns that characterized the debates over education forced ideas about the French nation, the French state, and French society into dialogue with one another. Designing a system of national instruction (or resisting such a design) entailed not only discussion of what attributes or knowledge the French people needed, but also thinking about the French state, its finances, its agents, its administrative powers, its relationship to civil society, and its power to compel (parents, children or students, instructors, and institutions alike). Ideas about education and its possible reform relied, explicitly or otherwise, on ideas about what the state was, what it could or should do, through whom it should act, and to what end it should do so.

In addition to this explicit politicization of education, these debates were also an example and an examination of the eighteenth-century "public sphere" that has attracted so much attention from historians.[16] They brought a range of political, cultural, and intellectual authorities and institutions into dialogue with one another, as government administrators raised and sought to answer questions being addressed in philosophical works banned by government censors, as academies prompted discussions to which individuals without official or academic credentials could contribute, and as the worlds of official and clandestine publishing interacted with a culture of correspondence that blurred the division between personal reflection and public participation in political affairs. The "public" was also the indirect subject of many of these debates, as the reform of educational institutions and practices promised to have consequences for who could engage in public debates and on what terms they could do so. To ask who ought to be educated and what sort of education they ought to receive was to ask also what that education ought to prepare or permit them to do, both professionally and as members of the political community. That is, it was to make the public sphere and the requirements for membership in the "public" points of debate and, potentially, dispute.

Despite all of the attention from Enlightenment thinkers, it was not until the last third of the century that the schools became a pressing and practical problem. The almost simultaneous appearance of Rousseau's *Émile* and expulsion of the Jesuits from Paris in 1762 led political administrators and public commentators to consider how new ways of thinking about education might translate into institutional and social reforms. Whether or not they had embraced the prospect of reforming education to promote social, political, or economic change, it seemed suddenly that changes were coming to the schools and, by extension, to French society. This was, as Marguerite Figeac-Monthus put it, an "effervescent moment" in French thought about education, and the expulsion transformed a debate that had been taking place "on the level of theoretical speculation" into one demanding concrete proposals for the solution of practical problems.[17]

This transformation revealed important fissures in the Enlightenment debate over education. These, in turn, reveal a crisis in Ancien Régime politics, a paralysis in the political imagination of those who considered reforming the formerly Jesuit institutions as the first step towards a new and national system of education. When eighteenth-century thinkers turned to the practical work of reforming the schools and reimagining French education – when they sought to bring the Enlightenment to bear on the society in which they worked and lived – they found that while a century of thought had identified several issues as clearly important to the work of reform, there was no clear path forward. They were left with dilemmas but not direction.

A similar dynamic emerged with the absolute monarchy's collapse and the coming of the French Revolution. Again, it was widely believed that the transformation of the schools and of the social order went hand in hand, though this time the order was reversed. After 1789, it was the reinvention of French politics and society that seemed to require changes in the schools, and the reform of education came to be seen as both an instrument and a necessary consequence of the changes sweeping France. As the Revolution gave rise to what Robert Darnton called a sense of "possibilism against the givenness of things," schools seemed like a necessary and natural bridge from the possible to the real.[18]

Confident that educational and political regimes needed to complement one another, aware of education's role in helping to establish and preserve any new social and political order that might come into being, but unable to foretell what that new order would be, participants in the revolutionary debates over education sought to navigate the path from an unstable present to an uncertain future. Their desire to establish a uniform system of education competed with the need to find short-term solutions to pressing and critical problems, to provide for students already in school, and to secure increasingly scarce resources (financial, material, and human alike). The result was a series of trial-and-error attempts to balance revolutionary ambition with practical necessity, to chart a course forward despite deep uncertainty and persistent instability. This was true, albeit in very different ways, for *philosophes*-statesmen like Charles-Maurice de Talleyrand-Périgord and Marie-Jean-Antoine-Nicholas de Caritat, marquis de Condorcet, and for provincial schoolmasters and local political administrators. The latter wrote missives to Paris requesting guidance, resources, or support, the former presented plans to fellow deputies distracted by constitutional concerns and the coming of war; in each case a revolution infatuated with the future found itself distracted and disoriented by a tumultuous present.

The French Revolution's most significant innovation regarding education was the idea of "public instruction," an ambition that transcended the pre-revolutionary distinction between moral education and technical instruction. "Public instruction" sought to situate the development of technical skills (such as reading, writing, and basic computation) within the cultural context of civic sociability and to establish a model of political engagement that relied upon the politically virtuous application of those skills. The citizens upon whom so many revolutionary ambitions depended would need to possess not only the requisite skills for participation in the public sphere and in political society, but also the sort of political sensibility and civic disposition that would make their participation conducive to the well-being of the society and of the body politic.[19] This is what Honoré de Mirabeau had in mind when he called for a system of national education that would "found the people's well-being on their virtues, and their virtues on their enlightenment."[20]

But public instruction was a pedagogical ambition, not a program, and its ideological contours were never entirely clear. This allowed the phrase to survive the ruptures and factionalization of revolutionary politics, and it has led historians to look past the concept's novelty, moving too quickly to the political or ideological conflicts by which it was apparently consumed. But the radical ambition of public instruction stemmed precisely from its pedagogical priorities (rather than ideological imperatives) and from its underlying (rather than overbearing) principles. Its importance relied upon expectations regarding how the new politics would work; how citizens would engage with one another, with the institutions of political discussion, and with the new political administration: politics would be contestatory, public, and responsive to the views and interests of the populace; political debate would take place across myriad venues and through a range of media, allowing a literate public to remain informed about and engaged in the process of collective self-governance; the legitimacy and sustainability of the new political institutions would depend in large part on the existence and engagement of an educated citizenry whose members were bound to one another by civic sentiments and public virtues. The oft-repeated claim that the legitimacy and success of the new political order would depend on education – on the cultivation and dissemination of particular skills, habits, and virtues among the citizenry – represented a revolutionary and radical proposition in 1789; it remains one still.

Establishing a system of public instruction in revolutionary France would prove a Sisyphean task, each bit of progress unsettled or overturned by social strife, economic instability, or political conflict. Nonetheless, it was a task to which deputies repeatedly turned and to which citizens across France sought to contribute. To understand how and why they did so, this book examines the first years of the Revolution, the period during which public instruction was first articulated and embraced. It focuses primarily on the years of the constitutional monarchy (1789–92), tracing and retracing the debates over education across a number of concerns and from a range of perspectives. Concentrating on such a brief period has its pitfalls, but it also allows us to recognize the contingencies that shaped revolutionary politics and the sometimes lurching path by which those politics proceeded. It offers us an opportunity to put the discursive and ideological currents of the Enlightenment and the Revolution in dialogue with the situational logic and circumstantial developments that shaped how individuals, groups, and institutions responded to political and social upheaval. It pushes revolutionary proposals and plans back into the material and political circumstances of their creation. And it prompts us to recognize citizens' efforts to understand and contribute to the pursuit of participatory, representative, and revolutionary politics, in situ and without a script.

The range of sources upon which this study draws – including philosophical treatises, legislative debates, and formal proposals for reform; government reports and administrative surveys; institutional records; political pamphlets; and hundreds of pieces of correspondence from institutions, political clubs, and individual citizens – reflects the vitality and the breadth of eighteenth-century debates over education. The "education question" preoccupied the most celebrated *philosophes* and the most obscure schoolmasters (though not necessarily in the same manner), the prospect that schools might contribute to social or political transformation enticed (or frightened) cultural critics and political authorities, and the challenge of reconciling new philosophical or political imperatives with material realities frustrated political and pedagogical authorities at the national, regional, local, and institutional levels. Likewise, navigating the shifting currents of revolutionary politics was a problem not just for legislators in the National Assembly (and then National Convention), but also for instructors, professors, students, parents, and citizens across France. The work of reimagining education so that it might promote and preserve a system of representative and participatory politics was undertaken at once in the academies, *collèges*, and universities, in the halls of the Assembly and the pages of the periodical and pamphlet press, in local reforms and regulations, and in the epistolary contributions of engaged citizens.

This book aims to recapture the dynamism of this polyvalent debate and to flesh out the ambitions and dilemmas that gave it meaning during this most turbulent of historical moments. After a brief prologue surveying the institutional landscape of education in mid-eighteenth century France, Chapter 1 traces an ambivalent strain in Enlightenment thought on education, a deep tension at the point of contact between seemingly limitless philosophical possibilities and the apparent limitations imposed by political and social realities. This tension is highlighted in the works of Rousseau and Helvétius, and in debates over female education and the gendered order of eighteenth-century life. In each case, writers struggled to make sense of divergent imperatives associated with nature and society, with "nature" serving – as it so often did in Enlightenment debates – as a critical mirror to society's shortcomings. More remarkable than this rhetorical juxtaposition and well-established trope, however, is the explicit function of the "social" and the "political" as a practical and persistent check on the possibilities apparently suggested by "nature." The result was an Enlightenment debate over education wherein a deep chasm separated the disappointing present from a nobler future, and the prospect of improvement was increasingly viewed in terms of crisis, cataclysm, and revolution, or with a sense of frustrated resignation.

A similar dynamic plays out in the more explicitly political and administrative sources reviewed in Chapter 2. After the expulsion of the Jesuits in 1762, *parlementaires*, members of the royal administration, administrators at the *collèges*, and commentators across France participated in a wide-ranging debate about the existing institutions and curricula, the prospects and ambitions that might drive educational reform, the desirability and practicality of a national system of education, and the relationship between the pedagogical and political orders. It was during these years that the desire for a system of "national education" was first articulated, the *agrégation* was established to prepare and certify instructors for the nation's schools, and the prospect of overhauling French education to reform or rejuvenate the French polity was seriously considered. And yet, for all that the 1760s and 1770s transformed the French debate over education, both by making it national and by wedding it to the practical concerns of specific institutions, the steps actually proposed and pursued indicate a relative paralysis in Ancien Régime politics, one that echoes the resignation noted in the Enlightenment texts from Chapter 1. Bringing together royal edicts and decrees, reports from parlementary commissions, and proposals from prominent political and pedagogical commentators, Chapter 2 finds that what historians have generally described as a programmatic consensus for reform that was then undermined by later political crises was, in fact, a deeply divided discursive and political field, one in which no path to national reform seemed plausible. This sense of crisis is reinforced in the text and fate of this period's most ambitious proposal to overhaul the educational and political infrastructure of France, the stillborn *Mémoire sur les municipalités* presented to Louis XVI by Pierre-Samuel Dupont de Nemours and Anne-Robert Jacques Turgot in 1775 (also discussed in Chapter 2).

Chapters 3 and 4 move us into the Revolution, situating the debate over education amid broader concerns about the nature and efficacy of representative government and analyzing the nascent idea of "public instruction" from its emergence as a revolutionary ambition through efforts to fulfill the constitutional promise of national education. They draw upon debates in the National Assembly and records from the myriad legislative committees involved in planning a national system of education (both before and after the centralization of these efforts with the creation of the Committee of Public Instruction in October 1791), and they present a reinterpretation of the proposals for reform presented by Talleyrand and Condorcet. These chapters argue for a new understanding of "public instruction" as a pedagogical and political ideal and, with that, a revised sense of education's role in regenerating France and in working towards a representative and participatory system of government.

Chapters 5 and 6 follow the debates over education beyond the halls of the Assembly, analyzing the proposals, exhortations, suggestions, and critiques submitted to the deputies by correspondents across France, as well as more local efforts to fulfill the promise of public instruction. Chapter 5 discusses the imagined role of letter-writing in representative government and analyzes the correspondence related to public instruction as both an example of and a reflection upon participatory politics. Chapter 6 focuses more specifically on letters and proposals submitted by people affiliated or associated with the schools and related institutions (representatives of the universities or *collèges*, individual instructors, professors, academicians, administrators, and students). Together, these chapters highlight how local populations contributed to the debates over education, experimented with possible solutions to political and practical problems, and worked towards a system of public instruction that they saw as central to the revolutionary project (even as that project changed over time).

Finally, Chapter 7 surveys what changed – and what did not – as the "education question" took on an explicitly republican form after September 1792. It draws again on the debates, reports, and decrees of national political authorities (this time the National Convention), as well as popular correspondence, institutional surveys, proposals from political clubs, reports of local experiments, and updates from local political administrators. While the festivals, dramatic productions, and public spectacles of these years are more familiar to historians, attempts to preserve, reform, or reinvent the schools continued to motivate legislators and citizens across France. These sources reveal a sustained and consistent attempt to establish a system of public instruction, one that people hoped would prepare the French for active and contributory citizenship, and they make clear that local attempts to reform education and establish a new political pedagogy persisted alongside the political centralization associated with the early Republic.

This book traces the debates over education from *philosophes* to deputies, and from deputies to citizens, teachers, administrators, and students across France, but it is not simply a history of diffusion. The problem of public instruction in the French Revolution was at once philosophical, political, and practical, and each of these elements facilitated and legitimized its own forms of discursive authority. Correspondents who wrote to the Assembly did so as full, if not equal, participants in the process of discussing, debating, and pursuing a new form of politics and a new sort of polity. They challenged the philosophical or political premises of revolutionary proposals, proposed measures to expedite or improve the deputies' work, lay claim to an authority grounded in practical experience (even as the political implications of that experience became problematic), and experimented with ways to reconcile legislative and material imperatives. Embracing their role in the reform of education, these correspondents embraced also the practical corollary to the sense of "possibilism" highlighted by Darnton: a "conviction ... that ordinary people can make history instead of suffering it."[21] A system of public instruction promised to clarify the principles and practices of revolutionary citizenship, a prospect that mobilized deputies, local officials, professors, instructors, students, and citizens, and in so doing offered each an opportunity to contribute self-consciously to the work of collective self-governance and the refashioning of French politics.

In the pages that follow, I aim to establish three points. First, that the debates following the expulsion of the Jesuits revealed a crisis in the political imagination of Ancien Régime France and, at the same time, established a set of practical concerns as central to the problem of educational reform. Second, that how revolutionaries thought about education was crucially important to how and why they thought representative government might work, and the resulting ambition – what they called "public instruction" – was a political pedagogy that transcended Ancien Régime categories and reflected a new way of thinking about political society and contributory citizenship. Finally, that the pursuit of "public instruction" was driven not only by ideological or political imperatives but also by trial-and-error attempts to solve practical problems, that it was molded by local efforts and experiments as well as national political currents and Parisian authorities. Recognizing this allows us to move beyond misleadingly linear narratives of political or institutional succession and to appreciate sustained efforts to design a system of public instruction even when deputies were distracted and the national governments' attempts were consumed by war and the Terror.

Taken together, these points suggest broader themes in the history of the Enlightenment, the Revolution, and the relationship between the two. Debates over education marked a clear point of contact between Enlightenment philosophy and eighteenth-century life, between the ideas and institutions that would shape French society and the French nation. Recognizing the ambivalence and uncertainty that underlay these debates reminds us that the Enlightenment's radicalism stemmed not (only) from the brilliance or clarity of *philosophes*' answers to abstract questions, but from the spectacular range of questions brought to bear on the social, political, cultural, intellectual, and institutional foundations of modern life, from the supposition that how such questions were answered would shape human society and the social future.

Engaging the Enlightenment as a fertile source of questions and collective concerns gives us a clearer sense of what was at stake in the "stormy" debates of the eighteenth century and why these debates mattered beyond the salon walls. It helps us to appreciate the dynamic processes by which Enlightenment debates arose and from which protagonists' arguments and positions emerged, and to note that these processes were shaped by practical, material, institutional, and circumstantial factors as well as political, philosophical, or ideological commitments.[22] Such an approach also allows us to better understand the relationship between Enlightenment debates and the ambitions, uncertainties, and conflicts of revolutionary politics. The revolutionaries inherited from the Enlightenment a sense that it might be possible to reform or even transform society, to regenerate it through concerted political action.[23] But the *philosophes* had not established a blueprint for such action or a prefigured set of ideological and political imperatives. Their legacy was, instead, a range of competing ideas about how society works, suggestions about how it might be refashioned, and arguments about where one might invest energy and attention in remedying the shortcomings of the present.[24] The revolutionaries would have to make what they could of this legacy, and they would have to do so amid the economic, political, and social upheaval that brought the Revolution into being; in this respect, the history of "public instruction" illustrates well the complex intersection of Enlightenment and Revolution.

The revolutionaries did not solve the problems left to them by their Enlightenment and Ancien Régime predecessors. In this sense, what follows is the history of a failure. More than thirty years of debate did not result in a model of public instruction that could promote and preserve a system of representative and participatory politics. By the end of the period discussed, most of the schools were in disarray, without funds and, in many cases, lacking teachers or students or both. While the Directory would reanimate many of the institutional ambitions of the late Ancien Régime and the early years of the Revolution, it did so without the earlier efforts' confidence that new schools would usher in a period of democratic sociability and political civility.

But this is also a history of how people in eighteenth-century France thought about, engaged with, and attempted to act upon the society in which they lived. Attention to their efforts helps us to think about what revolutionary legislators aimed to accomplish, what a broader populace hoped or expected the Revolution might achieve, and how they thought such changes might come about. It is a history of how new ways of thinking about education underwrote one of humanity's most ambitious attempts to reimagine political society and to reinvent political citizenship. It is a history of how modern politics was first pursued.

Notes

1 *Mercure de France, par une société de gens de lettres, novembre 1777*, no. 15 (Amsterdam, 1777), 164–165. This contest and the winning essay, written by Goyon d'Arzac, are discussed in Harvey Chisick, *The Limits of Reform in the Enlightenment: Attitudes towards the Education of the Lower Classes in Eighteenth-Century France* (Princeton, NJ: Princeton University Press, 1981), 10–15, *passim*.

2 Archives Nationales de France, Paris [hereafter AN], F/17//1309, dossier 1, no. 9, "Appel à l'opinion publique sur l'éducation nationale," 1 November 1791, submitted by M. de Wouves, 2–3.

3 Michael Fitzsimmons, *The Remaking of France: The National Assembly and the Constitution of 1791* (New York, NY: Cambridge University Press, 1994); William Rogers Brubaker, *Citizenship and Nationhood in France and Germany* (Cambridge, MA: Harvard University Press, 1992): 35–49; Elisabeth G. Sledziewski, *Révolutions du sujet* (Paris: Méridiens Klincksieck, 1989).

4 R. R. Palmer, *The Improvement of Humanity: Education and the French Revolution* (Princeton, NJ: Princeton University Press, 1985); Harvey J. Graff, *The Legacies of Literacy: Continuities and Contradictions in Western Culture and Society* (Bloomington, IN: Indiana University Press, 1987), 266–267.

5 Vincenzo Ferrone, *The Enlightenment: History of an Idea*, trans. E. Tarantino (Princeton, NJ: Princeton University Press, 2015), xi. Emphases in the original.

6 Roger Chartier highlights a similar retrospective coherence and "origins story" at work in the revolutionaries' own relationship to the "Enlightenment." Roger Chartier, *The Cultural Origins of the French Revolution*, trans. L. Cochrane (Durham, NC: Duke University Press, 1991), 5.

7 The phrase is taken from Reinhart Koselleck, *Futures Past: On the Semantics of Historical Time*, trans. Keith Tribe (New York, NY: Columbia University Press, 2004), 50–51.

8 Dan Edelstein, *The Enlightenment: A Genealogy* (Chicago, IL: University of Chicago Press, 2010), 83–84; Anne Goldgar, *Impolite Learning: Conduct and Community in the Republic of Letters, 1680–1750* (New Haven, CT: Yale University Press, 1995), 239.

9 Peter Gay, *The Enlightenment: The Science of Freedom* (New York, NY: W.W. Norton & Co., 1969), 501–502.

10 Chisick, *The Limits of Reform in the Enlightenment*, 77, 91.
11 John C. O'Neal, *The Authority of Experience: Sensationist Theory in the French Enlightenment* (University Park, PA: The Penn State University Press, 1996), 13-59; Natasha Gill, *Educational Philosophy in the French Enlightenment: From Nature to Second Nature* (Farnham: Ashgate, 2010); John W. Yolton, *Locke and French Materialism* (New York, NY: Oxford University Press, 1991).
12 Jan Goldstein, *The Post-Revolutionary Self: Politics and Psyche in France, 1750-1850* (Cambridge, MA: Harvard University Press, 2005), 36; also, Chisick, *The Limits of Reform in the Enlightenment*, 38-39.
13 On this, see Keith Michael Baker, "Enlightenment and the Institution of Society: Notes for a Conceptual History," in Willem Melching and Wyger Velema (eds), *Main Trends in Cultural History: Ten Essays* (Atlanta, GA: Rodopi, 1994): 95-120; Edelstein, *The Enlightenment*, 32-34.
14 David Bell, *The Cult of the Nation in France: Inventing Nationalism, 1680-1800* (Cambridge, MA: Harvard University Press, 2001), 3-5.
15 Ibid., 145.
16 Most famously Jürgen Habermas, *The Structural Transformation of the Public Sphere: An Inquiry into a Category of Bourgeois Society*, trans. Thomas Burger (Cambridge, MA: Harvard University Press, 1989). Also Keith Michael Baker, *Inventing the French Revolution: Essays on French Political Culture in the Eighteenth Century* (Cambridge: Cambridge University Press, 1990), esp. 167-199; James Van Horn Melton, *The Rise of the Public Sphere in Enlightenment Europe* (Cambridge: Cambridge University Press, 2001).
17 Marguerite Figeac-Monthus, *Les Enfants de l'Émile? L'effervescence éducative de la France au tournant des XVIIIe et XIXe siècles* (New York, NY: Peter Lang, 2015), 5; Roland Mortier, "The 'Philosophes' and public education," *Yale French Studies*, 40 (1968), 66.
18 Robert Darnton, "What was revolutionary about the French Revolution?" in Peter Jones (ed.), *The French Revolution in Social and Political Perspective* (London: Arnold, 1996), 27.
19 Sledziewski, *Révolutions du sujet*; Susan Maslan, "The dream of the feeling citizen: law and emotion in Corneille and Montesquieu," *SubStance*, 35:1 (2006), 79-81; Thierry Ménissier, "République et fraternité. Une approche de théorie politique," in Gilles Bertrand, Catherine Brice and Gilles Montègre (eds), *Fraternité: Pour une histoire du concept* (Grenoble: Les cahiers du CHRIPA, 2012), 39-40.
20 Honoré Gabriel Riqueti, comte de Mirabeau, *Travail sur l'éducation publique, trouvé dans les papiers de Mirabeau l'aîné* (Paris: Imprimerie nationale, 1791), 73.
21 Darnton, "What was revolutionary about the French Revolution?," 29.
22 Jeffrey D. Burson, "Reflections on the pluralization of Enlightenment and the notion of theological Enlightenment as process," *French History*, 26:4 (2012):

524–537; Jonathan Israel, *Enlightenment Contested: Philosophy, Modernity, and the Emancipation of Man, 1670–1752* (New York, NY: Oxford University Press, 2006), 23–26.
23 Edelstein, *The Enlightenment*, 102–103.
24 Lynn Hunt, *Politics, Culture, and Class in the French Revolution* (Berkeley and Los Angeles, CA: University of California Press, 1984), 32–34, *passim*; Anthony Gottlieb, *The Dream of Enlightenment: The Rise of Modern Philosophy* (New York, NY: W. W. Norton & Co., 2016), 239–241.

Prologue
The educational "system" of eighteenth-century France

There was no "system" of education in Ancien Régime France. There was, instead, a patchwork of local arrangements, institutional traditions, corporate models, and individual accommodations. These ranged from private tutors and independent masters offering classes in their homes to the elite faculties of the French universities and the learned academies, with *petites écoles*, *collèges*, seminaries, provincial academies, and other such institutions in between. R. R. Palmer described the *collèges* as having "rigid institutional structures" but "hazy" boundaries; the description applies equally well to the "system" of education writ large.[1]

There were approximately 330 *collèges* in mid-eighteenth century France, and they enrolled roughly 48,000 male students, or one in fifty-two young men between the ages of 8 and 18.[2] The average *collège* had 100–200 students – although a few had a great many more – and they tended to be located in cities; every city of more than 5,000 inhabitants had at least one *collège*, and most of the smaller cities had one as well. While they were generally administered or staffed by the Church, they were overseen, financed, and supported by political authorities, often accounting for 10 percent of municipal expenses.[3]

Prior to their expulsion from Paris in 1762, and from all of France in 1764, the Jesuits administered more than 100 of the *collèges*, making them the most prominent of the teaching orders and among the most influential actors in eighteenth-century French education. Unsurprisingly, their expulsion brought with it increased scrutiny to the wide array of schools and to the relationships among them. With that in mind, and before moving in Chapters 1 and 2 to the ambivalence of Enlightenment ideas about education and the halting and uncertain efforts at reform that followed expulsion, this prologue will offer a survey of the educational and institutional terrain from which the Jesuits were suddenly absent.

The most elementary level of instruction, beneath the *collèges*, was carried out in a variety of *petites écoles*, elementary institutions offering a combination of religious instruction and some basic training in reading, writing, and arithmetic. These schools differed considerably in their material circumstances, pedagogical practices, and social, political, or religious affiliations. While their existence and accessibility varied by region and by social milieu, the eighteenth century saw sizeable increases in the number of *petites écoles* and in the number of students attending them. Precise numbers are notoriously difficult to establish, but such schools had become sufficiently common and sufficiently important to communities' social and religious lives to serve as a presumptive starting point for discussions of national education.[4]

The "infinite variety" among the *petites écoles* was a byproduct of their having been "created haphazardly over the course of centuries, amid a web of particular factors and local influences, [which] gave to each school its own particular physiognomy."[5] Despite this variety in institutional organization and affiliation, many of the *petites écoles* shared a basic curriculum. Students would begin their studies by memorizing and reciting catechistic dialogue, then learning to read – first learning their letters, then syllables, then words and phrases.[6] Traditionally, at least until the seventeenth century, students would learn to read first in Latin, and then in French, with bilingual editions to ease the transition from one to the other. From the late-seventeenth century on, the primacy of Latin was challenged by pedagogues, like Jean-Baptiste de La Salle, who argued that students ought to learn how to read first in French, and then in Latin only after they were competent in the vernacular. This remained a point of contention through the eighteenth century and into the Revolution, as language was increasingly thought to reflect and to nurture membership in a larger social, political, or religious community. After they could read (whether in Latin or French), students would learn to write by copying model letters or phrases written by their instructor. Finally, near the end of their time in the *petite école*, students would study arithmetic, learning to count either "*par les jets*" or "*par la plume*," that is, by counting tokens or writing numbers.[7]

Despite regulations requiring that boys and girls be educated separately, in practice many of the *petites écoles* were co-ed institutions, though the emphases and extent of education still differed by sex (e.g., girls were less likely than boys to be taught how to write).[8] Stronger on paper than in practice, the prescriptive separation of male and female education would prove important as the relationship among the state, the schools, and the French people was reconsidered and reimagined in the last years of the Ancien Régime and early years of the French Revolution. Presuppositions about the gendered nature of education and educational institutions would shape expectations about who could and should be prepared for contributive citizenship, and here inherited prescriptions mattered more than practical but unsanctioned experience.

Attendance at a *collège* was far less common than at a *petite école*. At the same time, while the *collèges* were often criticized as bastions of the privileged (a critique that would be more forcefully leveled during the years of the Revolution), they were not in practice reserved for the aristocratic or financial elites. Studying the enrollment registers for a handful of *collèges* in the seventeenth century, Jean de Viguerie claims that while approximately half of the students came from families of the social elite – the sons of gentlemen, *parlementaires*, lawyers, notaries, bourgeois *rentiers*, doctors, and the like – one-quarter were the sons of merchants, and the final quarter were sons of the laboring or artisan classes. No children of manual laborers or day workers attended these *collèges*. The social composition of the *collèges'* student body did not change dramatically from the seventeenth to the eighteenth century, although Viguerie does identify two noteworthy developments: during the eighteenth century, a few sons of day laborers joined the ranks, while the sons of the wealthiest part of the bourgeoisie – those whose fathers were royal officials, *parlementaires*, or successful *négociants* – left them.[9] These wealthier families often chose to hire private tutors to educate their children at home.[10] These demographic shifts in the student populations contributed to the idea, at least among some commentators, that the *collèges* might serve as instruments of social advancement rather than exclusion. While it is unclear if access to the *collèges* actually translated into increased social mobility, this possibility would emerge as an important consideration in the post-expulsion debates.[11]

Broadly speaking – and recognizing that there were curricular variations across schools and over time – each of the *collèges* would offer one of two courses of study, either a six- or an eight-year program, and they were known as either *collèges d'humanités* (six-year) or *collèges de plein exercice* (eight).[12] The *collèges de plein exercice* were generally located in larger towns and cities, while *collèges d'humanités* tended to have fewer students and to be located in smaller towns.[13] Correspondingly, the *collèges de plein exercice* tended to draw from a greater geographical radius, although even they drew the vast majority of their students from within thirty or forty kilometers.[14] The two sorts of *collèges* shared a general curriculum for the first six years, which would start with the VIe class, focused primarily on grammar and the rudimentary acquisition of Latin, and culminate in the Ier, also known as Rhetoric. The education they received was intended to "form Christian gentlemen by teaching religion and morality through acquaintance with Christian authors ... [by having] students memorize passages dictated by the teachers and write themes, all on noncontroversial subjects and primarily in Latin."[15] By the time students completed their course in Rhetoric, they were expected to have eloquent command of the spoken as well as written word, although the former was a relatively recent and vocationally motivated development intended to "prepare young men to be fluent advocates in a courtroom, convincing advisers in a royal council, or eloquent preachers if they later joined the pastoral clergy."[16] At the *collèges de plein exercice*, students could continue after Rhetoric to two years of Philosophy (which might include some study in the physical and natural sciences).[17] Generally, those students who stayed through Philosophy intended to then enroll in one of the higher university faculties, although even in the *collège de plein exercice* many students left after their year of Rhetoric.

Students who continued to one of the twenty-three French universities would pursue a degree in one of the four major faculties: the Arts, Law, Medicine, and Theology. The relationship between universities and *collèges* varied, as some *collèges* were associated with universities (often constituting the Faculty of Arts), creating a somewhat blurred boundary between secondary and higher education. Other *collèges*, including those overseen or administered by religious orders, had no affiliation with a university. The post-expulsion debates would envelope both sorts, calling into question the pedagogical, practical, and political logic of each arrangement.[18]

Universities and *collèges* occupied a prominent but liminal position in Ancien Régime society. They were generally urban institutions, and yet they were often experienced and imagined at a remove from the cities around them. They occupied ranks in both secular and ecclesiastical hierarchies, and so had to reflect the interests of both Church and State as they navigated the often complicated relationship between the two.[19] University faculties accrued both fame and prestige from their (often long) histories, and their graduates gained both status and opportunity from their degrees, but the universities themselves came under increasingly fierce (though sometimes unwarranted) attacks for being moribund, antiquated, and slow to embrace changing philosophical, pedagogical, or scientific priorities.[20] New ideas about the public function of knowledge, about the practical value of education, and about the political implications of each brought renewed attention and increasingly public challenges to the Ancien Régime's universities and *collèges*.

While data are not readily available for many aspects of university life in the eighteenth century, it seems that the demographic make-up of university students varied considerably among the twenty-three universities. With the exceptions of Toulouse, with just over 1,000 students, and Paris, with approximately twice that number, the universities were generally quite small – numbering between three and four hundred students – and they drew their students from a relatively limited geographical radius.[21] These students were being prepared for legal, medical, state-bureaucratic, and clerical careers, and a degree from one of the higher university faculties was *de rigueur* for entrance into the elite ranks of those professions. This preparatory function led royal administrations from Louis XIV on to take an active interest in the universities, pressing them to offer a more "practical" education, one that would better serve the social, political, and economic interests of the State.[22] The universities also served, though sometimes indirectly, as conduits for developments in the sciences and philosophy, participating in the dissemination and cultivation of Enlightenment ideas despite their later reputations as intellectually stagnant or antiquated institutions.[23]

As maps of early modern cities and images of early modern schools make clear – with schools located near the heart of the city but each *collège* and faculty walled off from its environs – these institutions were at once part of and apart from the city around them. Their geographical and architectural markers reflected the particular corporate and civic identity of the schools, a status reflected in the lives and rituals of the faculty and of the students. Faculty and students wore distinctive academic dress, worshiped as a corporate body, celebrated private festivals, and sent representatives to serve as honored guests at public celebrations. They also enjoyed privileges such as exemption from royal and municipal taxation, the judicial right of *committimus*, which allowed professors and students to re-locate trials in which they were concerned to the local jurisdiction of the university and, for university graduates, the *droit de gradués*, or right of first refusal over some benefices during three months of the year.[24] These privileges and traditions marked the university (and many of the *collèges*) as "a city within the city," a status that would sometimes serve them well, though it could also lead to their neglect or, as in the Revolution, leave them vulnerable to attack.[25]

The schools' position, at once removed from and central to Ancien Régime society, was increasingly – if often quietly – challenged by political and cultural developments. This was particularly true after 1724, when Louis XV began sending royal *intendants* into the schools. While the *intendants* did not explicitly encroach upon the authority or influence of the clergy running the schools, they did exert some influence on administrative and financial matters.[26] This was the case through mid-century, until finally the expulsion of the Jesuits offered political authorities an opportunity – should they want it – to exert a far greater influence upon Ancien Régime schools. Deciding whether or not to seize such an opportunity led political and pedagogical authorities to think again about the role of education in people's lives, and about the promise or peril of employing the schools to reform, reinforce, or reimagine the contours of French society. In short, it forced them to consider if and how to bring Enlightenment ideas to bear on social, political, and institutional realities.

Notes

1 Palmer, *The Improvement of Humanity*, 12.
2 Roger Chartier, Marie-Madeleine Compère, and Dominique Julia, *L'Éducation en France du XVIe au XVIIIe siècle* (Paris: Société d'Édition d'enseignement Supérieur, 1976), 188–190.
3 Jean de Viguerie, *L'Institution des enfants: L'Éducation en France XVIe-XVIIIe siècle* (Paris: Calmann-Lévy, 1978), 71–77.
4 For attempts to make sense of data regarding education (and literacy) in the eighteenth century and the place of the schools in Ancien Régime communities, see Maurice Gontard, *L'Enseignement primaire en France de la Révolution à la loi Guizot* (1789–1833): *Des Petites Écoles de la monarchie d'ancien régime aux écoles primaires de la monarchie bourgeoise* (Paris: Société d'Édition 'Les Belles Lettres', 1959), 16–22; Viguerie, *L'Institution des enfants*, 77–94; Chartier, Compère, Julia, *L'Éducation en France du XVIe au XVIIIe siècle*, 92–105; François Furet and Jacques Ozouf, *Reading and Writing: Literacy in France from Calvin to Jules Ferry* (Cambridge: Cambridge University Press, 1982), 34–50; Palmer, *Improvement of Humanity*, 10–12; Karen E. Carter, *Creating Catholics: Catechism and Primary Education in Early Modern France* (Notre Dame, IN: University of Notre Dame Press, 2011), 13–16, 202–212.
5 Gontard, *L'Enseignement primaire en France*, 16; see also Jean Morange and Jean-François Chassaing, *Mouvement de réforme de l'enseignement en France, 1760–1798* (Paris: Presses universitaires de France, 1974), 21;

Ferdinand Brunot, *Histoire de la langue Française: Des Origines à nos jours*, T. VII: *La Propagation du français en France jusqu'à la fin de l'Ancien Régime* (Paris: Armand Colin, 1967), 132–139; Michel Froeschlé, *L'École au village: Les Petites Écoles de l'Ancien Régime à Jules Ferry* (Nice: Serre, 2007), 9–24.

6 Viguerie, *L'Institution des enfants*, 157; Carter, *Creating Catholics*, 58–60.
7 Viguerie, *L'Institution des enfants*, 141–157.
8 Karen E. Carter, "'Les garçons et les filles sont pêle-mêle dans l'école': gender and primary education in early modern France," *French Historical Studies*, 31:3 (2008): 417–443. As Carter notes, the disconnect between regulations and practices makes a proper estimate of how many children were educated very difficult, particularly when estimating how many girls learned how to read even if not write.
9 Viguerie, *L'Institution des enfants*, 120–122. Similar results are to be found in Willem Frijhoff and Dominique Julia, *École et société dans la France d'Ancien Régime. Quatre exemples: Auch, Avallon, Condom et Gisors* (Paris: Armand Colin, 1975).
10 Viguerie, *L'Institution des enfants*, 35–36.
11 Ibid., 120–121. Frijhoff and Julia argue that even when present, this hope was rarely realized. Frijhoff and Julia, *École et société dans la France d'Ancien Régime*, 84.
12 On the variations of curricula, see Daniel Mornet, *Les Origines intellectuelles de la Révolution française, 1715–1787* (Lyon: La Manufacture, 1989), 63, 177.
13 Viguerie, *L'Institution des enfants*, 78.
14 Chartier, Compère, Julia, *L'Éducation en France du XVIe au XVIIIe siècle*, 191.
15 Charles R. Bailey, *French Secondary Education, 1763–1790: The Secularization of ex-Jesuit Colleges* (Philadelphia, PA: The American Philosophical Society, 1978), 4.
16 Palmer, *The Improvement of Humanity*, 16.
17 Bailey, *French Secondary Education*, 4; Palmer, *The Improvement of Humanity*, 18. Palmer claims that during the closing decades of the *ancien régime*, 5,000 young men would be studying physics during any given year. Of the approximately 330 *collèges*, 85 had a professor of physics in 1761.
18 Morange and Chassaing, *Mouvement de réforme de l'enseignement en France*, 22.
19 Gaël Rideau, "Un corps séparé: L'Université et les pouvoirs urbains à Orléans aux XVIIe et XVIIIe siècles," in Thierry Amalou and Boris Noguès (eds), *Les Universités dans la ville: XVIe-XVIIIe siècle* (Rennes: Presses universitaires de Rennes, 2013), 81–99. This was most conspicuously evident in the controversies and conflicts surrounding the papal bull *Unigenitus*, which divided not only Jesuits and Jansenists, but also faculties at French *collèges* and universities, and which led the faculty at the University of Paris, and the theologians at the Sorbonne, to oppose the will of both king and pope. On this, see

Palmer, *The Improvement of Humanity*, 45–46; Dale Van Kley, *The Religious Origins of the French Revolution: From Calvin to the Civil Constitution, 1560–1791* (New Haven, CT: Yale University Press, 1996), 135–190.

20 L. W. B. Brockliss, *French Higher Education in the Seventeenth and Eighteenth Centuries: A Cultural History* (Oxford: Clarendon Press, 1987); Alan Charles Kors, *D'Holbach's Coterie: An Enlightenment in Paris* (Princeton, NJ: Princeton University Press, 1976), 180–182; Edelstein, *The Enlightenment*, 79–91.

21 Brockliss, *French Higher Education*, 17–26.

22 For example, the establishment of university chairs in French civil law in the 1670s and the effort to validate and broaden the study of medicine undertaken in 1707. Viguerie, *L'Institution des enfants*, 85–86.

23 Brockliss, *French Higher Education*, 350–370; Kors, *D'Holbach's Coterie*, 180–182; Edelstein, *The Enlightenment*, 86–91.

24 Brockliss, *French Higher Education*, 52–53; Viguerie, *L'Institution des enfants*, 102–103; Rideau, "Un corps séparé," 86–87.

25 Viguerie, *L'Institution des enfants*, 77; Brockliss, *French Higher Education*, 15.

26 Gontard, *L'Enseignement primaire en France*, 14.

1

Education and an ambivalent Enlightenment

As Peter Gay noted almost half a century ago, ideas about education were central to the theory, ambitions, and experience of the Enlightenment.[1] *Philosophes* and fellow travelers concerned themselves to an extraordinary degree with education and its power to shape people's character, capacities, and lives, to influence who they were individually and altogether. What people could and should learn, by whom they should be taught and how much instruction they should receive, where and to what end they should be educated: these were questions that cut across the national, intellectual, scientific, and denominational fault lines of Enlightenment exchange. They were questions that forced Enlightenment thinkers to consider the underlying principles and human implications of their ideas and, insofar as debates over education became debates over the schools, they forced eighteenth-century authorities and institutions to engage with new ways of thinking about what they did and why.

These debates were shaped in critically important ways by sensationist philosophies of epistemology and psychology, especially those inspired by the late-seventeenth-century work of John Locke (*An Essay Concerning Human Understanding* (1689) and *Some Thoughts Concerning Education* (1693)) and spread through France in the works of Voltaire, Étienne Bonnot de Condillac, and others.[2] Sensationism denied the existence of innate principles or ideas, holding instead that the mind at birth is a tabula rasa – or blank slate – and that all cognition derives ultimately from sensory experience of the external world. More broadly, this meant that a person's character, habits, intellect and, in the philosophy's more radical forms, capacities were the result of experience and education (broadly conceived). It seemed to follow from this view that familial, pedagogical, and social environments could be designed to influence people's character – both individual and collective – and to promote particular social, political, or cultural norms.[3] Drawing on the works of Fénelon, Locke, Charles Rollin, and others, theorists and reformers came to emphasize the entangled nature of pedagogical and political regimes and worked to design an order in which each would complement and complete the other.[4] These writers aimed to "link education to political and social transformation," sought to establish pedagogical practices that would nurture desirable social or political habits, and argued about which social and political habits were, in fact, desirable.[5]

These ideas were reinforced by changes in the practical organization of the schools. During the eighteenth century, the ages at which students entered and the rate at which they progressed through the *collèges* became more uniform, helping to normalize a specific trajectory of studies and student life. The change was, in some cases, striking. During the seventeenth century at the Jesuit *collège* in Châlons-sur-Marne, five or six years could separate the youngest from the oldest members of a class: students in the V^e ranged from age 10 to 15, and from 13 to 18 in the IIIe. According to Chartier and Julia, however, "this heterogeneity was progressively reduced during the eighteenth century ... [as] the 'pyramid of ages' within each class showed a tendency to stabilize around a 'normal' age: 10 or 11 for the VIe, 11 or 12 for the V^e, etc." They note that this "eliminated the most visible – if not necessarily the most important – difference between the students ... [and] was an essential condition for the *collège* to be considered a moral sphere in which success indicates merit and where, with discipline and hard work, one can achieve excellence."[6] The movement towards uniformity within a class and within a school was an essential condition not only for a meritocratic conception of the *collège*, but also for an understanding of education as formative for students' characters during their maturation from child to adult and, consequently, for the idea that one might use education to define, reform, or solidify social mores and practices.

This interpenetration of political and pedagogical concerns is most famously evident in the mid-century works of Montesquieu and Charles Duclos, though it had taken shape during the second quarter of the eighteenth century. That quarter-century saw the convergence of educational thinking around a number of points and priorities, among them a desire to reconcile models of individual morality and the pursuit of the collective good and a related sense that the benefits of education were to be both nurtured and realized in society (rather than exclusively in private or in the soul).[7] Unlike the Scholastic model of education, which sought to help students "achieve detachment from the sinful world by immersion in a formal and not commonly used language and ... gain humility through constant, difficult study," eighteenth-century thinkers increasingly argued that "children should be educated in the world rather than cloistered from it and taught about society rather than tossed into it unprepared."[8] This transition reached a logical climax of sorts in Duclos's 1751 *Considérations sur les moeurs de ce siècle*, in which Duclos claimed that eighteenth-century France was well equipped with institutions offering the sort of "instruction" that could train "savants and artists of every sort," but was woefully lacking the sort of "education" needed to "form men," to "raise them to live one for another," and to establish among them a collective "*morale de l'utilité*."[9]

Mid-century calls for an educational system that would be useful to both the students and society focused on several points. The most frequent were proposals that the *collèges'* curriculum and administrative structure be made uniform, that they be amended to include a greater emphasis on mathematics and the sciences, and that instruction be in French rather than Latin. These proposals reflected a growing sense that the schools and the public ought to inform and influence one another, a point that was reflected in the emergence and popularity of non-scholarly and "public" courses in specialized and useful subjects, including but not limited to architecture, chemistry, modern languages, and mathematics. The success of the "*cours public*" and "*cours spectacle*" (for which participants generally had to pay), indicated the popular embrace of new ideas and expectations regarding education, as well as a growing sense that education could benefit a non-academic public; they indicated, in short, a new "market" for education, one that pushed against the historical, institutional, and pedagogical logic underlying the *collèges* and universities.[10]

This relocation of education and its ambitions amplified arguments for the schools to implement a more "useful" curriculum and to make French, rather than Latin, the default language of instruction. Advocates of instruction in the vernacular claimed that the traditional education "substituted words for things" (running afoul of sensationist principles), failed to prepare students for civil society, and set them apart from the rest of their countrymen, that it cloistered them. Louis-René de Caradeuc de La Chalotais, whose *Éssai d'éducation nationale* is discussed in Chapter 2, quipped that "a foreigner to whom one explained the details of our education would imagine that France's principal goal was to populate

Latin seminaries, cloisters and colonies."[11] But establishing French as the language of instruction ran into resistance not only from pedagogical tradition, but also from the many dialects spoken across France, the regional languages known derisively as *patois*. Reformers hoped that the two problems – ancient and regional – might be solved simultaneously and that establishing French as the uniform and standard language of instruction would help to make it also the standard language of Frenchmen. This pursuit of linguistic unity was, for its advocates, a prerequisite for and first step towards the realization of a unified French culture, one wherein scholarly and social influences collaborated in shaping the characters of individuals and of the social collective.[12] Increasingly, the schools, their curricula, and their internal regulations were imagined as part of, and as preparations for, civil society rather than learned enclaves set apart from social affairs.

Montesquieu gave voice to this new paradigm in his claim that the "laws of education ... prepare us for civil life." When he extrapolated from this that "the laws of education will be therefore different in each species of government: in monarchies they will have honor for their object; in republics, virtue; in despotic governments, fear," he made clear a radical (and potentially troubling) consequence of the emerging consensus: if different types of governments depended on different sorts of educational systems to reproduce themselves, might not a change in education foment a change in government?[13] In light of the tremendous formative power ascribed to childhood education in eighteenth-century thought, and appearing at a moment when the foundations of French social and political life were subject to increasing criticism, condemnation, and reimagination, Montesquieu's work seemed to present an unsettling and double-edged prospect: any meaningful reform of education would almost certainly result in significant political change; at the same time, any political change would need an effective reform of education to succeed. By making explicit the political nature of the debate, Montesquieu dramatically raised the stakes of the "education question" and, in so doing, reaffirmed the importance of education in Enlightenment thought.

That education was important, few doubted. Far less consensus existed about what should be done with this almost uniquely powerful instrument of social, political, and moral influence. Due in part to the long-term optimism of texts like Condorcet's "Sketch for a Historical Picture of the Progress of the Human Mind" and the self-evident ambition of projects like Diderot's *Encyclopédie*, the debates over education are often presented as part of a confident Enlightenment's assertion of its historical mission. After all, Helvétius declared that "education can do anything," and programs for educational reform offered *philosophes* an apparently "reasonable way of accepting the world of the present without sacrificing the possibilities of the future."[14] The vision of human and social progress underlying such sentiments allowed Enlightenment thinkers to reconcile the promise of human intelligence and human agency with the shortcomings of the world around them. It also presented a venue for concrete and sustainable action to make that world a better and more "enlightened" one. And yet, a practical pessimism coursed through the Enlightenment debates, a sense that while much could be done, little would; Enlightenment philosophy transformed our sense of what education could do, but the *philosophes* were remarkably pessimistic about the prospects for reform.[15]

While Harvey Chisick and others have drawn our attention to the "limits" of the Enlightenment, the exclusions and ellipses in proposals for reform are just part of this break in eighteenth-century views of education.[16] The *philosophes*' pessimism was not only an indictment of self-interested or short-sighted rulers (though it was often that), nor was it a mere byproduct of the elitist contempt with which some *philosophes* viewed the peasantry (though, again, that was often present, as when Voltaire claimed that the "*canaille* … are not worthy of being enlightened," that for the popular, uneducated classes, "all yokes are proper");[17] this tension stemmed from a deeper sense that for all of the "progress" that had been achieved and all the possibilities suggested by new ways of thinking about education and about social relations, European societies were on the whole inert, uninterested, and often unjust. On this view, it was not just the illiterate who undermined programs for enlightened progress but also, and perhaps more problematically, the distracted, the selfish, and the petty. The result was an ambitious and sophisticated body of philosophical work revealing education's power as an instrument of social reform and improvement coupled awkwardly to complaints that it was only through conquest, cataclysm, or crisis that this instrument might be put to use. This would have important consequences for the legacy of Enlightenment debates over education, for the ambitions and expectations that shaped the Revolution, and for how the revolutionaries encountered the problem of reform after 1789.

To flesh out this tension in late-Enlightenment debates over if, how, and to what end education might transform society, we turn first to Rousseau and Helvétius, and then to debates over female education and the gendered foundations of the social order. These examples illustrate

Enlightenment ambivalence about education across apparently fundamental philosophical divides (in the case of Rousseau and Helvétius), and at the point of contact between natural and social states of human organization (in the debates over female education). In each case, Enlightenment thinkers faced the paralyzing gap between what they thought to be true and what they believed could be real.

Rousseau, Helvétius, and education's dim prospects in Ancien Régime France

The political and philosophical stakes of the debates over education, and the ambivalence to which these debates gave rise, are clear in the works of Jean-Jacques Rousseau and Claude-Adrien Helvétius, figures who came to represent both the possibilities and the divisive implications of Enlightenment thought about education and politics. The two are often juxtaposed in histories of educational philosophy and the Enlightenment, and understandably so. They exerted important, albeit often adversarial, influence upon one another, and the split between them represented a serious fissure in the *philosophe* approach to education and epistemology, a turning point in the perception and reception of sensationist and materialist philosophy in France. Their disagreements were fundamental and far-reaching, touching on the existence or nonexistence of innate ideas and traits, the purpose and efficacy of education, the relative importance of nature and what we might call "nurture," and the relationship among sensory experience, judgment, and knowledge (at its root, the Rousseau–Helvétius controversy stemmed from the conflict between Helvétius's thoroughly materialist epistemology and Rousseau's attempt to preserve an active mental faculty by synthesizing Cartesian dualism, the existence of innate traits, and the empiricism of sensationist thought).[18] And yet, their views converged on a point that is central to understanding the debates over education and politics in the 1760s and 1770s: the tension between education's potential to influence and improve individuals and societies, on the one hand, and the sense that there was little hope of realizing that potential in eighteenth-century France, on the other. These two thinkers, among those most closely associated with Enlightenment ideas about the importance and influence of education, saw the prospect of meaningful educational reform as little more than a fantasy in Ancien Régime France.

Rousseau is at once a towering and a spectral figure in this history. The 1762 publication of *Émile* was an international event, and the work's embrace of experiential learning (and indictment of rote memorization) helped to shape debates over pedagogy and educative purpose in the ensuing decades, but its immediate influence on debates over the reform of schools was minimal (so much so that R. R. Palmer could plausibly claim that "*Émile* has nothing to do with schools"[19]). *Émile* gives us good reason to think that Rousseau saw his project as divorced from the sorts of social, institutional, and practical concerns that emerged with the Jesuits' expulsion. Rousseau wrote dismissively of the educational institutions and political concepts being debated in the 1760s: "I do not consider those laughable institutions we call *collèges* to be institutions of public education" and, more directly still, "public institutions do not exist, and can no longer exist, because there is no longer a Patrie, and there can no longer be citizens. These two words, Patrie and Citizen, should be erased from modern languages."[20]

And yet elsewhere he wrote of education in ways that are relevant to the practical (and institutional) debates over education and politics. In his 1755 "Discourse on Political Economy," published in the fifth volume of Diderot's *Encyclopédie*, Rousseau offered a variation of his condemnation of the modern state, modern society, and modern education ("Since the time the world was divided into nations too large to be governed well, [public education] has not been practicable"[21]), but he also emphasized education's role in shaping and preserving civil society. In describing how private wills might be brought into conformity with the general will, he claimed that "it is not enough to say to the citizens: be good. They must be taught to be so" and, later, "public education under the rules prescribed by the government and under the magistrates put in place by the sovereign, is ... one of the fundamental maxims of popular or legitimate government." He described education as "the state's most important business."[22]

Of course, this was still an abstract claim rooted in examples from Antiquity (he cites the Cretans, the Lacedaemonians, and the Persians), and so entirely reconcilable with his later approach in *Émile* and his despair about modern circumstances. The argument that modern states should, in fact, devote their energies to the establishment of institutions of public education awaited clearer articulation in his *Considerations on the Government of Poland*.

His advice to the Poles reveals important points in how Rousseau thought about the practices and practicalities of public education. Facing the prospect of partition in the late 1760s and early 1770s, Rousseau encouraged the Poles to design a national system of education so as to "give the national form to souls, and direct [the people's] opinions and their tastes so that they will be patriots by inclination, by passion, by necessity."[23] This imperative was followed by more practical points, including suggestions that only Poles (and preferably married Poles) be hired as instructors, that political authorities oversee the curriculum, and that students of different social stations be educated in common to foster a sense of shared identity and purpose. He suggested that the curriculum include public games where students could be encouraged to work together and to compete for public acclaim, and he sought to "accustom [students] early to regulation, to equality, to fraternity, to competition, to living under the eyes of their fellow citizens and to desiring public approval." He even invoked the French schools as an example that might be emulated, at least on the establishment of scholarships to allow some poor students to pursue their studies.[24]

In fleshing out his proposals for Poland, Rousseau also invoked the Swiss, highlighting a practice in schools in Berne that anticipates an important element of revolutionary proposals for public instruction. He describes an arrangement in which students' lives at the school served as microcosms of the social and political world, offering an "apprenticeship for life" that was at once realistic and safe from the corruptive pressures and impressions of adult society. Rousseau claimed that the exercise, known as "the external State," offered a

> miniature copy of everything that makes up the government of the Republic: a Senate, the Principal Magistrates, the Officials, the Bailiffs, the Orators, lawsuits, judgments, solemnities. The external State even has a little government and some revenues, and this institution, authorized and protected by the sovereign, is the nursery of the Statesmen who one day will direct public affairs in the same employments they first exercised only as a game.[25]

Even if such an education could not by itself guarantee the success or preservation of the polity, its absence virtually ensured further decline and degeneration. Rousseau made the point directly, writing:

> Direct the practices, the customs, the morals of the [people] in this spirit of education, you will be developing in them that leaven that is not yet made flat by corrupt maxims, by worn-out institutions, by an egotistical philosophy that preaches what is deadly ... Without these precautions expect nothing from your laws. However wise, however farsighted they might be, they will be evaded and vain, and you will have corrected some abuses that wound you, only in order to introduce others that you will not have foreseen.[26]

While this admonition is more cautionary than reassuring, it nonetheless points towards an affirmative role for education in modern societies.

For Rousseau, incorporating the sort of political apprenticeship offered in Berne into a national system of education seemed to offer a practical sense of how one might try to reconcile public education and representative governance in a polity larger than ancient city-states. If *Émile* (and the *Social Contract*) gave us good reason to think that Rousseau had despaired of modern politics and of public education, his "Discourse on Political Economy" and *Considerations on the Government of Poland* suggest that this despair was tempered by considerations both abstract, in the former, and practical, in the latter.

How, then, should we think of Rousseau's views on education and modern politics? Here the apparent imbalance between circumstances and remedies in the Polish case may offer a clue. Rousseau's suggestions did little to guard against the diplomatic crises and hostile neighbors threatening Poland. Given the situation in which the Poles found themselves, it is hard to imagine what immediately "useful" advice he could have given. Perhaps, then, it was the severity of the crisis that directed Rousseau's attention to the civic and interpersonal aims of education, allowing him to think about the problems of civil society in modern terms. Because Poland's social and political institutions were unlike their European counterparts in the eighteenth century, and because their transformation (or disappearance) seemed imminent, the Polish case gave Rousseau a chance to pursue in relatively specific terms an otherwise speculative line of inquiry into the nature of modern political communities and citizenship, the *Considerations on the Government of Poland* thus serving as an indirect and implicit counterpoint to the abstraction of *The Social Contract*.[27] For France, however, Rousseau expressed no sense that its institutions, traditions, or circumstances might so rapidly change, and his often disparaging commentary on French society offers little reason to think that he saw pedagogical, political, or social reform anywhere on the horizon.[28]

This sense that the realities of French society closed off the vast possibilities opened up by new ways of thinking about education is less often associated with Helvétius, who famously claimed that "education can do anything," than it is with Rousseau, who sent Émile away from society so that he might receive a decent education. And yet Helvétius's works is shaped by a similar resignation, a similar recognition that what was suggested by philosophy was likely precluded by the social and political condition of Louis XV's France.

Combining radically sensationist views of the mind with a utilitarian approach to politics, Helvétius's works presented a world in which education was saturated with social and political significance and social and political circumstances were inescapably educative. The corollary to his claim that education can do anything was, as a result, a sense that education takes place everywhere.[29] These points were central to his 1758 work, *De l'Esprit*, and then to his later *De l'Homme*, written between 1766 and 1769 but not published until 1772, a year after Helvétius's death.[30]

De l'Homme was intended as both a defense and an expansion of *De l'Esprit*, which had aroused the ire of the dauphin, had been condemned by the authorities at the Sorbonne and the Parlement of Paris, and was criticized as either unoriginal, false, or dangerous by a number of prominent *philosophes* (Voltaire and Rousseau among them); the condemnations were so frequent and fervent that Helvétius would comment in a letter to David Hume that "the Inquisition [had] left Spain, and come to France."[31] Despite having recanted the views expressed in *De l'Esprit* on more than one occasion – first in August 1758, in a letter to the Jesuit Père Plesse, then in a letter to Malesherbes, and again in January 1759, to the Parlement of Paris[32] – Helvétius began *De l'Homme* by defending the earlier work, declaring in the preface, "if I do not renounce any of the principles that I established in *De l'Esprit*, it is because those appear to me to be the only reasonable options, the ones which, since the publication of that book, enlightened men have come to adopt."[33] In addition to his radically sensationist epistemology, these principles included the claim that man was motivated only by self-interest (or "self-love"), that man and society were both capable of being improved, and that public utility ought to be the standard against which all actions and legislation are measured. The result was more than a work of philosophy (although it was certainly that); it was also a provocation, a political tract, and an attempt to complete the work begun in *De l'Esprit*.

Helvétius's work emphasized education's role in shaping society, culture, and politics and, no less, the role of society, culture, and politics in giving substance to education. Thus it followed that the reform of education could not be undertaken alone, nor could it be relied upon to independently produce social or political reforms; instead, what was needed was a study of "[men's] hearts, of the human spirit, and of its diverse operations" so that new laws and new institutions could contribute to the "progress of the sciences, of morality, of politics, and of education."[34]

Helvétius claimed that "man is nothing but the product of his education" and that an individual's talents and virtues are acquisitions rather than products of his or her natural "organization."[35] The acquisition of those talents and virtues followed from sensory experience and the motivating force of "*amour de soi.*" While "self-love" – or "self-regard" – was not an innate trait it was, Helvétius thought, an "immediate consequence of [man's] physical sensibility, and, by consequence of that, common to all and inseparable from man's being."[36] On this view, people were "motivated only in their own self-interest," though this did not necessarily mean that they would act selfishly or contrary to the public good.[37] Like Montesquieu, Rousseau, and others, Helvétius thought that one's sense of "self-interest" was molded by "the education one received, the government under which one lived, and the different situations in which one found oneself."[38] Shaping how one thought about his or her self-interest was among the most important elements of that person's education, and getting it right required the combined influence of schools, government, and social forces.[39]

To steer the individual's "interest" towards virtue it was necessary to establish circumstances in which virtue was rewarded. As Helvétius wrote in volume II of *De l'Homme*, "spirit and talent are nothing more than the product of men's desires and circumstances. The science of education can thus be reduced to placing men in a position which leads them to acquire the desired talents and virtues."[40] While many influences shaped an individual's character, it was the form of government under which one lived that was most important. "If men who are honest, loyal, industrious, and humane under a free government, are base, dishonest, vile, without genius and without courage under a despotic government, the difference in their character is the effect of the different education received under one of these governments or the other."[41] And again, near the end of *De l'Homme*, "whether an education is good or bad is determined almost entirely by the laws."[42]

This attention to social and political circumstance led Helvétius to emphasize *émulation* as a pedagogical complement to self-interest.[43] Emulation was, like self-interest, a motivating force that could push people towards good or ill. Here Helvétius offered a grim assessment of the education being offered in the schools, asking "how does one prove to a student that it is by the services he renders to his country that he can win public esteem and celestial glory? what models are put forward for him to imitate? a monk, a fanatical and lazy dervish, whose intolerance leads to trouble and devastation for empires."[44] Helvétius argued that secular and religious authorities had not only different but conflicting interests, and so it was never in the interests of the citizenry or of the state to give religious authorities control over the schools.[45] Religious orders in particular were "animated by an interest contrary to the public good."[46]

While state control was particularly important, the successful reform of education would require action well beyond the walls of the school. Indeed, Helvétius thought that students' real education began when they left the schools:

> It is upon leaving the *collège*, upon entry into the world, that one's 'adolescent' education begins ...
> This is when he receives his most lasting instruction, when his values and his character will take shape, when he is finally free and is most himself, and the passions excited in his heart will determine his habits and, often, the way he will conduct himself throughout his life.[47]

At this point the pupil's primary "instructor" changes; it is no longer the schoolmaster, professor, or tutor, but the government under which he or she lives and the society into which he or she enters.

This ambient "instructor" was itself subject to change over time as nations and societies, like individuals, developed their character as a result of experience: "Each nation has its particular manner of seeing and of sensing, and this manner forms its character; and among all peoples, whether that character changes all at once, or is altered little-by-little, will depend upon the suddenness or subtlety of changes in the form of government, and so in public education."[48] Here Helvétius's argument resists linear explanations of how political, social, and pedagogical change relate to one another. Education was at once the source of social custom and was shaped by social custom; it was the foundation of a government's power and was a product of that government's nature; it needed to be based upon clear and universally applicable principles, maxims, and practices and was, at the same time, beyond any puppet-master's control. Because education was everywhere, it resisted the efforts of those who would dictate its every element, undermined the possibility that two individuals could ever receive the same education, and thwarted efforts to form the people in a mold of their ruler's (or, on a smaller scale, instructor's) making.[49]

If education resisted complete control, it could still be improved, though this would be an immense undertaking. The difficulties stemmed from Helvétius's view of the feedback dynamics among social, political, and pedagogical institutions, a dynamic that was evident in his discussion of language and civic morality. He bemoaned the confused understandings of words such as *"Bon," "Intérêt,"* and *"Vertu,"* misunderstandings he thought of as both symptoms and causes of moral decay in eighteenth-century Europe. Addressing this problem would require not only the prescriptive improvement of language (through a more perfect dictionary, which could give a settled meaning to the words), but also social reforms that might align the interests of the individual with public pride and the public recognition of virtue.[50] The same was true of education, the reform of which would demand (and produce) changes in both the schools and in French society.

And this is where Helvétius's nearly infinite faith in the power of education exhausted itself. For a program of educational reform to succeed, for it to produce the sorts of "brave, industrious, enlightened, and virtuous" citizens that bring glory to empires, France and French society would need to be reinvented all at once. France would have to experience a radical break, a political, social, and cultural rupture that could redirect the nation's momentum so that the formal and informal dynamics of everyday life might serve the public and common good.

Helvétius saw no such "salutary crisis" in France's future, warning instead that French society was killing itself "through consumption." Like Rousseau, Helvétius could only imagine educational reform as the complement to, or the result of, a broader social convulsion; it was, he thought, only by being "conquered" that France might be set free.[51]

From revolution to resignation in rethinking female education

Helvétius and Rousseau were far from alone in their sense that philosophical and political possibilities had to be calculated very differently. If anything, the differences, and the risks, in abstract and social calculations were even more prominent in concurrent debates about female education. Here education promised (or threatened) to transform the relationship between the sexes, overturn the hierarchies of French life, and break the supposed link between the "natural" and the "social" orders. In the debates over female education, sensationist ideas about experience, education, the self, and society brought the dictates of nature, nurture, and necessity into conflict with one another and, in so doing, revealed the ambivalence underlying Ancien Régime ideas about pedagogical reform.

Debates over female education are a particularly valuable site for thinking through Enlightenment ideas and uncertainties about education and the prospect of reform. Participants in these debates frequently invoked and built upon the distinction between natural and social states of being, presenting their arguments as a clear complement and (sometimes explicit) corollary to early modern debates over the social contract.

This was true of arguments that posited natural differences (and hierarchy) between the sexes as well as those that asserted a natural equality of the sexes, attributing gender inequality in modern life to social and cultural forces. The centrality of this natural–social nexus, together with seventeenth- and eighteenth-century reconsiderations of how motherhood and family structure shaped the social and political orders, marked the debates over female education as a critical point in the Enlightenment's consideration of how education might reinforce, reform, or radically transform eighteenth-century life. In that, they revealed in remarkably explicit and self-conscious terms the tension between the emancipatory and exclusionary impulses at work in Enlightenment thought.

This is particularly evident in Pierre-Ambroise-François Choderlos de Laclos's *Des Femmes et de leur éducation*. Laclos, best known for his 1782 novel, *Les Liaisons dangereuses*, began work on *Des Femmes* in the 1780s in response to a question, posed again by the Academy at Châlons-sur-Marne: "How might girls' education be perfected?"[52] That Laclos's answer would include a broader consideration of politics and society was made clear with his epitaph, which he drew from Seneca: "*Le mal est sans remède quand les vices se sont changés en mœurs.*"[53] Despairing, along with his Roman predecessor, Laclos concluded that "it [was] impossible to improve the education of girls" in eighteenth-century France.[54]

Laclos claimed that female education could not be improved because there was nothing upon which to build. He described the purpose of education as the "development of the individual's faculties towards the service of the social good."[55] Because the laws and customs of eighteenth-century France precluded women from positions that might serve the public good, their education was, within that society, impossible. The situation was worse than that though, as Laclos claimed that the circumstances of women's lives forced them to rely upon seduction to protect themselves and to pursue their interests. Because her livelihood and place in society depended upon her ability to seduce, and so to exercise men's imaginations rather than develop her own faculties, "woman" found herself at once oppressed and degraded, "[her] oppression lead[ing] to the stunting of her intellect and, in a second stage, to moral decay."[56] Without opportunities to contribute to the public good, and "enslaved" by their environment, women could not be educated, and so the improvement of their education was a nonsensical question.

Laclos described the inequality between the sexes as an historical, rather than natural, phenomenon. He attributed the unequal status of the sexes to the establishment of a social contract based upon force and inequality, one to which women had "conceded, but never consented."[57] He then distinguished between the circumstantial impossibility of improving female education and the question of female education as such. Perhaps, he conceded, female education could be improved, though doing so would require a "revolution" in the organization of society and in the relationship between the sexes. Addressing women – rather than the male academicians in Châlons-sur-Marne – Laclos wrote: "do not wait for the help of men, who are the authors of what ails you ... the only way to escape your enslavement is by a great revolution. Is this revolution possible? That you must decide, as it is upon your courage that the answer depends."[58] Of course, even on Laclos's own terms, this call to upend the social and sexual order offered little sense of what might actually be done, the prospect and pursuit of such an upheaval awaiting the deployment of a female agency that Laclos had himself written off as impossible under the prevailing circumstances. Nonetheless, he had staked out a rhetorical connection between the rejuvenation of nature and the coming of revolution, between the prospect of female education and the overthrow of French society.

By the time Laclos wrote the final essay of *Des Femmes et de leur éducation* in the late 1790s, even the rhetoric of social or sexual upheaval had disappeared from his work, and his enthusiasm for revolutionary change had waned considerably. In that third essay, Laclos tempered his continued calls for women to be educated in a broad range of subjects (including the natural and experimental sciences), warning that as their studies progressed, instructors would be called upon to provide "more moderation than encouragement," lest their pupils get carried away.[59] He concluded with the hope that the curriculum he described would leave the female pupil better educated, happier, and with the "good sense never to show her knowledge except among her closest friends, in confidence, so to speak."[60]

A similar tension between radical possibilities and conservative conclusions is evident in the pre-revolutionary works of Louise d'Épinay and Stephanie-Felicité de Genlis, suggesting a broader dilemma underlying Enlightenment debates over female education.[61] Indeed, their works illustrate the considerable ambivalence that followed from the entanglement of new ideas about education and the gendered underpinnings of Ancien Régime life.

Neither Genlis nor Épinay were *salonnières* in the proper sense, though they were each prominent and important figures in the Ancien Régime's Republic of Letters.[62] Mme de Genlis was a famously combative "woman of letters" who wrote prodigiously, engaged in intellectual battle with Rousseau and the *philosophes*, and claimed in her memoirs that she had almost been the first female member of the Académie française (roughly 200 years before Marguerite Yourcenar's election). She was the only woman to serve as *Gouverneur des enfants d'Orléans* and was, according to Samia Spencer, "probably the eighteenth century's most prominent and outstanding educator."[63] Likewise, Mme d'Épinay was a distinguished novelist and pedagogue, a friend and correspondent of many *philosophes*, and a patron (and later adversary) of Rousseau's. In 1783 she won the Montyon Prix d'Utilité, awarded by the Académie française to the year's best and most useful book (she won for the expanded second edition of *Conversations d'Émilie*, much to the chagrin of Genlis, who expected to win for *Adèle et Théodore*).[64]

Genlis and Épinay each argued that men and women are equal by nature, and they each attributed the sexual and gendered hierarchies of the Ancien Régime to social custom and cultural conditioning. As Genlis wrote in *Les Veillées du château*: "[had] all the arts ... been less the fruits of education and study than the happy gifts of nature, there is no doubt but there would have existed a perfect equality between men and women."[65] More directly, Épinay claimed in a letter to Abbé Ferdinando Galiani that "men and women possess the same constitution and nature."[66] In light of this natural equality, they each claimed that a more just society would provide women access to better and more varied courses of study as well as opportunities to make use of their talents, to have their accomplishments recognized publicly. In the end, however, each counseled young girls to foreswear their ambitions and to resign themselves to what Genlis described as a "monotonous and dependent life."[67] It seemed that the natural and the social worlds had to be reckoned differently, and the latter rendered the former maddeningly irrelevant.

This was particularly clear in the fate of Épinay's "*Fille Amazone*," who appeared in the first edition of *Les Conversations d'Emilie*. The story is about a young girl named Adélaïde whose family leaves the city for the countryside. The education she then receives includes activities normally off-limits to young girls, and she becomes adept at horseback riding, hunting, and similarly physical pastimes. Adélaïde thrives, and the story highlights the chasm between the opportunities afforded to girls by nature and those offered by eighteenth-century society, a point that was reinforced by its description as a replacement for the tale of the "inconsequential girl" in Emilie's curriculum.[68] As Mary Trouille notes, the "*Fille Amazone*" presented Emilie, and so Épinay's readers, with "an androgynous model" that was supposed to make clear that the "physical, mental, and emotional weakness of her female contemporaries was culturally conditioned."[69]

But the tale did not reappear in the new edition of 1783 (for which Épinay won the Prix Montyon), having been replaced by the tale of "*La Mauvaise Fille*," which presented "a model much closer to the traditional 'feminine' ideals of modesty, docility, and charm."[70] In this case, parental attention and discipline served to restrain a young girl's precocity, allowing her finally to marry (albeit belatedly, because of her poor disposition as a child), and so to "settle advantageously" as her "superior" and more obedient cousin had already done.[71] The young girl learned, much as Emilie was now supposed to learn, that "the first element of happiness ... must be to do one's duty, and be satisfied with oneself."[72] Épinay closed by warning her young pupil:

> We [women] run great risks in deviating from the beaten track. It requires much confidence to establish an opinion, unsupported by success, in preference to those instructions which are consecrated by public wisdom. It is evidently more expedient to follow common experience, than to commit an irreparable error, by attempting, without success, an untried experiment.[73]

There was, it seemed once again, little reason for women to look beyond their "private" and domestic concerns.[74]

This reinscription of female education into a primarily – perhaps even exclusively – domestic range of activities resonated in a cultural moment during which, as Habermas famously noted, political debate supplanted literary discourse and politics became increasingly associated with the work of an adjudicating (and male) public.[75] This shift is easily overstated, and we should guard against an excessive and "false opposition between public and private spheres," but the simultaneous politicization of debates over (male) education and domesticization of debates regarding female education both reflected and reinforced a broader cultural process whereby contributive citizenship was codified as a male phenomenon.[76] One result of this was the institutionalization of a gendered concept of political practice at a moment when such practices were otherwise subject to critical reconsideration. If schools were increasingly imagined as part of a multi-faceted apprenticeship for civil and political society, the reaffirmation of schools as exclusively male spaces presumed and prefigured an important limitation on the political imagination of the late eighteenth century.

But coherence and consensus about the political and social role of education remained elusive even within such limitations. Enlightened debates over the purposes and practices of education had helped to establish schools as potentially "national" institutions and to entangle the prospect of educational reform with fundamental questions about the character of French society, the nature of the French polity, and the powers of the French state. The question of what to do with the schools, and with it these deeper questions about France and its future, became more explicit and more urgent after the Jesuits' expulsion, and when *parlementaires*, members of Louis XV's government, and the new administrators of the formerly Jesuit institutions turned to the practical work of reform after 1762, they did so as heirs to, and participants in, this ambivalent Enlightenment discourse. The result was a debate in which the stakes seemed immense and the path forward not just unclear, but perhaps too treacherous to pursue.

Notes

1 Gay, *The Enlightenment*, 501–502.
2 Ibid., 501–516; O'Neal, *The Authority of Experience*, 13–59; Yolton, *Locke and French Materialism*.
3 Chisick, *The Limits of Reform in the Enlightenment*, 38–39.
4 Marcel Grandière, *L'Idéal pédagogique en France au dix-huitième siècle* (Oxford: Voltaire Foundation, 1998).
5 Gill, *Educational Philosophy in the French Enlightenment*, 117–137.
6 Chartier, Compère, Julia, *L'Éducation en France du XVIe au XVIIIe siècle*, 194.
7 Gill, *Educational Philosophy in the French Enlightenment*, 117.
8 Bailey, *French Secondary Education*, 4; Gill, *Educational Philosophy in the French Enlightenment*, 137.
9 Charles Pinot-Duclos, *Considérations sur les mœurs de ce siècle* (Paris, 1784), 20; Carole Dornier, "Morale de l'utilité et lumières françaises: Duclos, Considérations sur les mœurs de ce siècle (1751)" *Studies on Voltaire and the Eighteenth Century* (SVEC), 362 (1998): 169–188.
10 Bruno Belhoste, "Un espace public d'enseignement aux marges de l'université: les cours public à Paris à la fin du XVIIIe siècle et au début du XIXe siècle," in Amalou and Noguès (eds), *Les Universités dans la ville*, 217–234.
11 Louis-René de Caradeuc de La Chalotais, *Essai d'éducation nationale, ou Plan d'Études pour la jeunesse* (1763), 16.
12 Louis Trenard, "L'Enseignement de la langue nationale: une réforme pédagogique, 1750–1790," in Donald N. Baker and Patrick J. Harrigan (eds), *The Making of Frenchmen: Current Directions in the History of Education in*

France, 1679–1979 (Waterloo, Ontario: Historical Reflections Press, 1980), 99.
13 Charles Baron de Montesquieu, *The Spirit of the Laws* (New York, NY: Cosimo Press, 2011), 29.
14 Gay, *The Enlightenment*, 498–499.
15 The "strong streak of pessimism" that ran through Enlightenment hopes for "progress" is noted by Jonathan Israel, *A Revolution of the Mind: Radical Enlightenment and the Intellectual Origins of Modern Democracy* (Princeton, NJ: Princeton University Press, 2010), 3.
16 Chisick, *The Limits of Reform in the Enlightenment*; Gay, *The Enlightenment*, 517–528.
17 The quote is from a 5 January 1767 letter to Frederick II of Prussia. Voltaire (François-Marie Arouet de), *Œuvres complètes de Voltaire* T. 41 (Paris: L. Hachette, 1876–1900), 171–173.
18 On this debate, see Gill, *Educational Philosophy in the French Enlightenment*, 163–225; Jean H. Bloch, "Rousseau and Helvétius on innate and acquired traits: the final stages of the Rousseau-Helvétius controversy," in *Journal of the History of Ideas*, 40:1 (1979): 21–41.
19 Palmer, *The Improvement of Humanity*, 52.
20 Jean-Jacques Rousseau, *Émile, ou de l'Éducation* in *Œuvres de J.J. Rousseau*, T. XVIII (Amsterdam, 1773), 9.
21 Jean-Jacques Rousseau, "Discourse on Political Economy" in *Rousseau: Basic Political Writings*, ed. Donald A. Cress (Indianapolis, IN: Hackett, 1987), 126.
22 Ibid., 121, 125–126.
23 Jean-Jacques Rousseau, "Considerations on the Government of Poland," in *Rousseau: The Plan for Perpetual Peace, On the Government of Poland, and other Writings on History and Politics*, ed. Christopher Kelly (Hanover, NH: Dartmouth University Press, 2005), 179.
24 Ibid., 180–181.
25 Ibid., 181–182.
26 Ibid., 182.
27 Such a reading of Rousseau's essay on Poland is proposed in Willmoore Kendall, "Introduction," in Jean-Jacques Rousseau, *The Government of Poland*, trans. Willmoore Kendall (Indianapolis, IN: Hackett, 1985), xiii–xxx.
28 Carter, *Creating Catholics*, 82.
29 Mordecai Grossman, *The Philosophy of Helvétius, with Special Emphasis on the Educational Implications of Sensationalism* (New York, NY: Columbia University Press, 1926); Ian Cumming, *Helvetius: His Life and Place in the History of Educational Thought* (London: Routledge, 1955); for a comparison of Helvétius's sensationism to other eighteenth-century versions, see O'Neal, *The Authority of Experience*, 84–101.

30 Claude-Adrien Helvétius, *De l'Homme, de ses facultés intellectuelles, et de son éducation* (Londres, 1773) ed. Geneviève Moutaux and Jacques Moutaux (Paris: Librairie Arthème-Fayard, 1989). The arrangements made for the publication of *De l'Homme* prior to Helvétius's death are discussed in David Smith, *Bibliography of the Writings of Helvétius* (Ferney-Voltaire, France: Centre International d'Étude du XVIIIe siècle, 2001), 289–299.
31 This letter is quoted in Smith, *Bibliography of the Writings of Helvétius*, 289.
32 Cumming, *Helvetius*, 82–86.
33 Helvétius, *De l'Homme*, vol. 1, 9.
34 Ibid., 44.
35 Ibid., 45–46.
36 Ibid., 337.
37 Everett C. Ladd, Jr., "Helvetius and D'Holbach: 'La Moralisation de la politique'," *Journal of the History of Ideas*, 23:2 (1962), 222. On interest as a potential instrument for social, and even individual (or moral), improvement during the eighteenth century, see Albert O. Hirschman, *The Passions and the Interests: Political Arguments for Capitalism before its Triumph* (Princeton, NJ: Princeton University Press, 1977).
38 Helvétius, *De l'Homme*, vol. 1, 337.
39 Ibid., 227–236.
40 Helvétius, *De l'Homme*, vol. 2, 882.
41 Ibid., 880.
42 Ibid., 926.
43 Ibid., 889. On emulation more generally, see Olivier Ihl, *Le Mérite et la République: Essai sur la société des émules* (Paris: Gallimard, 2007); John Iverson, "Introduction," to the Forum on "Emulation in France, 1750–1800," *Eighteenth Century Studies*, 36:2 (2003): 217–223.
44 Helvétius, *De l'Homme*, vol. 1, 89.
45 Ibid., 81.
46 Ibid., 237.
47 Ibid., 69.
48 Ibid., 327–330.
49 Gay, *The Enlightenment*, 513–514; this is a point that has occasioned considerable misunderstandings of Helvétius's thought, which is too often characterized as proto-totalitarian in its implications. See, for example, Xavier Martin, *Human Nature and the French Revolution: From the Enlightenment to the Napoleonic Code*, trans. Patrick Corcoran (New York, NY: Berghahn Books, 2001).
50 Helvétius, *De l'Homme*, vol. 1, 229–232.
51 Ibid., 11.
52 Pierre-Ambroise-François Choderlos de Laclos, "Des Femmes et de leur éducation," in Laclos, *Oeuvres complètes*, ed. Laurent Versini (Paris: Bibliothèque

de la Pléiade, 1979), 387–443. According to Versini, the third essay was not written until later, probably sometime between 1795 and 1799.
53 Ibid., 389.
54 Ibid., 389–390.
55 Ibid., 390.
56 Lieselotte Steinbrügge, *The Moral Sex*, trans. Pamela E. Selwyn (New York, NY: Oxford University Press, 1995), 84. For Laclos's description of this process, see Laclos, "Des Femmes et de leur éducation," 421.
57 Laclos, "Des Femmes et de leur éducation," 390–391; 419–421.
58 Ibid., 390–391.
59 Ibid., 439–443.
60 Ibid., 443.
61 Adrian O'Connor, "Nature, nurture, and the social order: imagining lessons and lives for women in Ancien Régime France," *French Politics, Culture & Society*, 30:1 (2012): 1–22.
62 Dena Goodman, *The Republic of Letters: A Cultural History of the French Enlightenment* (Ithaca, NY: Cornell University Press, 1996), 75. Goodman writes of Épinay's home as a "haven for her philosophe friends, but never a salon in the formal sense." Mary Trouille seems to reject this distinction when she writes of "D'Épinay's triumph as a salonnière." Mary Trouille, "La Femme mal mariée: Mme d'Epinay's challenge to *Julie* and *Emile*," *Eighteenth-Century Life*, 20:1 (1996), 61, n. 4.
63 Samia Spencer, "Women and Education," in Samia Spencer (ed.), *French Women and the Age of Enlightenment* (Bloomington, IN: Indiana University Press, 1984), 91.
64 That two such important works about education, both written by women, should compete for the Prix Montyon in the same year points to both the centrality of education in considerations of public "utility" and the prominence of women within the public discussion of pedagogical questions. This point is underlined in Isabelle Brouard-Arends, "Les Géographes éducatives dans Adèle et Théodore de Madame de Genlis," in Nathalie Ferrand (ed.), *Locus in fabula: La Topique de l'espace dans les fictions françaises d'Ancien Régime* (Leuven: Peeters, 2004), 573.
65 Stéphanie Félicité, comtesse de Genlis, *Les veillées du château, ou cours de morale à l'usage des enfans*, vol. 2 (Dublin: Chez Wogan et Jones, 1795), 260–261.
66 Mme d'Épinay à Abbé Ferdinando Galiani, 14 mars 1772, in Ferdinando Galiani, Louise d'Épinay, *Correspondance*, vol. III, mars 1772–mai 1773, ed. Georges Dulac and Daniel Maggetii (Paris: Persée, 1992), 33.
67 Stéphanie Félicité, comtesse de Genlis, *Adèle et Théodore, ou Lettres sur l'éducation; contenant tous les principes relatifs aux trois différens plans d'éducation des princes, des jeunes personnes, & des hommes*, vol. 1 (Paris: Lambert, Baudouin, 1782), 43–44.

68 Louise Florence Pétronille Tardieu d'Esclavelles, marquise d'Épinay, *Les Conversations d'Emilie*, ed. Rosena Davison (Oxford: Voltaire Foundation, 1996). The tale of the "*Fille Amazone*" reappeared in the posthumously published 1788 Belin edition. The first five conversations of that edition are included as the second appendix to Davison's presentation of *Les Conversations d'Emilie*, the main text of which reproduces the 1782 edition. The "*Fille Amazone*" appears in the fourth conversation. Épinay, *Les Conversations d'Emilie*, 460–470. On the "Amazon Heroine" as a literary device, and its post-Fronde decline, see Joan DeJean, *Tender Geographies: Women and the Origins of the Novel in France* (New York. NY: Columbia University Press, 1991), 53.

69 Mary S. Trouille, "Louise d'Epinay: Lettre à Galiani (14 mars 1772); Les Conversations d'Emilie (1773)," in Anne R. Larsen and Colette H. Winn (eds), *Writings by Pre-revolutionary French Women* (New York, NY: Routledge, 2000), 512–513.

70 Ibid., 513.

71 Épinay, *Les Conversations d'Emilie*, 86–87.

72 Ibid., 107.

73 Ibid., 242.

74 At the same time, these "domestic" roles could empower women as "linchpins" for the production, reproduction, or reform of social and political systems. See Jennifer Popiel, *Rousseau's Daughters: Domesticity, Education, and Autonomy in Modern France* (Durham, NH: University of New Hampshire Press, 2008); Lesley H. Walker, *A Mother's Love: Crafting Feminine Virtue in Enlightenment France* (Lewisburg, PA: Bucknell University Press, 2008); Annie K. Smart, *Citoyennes: Women and the Ideal of Citizenship in Eighteenth-Century France* (Newark, DE: University of Delaware Press, 2011). It remained, however, for their brothers or sons to translate the work of the home into social and political realities.

75 On the political and literary public spheres, see Habermas, *The Structural Transformation of the Public Sphere*, 51–56; for this as a gendered phenomenon associated with the ascent of public opinion, Goodman, *The Republic of Letters*, 233–280.

76 Dena Goodman, "Public sphere and private life: toward a synthesis of current historiographical approaches to the old regime," *History and Theory*, 31:1 (1992), 1.

2

National education: promise and paralysis

In April 1762, when the Parlement of Paris ordered the Society of Jesus to relinquish control of the thirty-eight *collèges* it administered within the Parlement's jurisdiction, it set off a tremendous debate about the purpose, personnel, and politics of French education. When, four months later, the Parlement expelled the Jesuits altogether and, two years after that, Louis XV expelled the order from all of France, it became apparent that the debate over education would become national in scope and that it would require a long-term solution.

The expulsion of the Jesuits, first from Paris, then from France, created an institutional void that would demand government attention and offer an opportunity, for those so inclined, to imagine a dramatic overhaul of education in France.[1] The Jesuits had controlled 111 *collèges* prior to 1762, about 30 per cent of the national total (roughly 330).[2] Their expulsion removed approximately 1,250 Jesuits from the schools, raising questions about how and by whom the next generation of Frenchmen would be educated.[3] These concerns quickly reached beyond the classroom walls, leading to questions about the purpose and value of education, its function in French society, and its influence on the social and political orders.[4] The debates that followed drew upon a century's worth of thought regarding education, putting pressure on the competing impulses at work in Enlightenment ideas about education and weakening, at least temporarily, the sense that political circumstances or institutional traditions precluded dramatic changes to the schools and to French society. They also marked an important moment in the Enlightenment debates over education and the relationship between education and eighteenth-century society, especially in France. The almost simultaneous appearance of Rousseau's *Émile* and the expulsion of the Jesuits reinforced education's place in Enlightenment thought and France's position at the center of debates over education's social, political, and cultural work.[5] That these coincided with the end of the Seven Years War, and with efforts to reckon the implications of such a devastating loss, helped to establish the post-expulsion debates as a truly national controversy: these years saw a convergence of intellectual, political, and institutional crises that promised to challenge "basic concepts about authority, tradition, religion, science, and power," and to do so in potentially epoch-altering ways.[6]

The intensity of this controversy is indicated, albeit imprecisely, in the frequency with which works related to education were published before and after this moment: in the years from 1715 to 1759, fifty-one works were published in France on the subject of education; between 1760 and 1789, 161 such works appeared, thirty-two of them between 1762 and 1765. These texts both reflected and reinforced a sense that proposals regarding education were entangled with ideas about the nature and future of French society; as a result, these debates "preoccupied both the political and intellectual elites of the country."[7] They also revealed deep anxieties and uncertainties about the role of the public in French politics, the relationship between the State and the people, and the mutability or immutability of the social order.[8] As Dominique Julia and Roger Chartier note, the post-expulsion debates over education "reveal[ed] the crisis of a whole culture."[9]

This is a particularly interesting crisis, as there was – at least initially – little direct conflict between the various parties as they charted a post-Jesuit course of reform; indeed, education appeared to be one of the topics on which the relationship between the Parlement of Paris and the Crown "bordered on partnership" during the 1760s.[10] There was also a remarkable degree of consensus, if not quite unanimity, about the sorts of curricular reforms that were needed, with frequent calls for expanded education in French (rather than Latin), greater attention to the natural sciences and mathematics, and an increased focus on "useful" subjects. Despite this, the debates that followed the Jesuits' expulsion would reveal a very real crisis, one that was not of, but rather *about*, the French state, the composition of French society, the character of the French nation, and the relationship between such abstract entities and the institutions of everyday life.[11] It was about the prospect of politics and the composition of the polity, and the issues to which it gave rise were at once metaphysical and practical, philosophical and political. These years presented France with a fundamental crisis, not in the sense of a catastrophe or controversy to be survived or overcome, but "in the sense of reaching a crucial point" where decisive or further action "would tip the scales" towards one future or another.[12]

Recognizing the nature of this crisis is important, as it draws our attention to inaction as well as action, to indecision and half-measures as well as points of conflict or explicit contestation. The sudden absence of the Jesuits from the *collèges* would force political and pedagogical authorities to respond, and so reveal their priorities, defend the breadth (or limits) of their plans, and give voice to their sense of how the schools figured into the national and collective future. As Maurice Gontard has noted, institutions such as schools "bear the seal of the philosophical, religious, and moral ideas of their epoch, and reflect that epoch's conceptions of man and his destiny, of the state and its purpose."[13] The post-expulsion reforms, both those that were proposed and those that were pursued, reveal a society paralyzed by indecision, a society unable to articulate a coherent vision of its future.

In contrast to the scandals and *causes célèbres* of eighteenth-century politics, this was a relatively quiet affair. In fact, the prospects for a meaningful and perhaps national reform of education seemed good in the immediate wake of the Jesuits' expulsion, and the Parisian *collèges* were quickly redesigned in ways that had apparent implications for the rest of France. Given that the Parlement of Paris set the crisis in motion by expelling the Jesuits, it was perhaps fitting that the first changes were driven by that body.[14]

Designing a "nursery" in Paris

In August 1762, four months after expelling the Jesuits from Paris, the Parlement took up two important questions concerning the *collèges* within its jurisdiction. First, on 6 August, they called for the execution of earlier orders for non-Jesuits to take over teaching responsibilities at thirty-eight *collèges*, and for municipal authorities to assume oversight of thirty-seven of those thirty-eight, thereby granting to those authorities the right and responsibility to obtain teachers (as royal property, the *collège* at La Flèche had to await royal action).[15] Later in the month, the Parlement took up the question of what to do with the Collège de Lisieux, a University of Paris affiliate that had not been run by a religious order but needed a new site because it was being displaced by the church of Saint-Geneviève. On 7 September 1762, the Parlement ordered that the *collège* be moved into the vacant buildings of the formerly Jesuit Collège Louis-le-Grand and that Louis-le-Grand be re-established as the principal *collège* of the University of Paris. In so doing, the *parlementaires* indicated that the post-Jesuit reforms would include institutions that had not been run by the Jesuits and that they might aim at something grander than merely compensating for the absent order. These seemed to represent a first step towards reimagining secondary education in France.[16]

During this initial flurry of activity by the Parlement, the royal administration did little. Louis XV's government did not intervene until 2 February 1763, when it issued what has become known as the "February Edict." In this edict, the royal government presented the preservation of knowledge and the improvement of education as important projects, describing them as among "the most solid and durable foundations of the State's prosperity."[17] The edict noted that these were projects to which many had contributed, but also that they were fundamentally dependent upon the will of the monarchy. Despite its praise for religious, municipal, and academic authorities, the February Edict presented not just the success but the very existence of educational institutions as a result of royal *bienfaisance*, claiming that "without the consent of kings" – Louis XV's or that of his predecessors – "no schools could be established within the kingdom."[18] In at least this sense, then, the February Edict seemed to represent an aggressive "act of centralization" by the Crown.[19]

And yet the nature of this centralization was unclear. Louis XV ordered that control over all *collèges* not administered by a religious order or affiliated with a university be made uniform under the authority of local boards, thereby undercutting the Parlement's earlier decision to grant control of those institutions to municipal authorities.[20] These boards would consist of the city's archbishop or bishop, the Court's president and attorney general, two municipal officials, two local notables, and the principal of the *collège*, and they would be responsible for the hiring and firing of teachers (except for professors of Theology, who would be chosen by their ecclesiastical superiors), and also for the day-to-day regulations, disciplinary measures, and financial administration of the schools.[21] The February Edict overruled the Parlement of Paris, side-stepped the municipal authorities to which the Parlement had entrusted the *collèges*, and called for a uniform system of educational administration. But it did not describe or establish a nationally centralized set of administrative rules or regulations and, as Jean Morange and Jean-François Chassaing point out, the system it created was one in which "neither the Church nor the King were particularly well represented."[22] Despite the claims of royal primacy and the rhetoric of centralized authority, the monarchy's first important intervention into the post-expulsion reform of education failed to indicate clear lines of political oversight or to establish a set of administrative principles and practical guidelines for the local boards to follow.

Conflicting proposals regarding oversight of the ex-Jesuit *collèges* notwithstanding, there were important points of convergence in the efforts undertaken by the Parlement and those outlined in the February Edict. This is particularly true with respect to Collège Louis-le-Grand, in which both the royal and parlementary authorities invested a great deal – both materially and symbolically – as a model and centerpiece for post-Jesuit reform.[23] The exceptional status of this *collège* was made clear in a parlementary commission's report of 12 November 1763 and in letters patent issued by Louis XV nine days later. These letters patent, which Charles Bailey describes as "surely the most important royal action on a single college in the eighteenth century," made Louis-le-Grand the focal point of the "education question" by establishing it as the central institution of the University of Paris, supporting it with a royal foundation, and declaring that its purpose was to provide both instructors and a model for *collèges* across France.[24] The royal instruction drew both directly and explicitly upon the parlementary report, and it represents the high point of royal–parlementary cooperation in the post-expulsion reform of education in France. To better understand the nature of that cooperation, we start then with the parlementary commission and its plan for reform.

On 4 February 1763, two days after receiving the February Edict, the Parlement of Paris established two commissions to prepare for the reform of the *collèges de non-plein exercice* under its jurisdiction. The first commission, composed of the rector of the University of Paris and five of his predecessors, was asked to examine the titles, accounts, and endowments of those *collèges* over the previous twenty years.[25] The second commission, composed of the anti-Jesuit and would-be financial reformer Pierre Philippe Roussel de la Tour, the Jansenist and soon-to-be Controller-General of Finances Clément-Charles-François de L'Averdy, and Barthélemy-Gabriel Rolland d'Erceville (whose *Compte rendu* will be discussed below), was asked to review the accounts and to present recommendations for reforming the *collèges*.

On 12 November, L'Averdy presented the report of this second committee, proposing that the *collèges de non-plein exercice* and their respective *bourses* be brought together and consolidated within Collège Louis-le-Grand.[26] He claimed that this plan promised a more efficient and more effective use of financial and institutional resources, a more manageable and more easily maintained administrative structure, and an improved education for students. L'Averdy's arguments made clear that these efforts were imagined as steps towards the wholesale reform of education in France, a prospect that seemed to follow from three key benefits promised by the proposed reorganization. Broadly speaking, these were an improved educational regimen, better financial organization (and so more operational *bourses*), and a long-term process of diffusion that promised both improvement and uniformity across France. By providing an improved education to an increased number of *boursiers*, the new *collège* could serve as a "nursery of masters for both Paris and the provinces," allowing the shared experiences and standards of the "nursery" to become normative for institutions across France.[27] Over time, L'Averdy hoped that this would improve schools across the country and lead people to "prefer the education offered by seculars to that offered by [religious] communities or congregations," thereby ensuring the success of a simultaneously secular and national system of education.[28]

L'Averdy's arguments were repeated almost verbatim in the 21 November letters patent. While this is not entirely surprising, given that L'Averdy was among those who helped draft these letters patent, it does indicate a considerable degree of influence for the parlementary commissioners. Indeed, the collaborative and cooperative nature of the process was emphasized in the letters patent: "We [the royal government] have determined to pursue this arrangement after having viewed the opinions of the most capable members of the University [of Paris], as well as those of the Parlement, who have, under our authority, reviewed this matter and regard this reorganization as the only means by which to reform the abuses which have crept into the *collèges* and to make the *bourses* of those *collèges* truly useful to the State."[29]

Like the report, these letters patent were presented as part of an initiative to reform and improve secondary education across France. They reaffirmed Louis-le-Grand's status as a model to which others should look when working towards the "reform or perfection of the *collèges de plein exercice* of the University and of the entire Kingdom."[30] More than just a model though, Louis-le-Grand would serve as an "abundant nursery" providing the "masters needed by the State."[31] The reform of Louis-le-Grand was presented as a means by which to simultaneously complete and compensate for the expulsion of the Jesuits and, at least implicitly, seemed to indicate the monarchy's desire to break French education's dependence upon religious orders.

This sense of the government's plan, and Louis-le-Grand's role in realizing that plan, was reinforced with the establishment of the *agrégation* in May 1766. In the accompanying letters patent, Louis XV called for royal subsidies to support sixty *docteurs agréges* during a year-long course of study at Louis-le-Grand, after which they would spend an additional two years as assistants in the Faculty of Arts at the University of Paris.[32] Open to *maîtres-ès-Arts* from any French university, but closed to Regulars, the *agrégation* gave institutional force to L'Averdy's call for a national and secular approach to the problems created by the Jesuits' expulsion. And so, when the first *concours* opened on 11 October 1766, it seemed that the contours of a post-Jesuit program for educational reform had not only taken shape, but had started to bear fruit.[33]

The ambitions driving the reform of Louis-le-Grand and the establishment of the *agrégation* appeared far-reaching, though the benefits could only be realized over time. This delay made local authorities wary of embracing or relying upon these reforms, doubting that they would produce enough instructors. (As it turns out, they were right to be skeptical; the *agrégation* produced only 200 *agrégés* between 1766 and the outbreak of the Revolution in 1789.)[34] The delay has also contributed to the view among historians that the reforms of the 1760s were a lost opportunity, a cooperative and generally sound undertaking cut short and left "incomplete" by the political turmoil of the "Maupeou Revolution."[35] And yet, important as these reforms were, Louis-le-Grand was but one *collège*; similarly, while the *agrégation* was national in its ambitions, it was quite limited in its immediate reach. By contrast, the problems that followed from the Jesuits' expulsion were both national and pressing. Any adequate response to these problems would have to be more immediate, more emphatically national, and more ambitious in its identification, recruitment, training, and installation of instructors.

Realizing such a program would have required articulating and enacting a national system of education, establishing clearly who would oversee and administer schools across France, settling on who could and who could not serve as instructors in those schools, and defining for whom the schools were intended and what sort of education those pupils would receive. There were proposals on each of these points, but none of them were pursued in any concerted or consistent fashion, and while the reforms of 1762–66 were transformative for Louis-le-Grand and for the University of Paris, they were clearly inadequate as a response to the broader problems and opportunities that followed from the Jesuits' expulsion. The incongruous fit of the problem's scale, the ambition of the language in which the reforms were couched, and the relative modesty of the steps actually taken suggest that the reforms of the 1760s were not the incomplete result of cooperation, but an imperfect compromise fashioned in and for a divided and uncertain polity.

Competing voices and a chimerical consensus

The specious nature of the post-expulsion consensus becomes clear if we re-examine the proposals for reform offered by Louis-René de Caradeuc de La Chalotais, Louis-Bernard Guyton de Morveau, and Barthélemy-Gabriel Rolland d'Erceville, proposals that are often drawn upon to illustrate the harmony and unanimity of the post-expulsion debates.[36] While these authors agreed on many points, their proposals differed in fundamentally important ways. The points on which they disagreed were at the heart of the political debates of the 1760s and 1770s including, ultimately, the nature, purpose, and power of the French state.

That their differences should reveal competing views of the state is particularly important because each of the three was involved and influential in politics. La Chalotais was the royal attorney at the Parlement of Brittany, Guyton de Morveau was a member of the Parlement of Burgundy, and Rolland d'Erceville was President of the Parlement of Paris, a member of the parlementary commission discussed above, and, subsequently, a member of the *Bureau d'Administration* at Collège Louis-le-Grand. Because of these political roles, each of the three approached education as an issue that was at once philosophical, pedagogical, and political. La Chalotais, Rolland d'Erceville, and Guyton de Morveau recognized that how one addressed the question of "national education" would depend upon, and reveal, deeper social, political, and cultural commitments, and their works reinforced the interweaving of political and pedagogical concerns that had been taking place over the preceding generation. In their proposals we see three different views of the French state and three very different visions of French society, suggesting that the path forward for reform was far less clear than we might imagine it to have been and that the philosophical and political crises of the 1760s ran deeper than we have supposed.

While they agreed about many points of pedagogy and curriculum (emphasizing instruction in French rather than Latin, the importance of the sciences and mathematics, etc.), the views of French society and the French polity offered by La Chalotais, Guyton de Morveau, and Rolland d'Erceville differed in important and irreconcilable ways. This is perhaps clearest in their proposals for political oversight and authority over the schools: where La Chalotais proposed a robust system of monarchical oversight, including the formation of a royal commission responsible for the design and implementation of standardized practices across French *collèges*, Rolland proposed a system in which academic institutions were largely free from political interference, operating as an independent scholarly system under the symbolic but distant authority of the crown.[37] Guyton de Morveau rejected even the fig leaf of royal oversight, arguing that the monarchy had historically delegated oversight of the universities and *collèges* to the Estates-General which had, in turn, passed the responsibility on to the parlements.[38] Presented after the letters patent of November 1763, this invocation of the *thèse parlementaire* was a direct challenge to the monarchy's stated position and to the assumptions underlying proposals like those of La Chalotais and Rolland d'Erceville.[39]

These disagreements about oversight of the schools reflect deeper divisions in their views of French society, the French nation, and education's role as a point of contact among the populations and institutions that comprised the French polity. This is unsurprising given the reach attributed to education and educational institutions in eighteenth-century thought, but it is not for that any less remarkable, and La Chalotais, Rolland d'Erceville, and Guyton de Morveau offer three very different views of how, and to what end, the schools might shape the social, political, and economic future of France.

La Chalotais's *Essai* is structured around what Chartier and Julia call a "mercantilist" logic of education, one in which the social and personal benefits of education are finite and the expansion of educational opportunity dilutes or diminishes the benefits that each student can expect to obtain.[40] This logic was evident in La Chalotais's call for Louis XV to simultaneously reform and limit education, arguing for better but fewer schools offering a more useful education to a smaller pool of students. The goal was a system in which "each citizen [was] content enough with his lot to never feel forced to leave it."[41] Looking beyond social or professional hierarchy, this view seemed to reject the idea that schools might be used to inculcate a more coherent or uniform national culture. For La Chalotais, "nationalization" was a question of authority and uniformity rather than character and qualities. This led him, despite the virulent anti-Jesuitism and the anti-monasticism he expressed elsewhere, and despite a general preference for lay instructors, to embrace a pragmatists' indifference about the identity of teachers as long as a sufficient number with good morals could be found and put in classrooms and so long as political authorities determined which texts they used when teaching (the texts serving as a guarantee of the substance, if not style, of education).[42] On these conditions, he argued that Regulars, Seculars, and laymen should all be allowed to teach but, again, they should do so under the relatively direct supervision of royally appointed authorities.[43]

Guyton de Morveau broke from La Chalotais on both the social and civic premises of reform. Guyton described society as an aggregate of productive individuals who had interests both particular and shared, each of whom could make claims upon the resources and institutions of the state.[44] This was evident, among other places, in his proposal that each *collège* have a professor lecture to the general public on agricultural practices so that scholars might "work together with citizens of all social orders" and, in so doing, contribute to a "happy revolution" in the morals and lives of the people.[45] Looking beyond economic development, he also embraced the schools as incubators of a national community and, with that, identified instructors as de facto embodiments of the national character. He warned that it would "always [be] dangerous to hand over the *collèges* to Regulars" and, presenting the dispute over who should teach as a question of national identity, stressed that the choice was between those who were of the nation and those (i.e. Regulars) who were not.[46] He writes:

> for the good of the Nation, for the tranquility and strength of its constitution, who ought we to have as the authorities in the public schools: citizens born in the country in which they live, brought to patriotism by their sense of themselves as sons, as parents, as spouses, as fathers, attached to their place by both glory and interest ... or, a body of men isolated from the State, recruited from all over the world, devoted to a foreign power, subject to another discipline, dedicated to a life in which their adaptation to the religious spirit renders them incapable of adapting to the spirit of society?[47]

Turning schools over to Regulars would "introduce a contrast between the morals of the schools and the morals of the world, a contradiction that destroys every advantage of education, at least for those who are not called to the monastic life, which is the vast majority."[48] For Guyton de Morveau, the "advantages of education" were to be realized in the rejuvenation of civil society, in the development of affective bonds among the citizenry, and in the emergence of a French national character that was simultaneously molded and modeled by instructors who were bound to the state and to the nation by reason and by sentiment.

Writing several years later, Rolland d'Erceville declined to weigh in on whether there is an inherent incompatibility between membership in a religious order and the responsibilities of teaching in a national system of education. In fact, he claimed that the issue had been exhausted by La Chalotais and Guyton.[49] He did, however, endorse an expansive model of national education designed to serve the interests of the state (rather than those of the populace or of a narrowly circumscribed elite). He proposed a vast expansion of primary instruction, hoping that universal education might permit the government to cultivate talented students as future servants of the state and to reinforce the loyalty and obedience of even those who did not continue beyond the first years of schooling.[50] With this, Rolland thought that the monarchy might secure for itself a more efficient administration and a more devoted populace, making the work of governing easier on all fronts.

Of course, establishing a national system of primary instruction would require a national system for recruiting, training, and certifying instructors, and Rolland thought here that an expanded version of the *agrégation* might allow the monarchy to realize the ambitions it had supposedly embraced in the letters patents of November 1763 and in the reforms of 1766.[51] By the time he revised his manuscript in the years after the Maupeou Revolution, Rolland had come to regret the limited scope of the post-expulsion gestures towards nationalization. He was, it seems, among the first to identify the reforms of the 1760s as an incomplete endeavor and a missed opportunity.[52]

But Rolland's was an improbable plan. Questions about how to recruit, train, and retain a sufficient number of suitable instructors, like disputes over which political authority could legitimately oversee and administer the *collèges*, were among the most materially pressing and politically charged issues of the post-expulsion debates. As La Chalotais noted of the debate over who might be suitable (and unsuitable) as instructors: attempts to answer such questions in any definitive sense "would open the door to innumerable discussions ... [and] the debate would become interminable."[53] He was right, as these questions embroiled the debates over education in controversies over the relative powers of the monarchy and parlements and over the relationship between Church and State, controversies that had given rise to spectacular political conflicts and debilitating political standoffs in the 1750s, as they would again in the 1770s.

Expanding the reforms pursued in Paris to the rest of France would require either resolving those controversies or finding a way to circumvent them, a prospect that raises serious doubts about whether such an expansion was at all plausible. It seems more reasonable to suppose that the reforms of the 1760s remained "incomplete" because there was no path by which to implement them across France without enveloping the country in a renewed bout of controversy and conflict. The post-expulsion debates had revealed a paralyzing crisis in Louis XV's kingdom.

Physiocracy and the logic of political and pedagogical reform

Even before Rolland had published his lament that the reforms of the 1760s had not gone further, the landscape of pedagogical and political reform had been transformed in fundamental and revealing ways. The political turmoil that roiled the first years of the 1770s (and the last years of Louis XV's reign) shattered even the pretense that parlementary and royal authorities would cooperate to design a national system of education. This was evident in the crown's decision to return an increasing number of formerly Jesuit *collèges* to religious orders (and so abandon the processes of secularization and nationalization associated with the *agrégation*).[54] These years, and the fight over the so-called "Maupeou Revolution," also focused attention on the role of "public opinion" in French politics, contributing to a more immediately and more explicitly political tenor in the debates over education.[55] By the time Louis XVI succeeded his grandfather in 1774, it seemed that both the schools and the state were in crisis, and that each would need to be reimagined *in toto* for reform to succeed.

The sense of crisis, and the intermingling of pedagogical and political concerns, was particularly evident in the famous *Mémoire sur les municipalités* presented to Louis XVI by his Controller-General of Finances, Anne-Robert Jacques Turgot.[56] Written for Turgot by Pierre-Samuel Dupont de Nemours, the *Mémoire sur les municipalités* sought to provide Louis XVI with a roadmap for the start of his reign, including a plan for new administrative institutions that would allow him to escape the political controversies that had marked his grandfather's last years as king. It laid out an ambitious agenda for reimagining and redesigning the political infrastructure of Ancien Régime France, and Manuela Albertone is surely right when she notes that the *Mémoire* represents "one of the most significant moments in the French debate over political representation before the Revolution."[57]

Dupont de Nemours and Turgot offered Louis XVI a bleak assessment of the polity over which he was to reign: "The cause of [the present] ill,

Sire, goes back to the fact that your nation lacks a constitution. It is a society composed of different, poorly united orders, a people who have but few social bonds uniting them."[58] As Keith Baker points out, it was not a matter of "resorting to claims for a traditional constitution" but "on the contrary ... recogniz[ing] that the French monarchy quite simply lacked a constitution – lacked, that is, a regular and orderly structure – and had to be reconstituted in such a way as to make government simpler, more responsive to the needs of the people, and more effective in tapping the resources of society at large for the public welfare."[59]

According to Dupont de Nemours and Turgot, the lack of a constitution had led to significant problems for the French state not only in its ability to govern, but in its ability to govern legitimately, for without a constitution the king's authority had to be imposed in order for the state to accomplish even the most basic tasks. The need to deploy royal authority so often and so widely led to a virtual "state of war" between the king and his subjects, particularly on issues of taxation:

> [People] regard the exercise of royal authority for the collection of taxes that should serve to maintain the public order ... as something to which they must submit simply because they lack the strength to resist, and as something they would evade, should they discover a means by which to do so. Each searches to deny and to dodge their social obligations. Thus, the revenues to be collected cannot be discovered but imperfectly, and only by a sort of inquisition in which ... Your Majesty is at war with his own people. And in a war such as this ... nobody has an interest in the government's success ... There exists no public spirit, since people neither see nor know their common interest.[60]

Lacking a constitution, and governing a population unaware of its common interests, Louis XVI had only force, whether physical or legislative, upon which to draw.

In typically Physiocratic fashion, the remedy that Turgot and Dupont de Nemours identified for this absence of "public spirit" was to make known and to activate the general laws that govern society.[61] This involved two distinct but intimately related measures: first, the institutional reformation and reconstitution of the French government; second, the creation of a vast system of public education. The reformation of political institutions was intended to "create a decentralized administrative system for France" that would serve as a sort of "school of political participation, and, [at the same time,] give a constitution to France."[62] Political assemblies would give citizens a purposeful role to play as members of a larger political collective; a new system of education would ensure that citizens had the knowledge and skills necessary to participate in those assemblies. Together, they would prepare and enable citizens to meaningfully "exercise their right of [political] representation," leading them to see the national community in themselves and their neighbors, to recognize the harmonious relationship between their private and collective interests.[63] The result would be a sense of "public spirit" ensuring that widespread participation in local, regional, and national assemblies strengthened French society and worked to the benefit of Louis XVI's state.[64] Reform of the political and pedagogical orders thus went together; indeed, for Dupont de Nemours and Turgot, neither education nor political representation would be sufficient or, in a broader sense, possible, without the other.

Their proposal offered an echo of, and response to, Duclos's claim from twenty-five years earlier that French education failed to "form men" because it did not prepare them for civil society. Dupont de Nemous and Turgot complained that while there were well-established "methods and institutions for training geometricians, doctors, and painters, there [were] none for forming citizens."[65] To remedy this they proposed a Council of National Instruction to establish and maintain a uniform system of education in schools across the kingdom. This council, which would operate "in the public eye" and organize the schools "according to uniform principles," was to oversee the academies, universities, *collèges*, and *petites écoles* – that is, all levels of French education – and would make education accessible to everybody, down even to the "*dernières classes*."[66] It would aim to give French schools a common purpose and pedagogy, stipulating which texts were used and the order in which they were read. Over time, they aimed to elevate the "national tone," make the people "educated and virtuous," and instill in each student "the principles of humanity, of justice, of kindness, and of love for the State."[67] Ultimately, their goal was to produce "among all classes of society, men who were virtuous and productive, [who had] just souls and pure hearts, and who were zealous citizens."[68] It was, in short, to create a civically minded populace.

The education they proposed would extend beyond the classroom. In keeping with their emphasis on preparing the people for participation in political institutions, Dupont de Nemours and Turgot noted that the new political assemblies would also serve an educative function. While perhaps not terribly effective for educating children, the assemblies would "accustom [citizens] to occupying themselves with important and useful tasks, to participating in discussions over the means by which to create equality among families, and to intelligently and profitably administering and improving their districts... [ultimately] making them into sensible men."[69] The meetings of the assemblies would help to create bonds among families living in the same town or village, among neighboring villages, and among the various regions of France, familiarizing the people with the nation and making them more sympathetic to the needs and interests of their fellow citizens. Both in the classroom and beyond, the population would receive instruction in the individual's responsibilities "as a citizen, as a member of a family, and as a member of the State."[70] With that, Louis XVI's France might take on a civic, if not a written, constitution, and the work of "forming citizens" could begin.

Dupont de Nemours and Turgot argued that such a transformation – both in individuals and in the national tone – could be achieved in approximately ten years, when the first children to receive this education would enter society. These young adults would have an "informed zeal for [public] service and for their country ... [they] would submit to authority not out of fear, but out of reason, would support their fellow-citizens, and would recognize and respect justice, the primary foundation of any society."[71] The first cohort would both foreshadow and model the transformation of the French people. They would enter society as promissory representatives of a public that could participate in politics, adjudicate political disputes, and sustain the national community through good times and bad.

The ambivalent and uncertain legacy of the Ancien Régime

The *Mémoire sur les municipalités* illustrates clearly the social and political force attributed to education in eighteenth-century thought. That the Physiocrats' proposal had no demonstrable effect on the political or pedagogical policies of Louis XVI's government is an unsurprising reflection of the state of the "education question" during the last years of the Ancien Régime. Educational reform required a coherent and plausible vision for France's political future; whatever consensus there may have been on matters of curriculum or administration fell apart when this vision was required, when the consequences of reform were considered. Indeed, many who agreed with the Physiocratic premise – that public instruction and the public's participation in politics were related – arrived at radically different conclusions about what ought to be done. These commentators argued that instead of using an expanded system of education to prepare the people for politics, the best course was to limit both, to limit the people's education in order to limit their access to politics. For example, in his *Vues patriotiques sur l'éducation du peuple* (1783), Louis Philipon de la Madelaine distinguished between the sort of education that could – and should – be offered to "the people," and that which should not. After arguing that the people should, of course, be educated ("only imposters and tyrants would say otherwise"), Philipon clarified his position:

> I argue that the people ought to be educated, if by that one means they should learn those things which might have an influence upon their wellbeing, steer their souls towards virtue, and train their bodies for the different professions appropriate to them ...
> But if by "educating" the people one means instructing them in languages, in the sciences, in letters, or the *beaux arts*, then they should keep away from the people: ignorance is preferable. I know of no weapon more dangerous that could be put in the hands of the people.[72]

Because the people were obliged to do manual labor to make a living, physicality had become their "essential characteristic"; one could only do them harm by distracting them with a "taste for enlightenment" and "love of science," leading them to divide their time between labor and study or, worse still, inspiring in them a desire to abandon their manual labor altogether. Instead, people should be taught "that their suffering and obedience were in accordance with the Divine Will."[73] He made clear that obedience was the primary purpose at which he aimed, arguing that the state ought to take an interest in the education of the people for fear of the consequences that attend ignorance: "if one thinks of revolutions, it is the people who bring them about; it is the people who have nothing to lose, and so will risk everything."[74] Only a carefully crafted and narrowly circumscribed program of popular education could prevent this sort of dangerous politicization of the people.

Philipon de la Madelaine was by no means alone in so arguing. There were many who argued, whether during the 1760s (such as La Chalotais, or, for that matter, Voltaire) or, after the years of the Maupeou Revolution and through the 1780s (including Jacques Necker), that educating the poor was only worthwhile insofar as it kept them from disrupting the social or political order or from trying to intervene in political affairs.[75] Indeed, in 1781 Goyon d'Arzac won the essay contest announced four years earlier by the Académie des Sciences, Arts et Belles-Lettres in Châlons-sur-Marne and noted at the start of the Introduction – which asked contestants to specify the "best plan of education for the people" – having submitted an essay that warned about the dangers that followed from teaching the *bas peuple* to read and write (though here the awarding commissioner took issue with Goyon's argument, noting the importance of literacy for instructing the people in their duties and obligations).[76] As Desgalois de la Tour, president of the Parlement in Aix and *intendant* in Provence, put it in 1782, "I have always found that [schools] have no purpose in the villages. A peasant who can read and write gives up his agricultural work to learn or practice some profession, which is certainly for the worse."[77] When extended beyond the conservative tasks of strengthening religious sentiment, reinforcing social hierarchies, and inculcating reverence for the monarchy and political authorities, education threatened to disrupt the social and political order. So these commentators feared. And so some others hoped, at least to a point.

The years that followed would wildly surpass the fears and hopes of the Ancien Régime commentators who thought education might be used to reform or reimagine French society and the French state. With the outbreak of the French Revolution, Helvétius's "salutary crisis" seemed to have arrived as the collapse of the Ancien Régime forced people to reconsider what was possible, what was practical, and what was necessary in French politics. Unsurprisingly, then, the coming of the Revolution gave rise to a rejuvenated debate over education and an ambitious rethinking of the relationship among the schools, the people, and the state. All of a sudden the question was not whether or not politics and education would be reformed, but what sort of education might the new politics require, and to what sort of political and social order might a new education give rise?

Notes

1 This inclination was by no means universal. See Morange and Chassaing, *Mouvement de réforme de l'enseignement en France*, 72–77. On the expulsion of the Jesuits more broadly, see John McManners, *Church and Society in Eighteenth-Century France*, vol. 2: *The Religion of the People and the Politics of Religion* (New York, NY: Clarendon Press, 1998), 530–561.
2 McManners, *Church and Society in Eighteenth-Century France*, vol. 2, 509; slightly different figures are given in Chartier, Compère, and Julia, *L'Éducation en France du XVIe au XVIIIe siècle*, 188; and Palmer, *The Improvement of Humanity*, 45, which estimate that the Jesuits controlled 105 *collèges* prior to their expulsion. On the evolution from logistical problems to a wide-ranging

debate, see Dominique Julia, *Les Trois Couleurs du tableau noir: La Révolution* (Paris: Éditions Belin, 1981), 125, and Viguerie, *L'Institution des enfants*, 68.

3 Palmer, *The Improvement of Humanity*, 62–64; Dominique Julia, "Les Professeurs, l'église et l'état après l'expulsion des Jésuites, 1762–1789," in Baker and Harrigan (eds), *The Making of Frenchmen*, 459–460; Chisick, *The Limits of Reform in the Enlightenment*, 42.

4 Chartier, Compère, Julia, *L'Éducation en France du XVIe au XVIIIe siècle*, 188.

5 Chisick, *The Limits of Reform in the Enlightenment*, 42.

6 This view of controversy is described in Israel, *Enlightenment Contested*, 23–25. For the "crisis of confidence" that roiled France after the Seven Years War, see James C. Riley, *The Seven Years War and the Old Regime in France: The Economic and Financial Toll* (Princeton, NJ: Princeton University Press, 1986), 192–222.

7 Chartier, Compère, Julia, *L'Éducation en France du XVIe au XVIIIe siècle*, 208.

8 Gill, *Educational Philosophy in the French Enlightenment*, 229.

9 Chartier, Compère, Julia, *L'Éducation en France du XVIe au XVIIIe siècle*, 208, 214.

10 Julian Swann, "Politics: Louis XV" in William Doyle (ed.), *Old Regime France, 1648–1788* (New York, NY: Oxford University Press, 2001), 216.

11 Adrian O'Connor, "From the classroom out: educational reform and the state in France, 1762–1771," *French Historical Studies*, 39:3 (2016): 509–534.

12 This view of "crisis" is presented by Reinhart Koselleck, "Crisis," trans. Michaela W. Richter, *Journal of the History of Ideas*, 67:2 (2006), esp. 358.

13 Gontard, *L'Enseignement primaire en France*, 1.

14 Morange and Chassaing, *Le Mouvement de réforme de l'enseignement en France*, 51–56.

15 Bailey, *French Secondary Education*, 5–6.

16 Ibid., 6–7.

17 AN, M/198, no. 4, "Edit du Roi, Portant Règlement pour les Collèges qui ne dépendent pas des Universités. Donné à Versailles au mois de février 1763," (Paris, 1763), 1. See also Bibliothèque de la Sorbonne, Archives de l'Université de Paris (hereafter AUP), Carton 8, folder 8, no. 61, which contains the February Edict and both of the letters patent of 2 February 1763.

18 AN, M/198, no. 4, "Edit du Roi, Portant Règlement pour les Collèges," 2.

19 Viguerie, *L'Institution des enfants*, 88.

20 AN, M/198, no. 4, "Edit du Roi, Portant Règlement pour les Collèges," 3.

21 Ibid., 4, 5. On this, see Morange and Chassaing, *Le Mouvement de réforme de l'enseignement en France*, 58–60.

22 Morange and Chassaing, *Le Mouvement de réforme de l'enseignement en France*, 59.

23 Palmer, *The Improvement of Humanity*, 61–62.

24 Bailey, *French Secondary Education*, 19; the letters patent is available at AN, H/3//2528, no. 5.
25 AN, M/198 no. 6, "Extrait des Registres du Parlement, du 4 fevrier 1763," (Paris, 1763). The results of this review can be found at AN, M/198, no. 41, "Mémoire sur l'administration du Collège de Louis le Grand et Collèges y Réunis, depuis la moment de la réunion, jusqu'au premier janvier 1771," (Paris, 1778), 87-91. The same document is available at AN, H/3//2528, no. 8.
26 AN, M/198, no. 12, "Compte Rendu aux Chambres Assemblées, par M. de L'Averdy, concernant le réunion des Boursiers fondés dans les Colléges de non-plein Exercice sis en la Ville de Paris," 12 November 1763.
27 Ibid., 6, 12, 15.
28 Ibid., 12.
29 AN, H/3//2528, no. 5, "Lettres Patentes du Roi, Pour la translation & établissement dans le collège de Louis le Grand du collège de Lisieux, ainsi que des Boursiers des collèges de Paris où il ne se trouve plus de plein exercice, & du Tribunal, des Archives & des Assemblées de l'Université de Paris; portant règlement pour lesdits objets. Données à Versailles le 21 novembre 1763," (Paris, 1763), 3.
30 Ibid., 3-4.
31 Ibid., 2.
32 AN, M/198 no. 26, "Lettres Patentes du Roi, Concernant l'Emploi du vingt-huitiéme du Bail des Postes & Messageries, relativement à la Faculté des Arts de l'Université de Paris, & portant établissement de Docteurs agrégés dans ladite Faculté. Données à Versailles le 3 mai 1766," (Paris, 1766); Morange and Chassaing, *Le Mouvement de réforme de l'enseignement en France*, 66-67.
33 AUP, Registre 93, "Concours d'agrégation. Procès-Verbaux des séances du jury, 1766"; Julia, "Les Professeurs, l'église et l'état après l'expulsion des Jésuites," 460-461.
34 Palmer, *The Improvement of Humanity*, 62-64. For the ways in which local authorities and institutions sought to compensate for the absence of the Jesuits, see Bailey, *French Secondary Education*, 16.
35 The "incompleteness" argument is most clearly presented by Jean Morange in his "bilan de la réforme," Morange and Chassaing, *Le Mouvement de réforme de l'enseignement en France*, 88-89.
36 La Chalotais, *Essai d'éducation nationale*; Louis-Bernard Guyton de Morveau, *Mémoire sur l'éducation publique, avec le prospectus d'un collège, suivant les principes de cet ouvrage* (1764); Barthélemy-Gabriel Rolland d'Erceville, "Compte Rendu aux Chambres assemblées, par M. Rolland, des différens Mémoires envoyés par les Universités sises dans le Ressort de la Cour, en exécution de l'Arrêt des Chambres assemblées, du 3 septembre 1762, relativement au plan d'Étude à suivre dans les Collèges non dépendans des Universités, & à la correspondance à établir entre les Colleges

& Universités. Du 13 mai 1768," in Barthélemy-Gabriel Rolland d'Erceville, *Recueil de plusieurs des ouvrages de M. le président Rolland* (Paris: Chez P.G. Simon & N.H. Nyon, 1783). On their supposed unanimity, see Figeac-Monthus, *Les Enfants de l'Émile*, 22-23; Bailey, *French Secondary Education*, 5; "Guyton de Morveau," in Ferdinand Buisson (ed.), *Nouvelle Dictionnaire de pédagogie et d'instruction publique* (1911), available online at www.inrp.fr/edition-electronique/lodel/dictionnaire-ferdinand-buisson/document.php?id=2840 [accessed April 2017]; Gill, *Educational Philosophy in the French Enlightenment*, 230.

37 La Chalotais, *Essai d'éducation nationale*, 142; Rolland, "Compte rendu," 75; Morange and Chassaing, *Le Mouvement de réforme de l'enseignement en France*, 31-34.
38 Guyton, *Memoire sur l'éducation publique*, 3-5.
39 On the *thèse parlementaire*, see Roger Bickart, *Les Parlements et la notion de la souveraineté nationale au XVIIIe siècle* (Paris: F. Alcan, 1932); Durand Echeverria, *The Maupeou Revolution: A Study in the History of Libertarianism, France, 1770-1774* (Baton Rouge, LA: Louisiana State University Press, 1985); Baker, *Inventing the French Revolution*; David Hudson, "In defense of reform: French government propaganda during the Maupeou Crisis," *French Historical Studies*, 8:1 (1973): 51-76; Van Kley, *The Religious Origins of the French Revolution*, esp. 249-302.
40 Chartier, Compère, Julia, *L'Éducation en France du XVIe au XVIIIe siècle*, 196.
41 La Chalotais, *Essai d'éducation nationale*, 28, 33.
42 Ibid., 143-144. For La Chalotais' general preference for lay instructors, see Ibid., 17-19. For his attacks on the Jesuits, see Louis-René de Caradeuc de La Chalotais, *Compte rendu des Constitutions des Jésuites... les 1, 3, 4, et 5 décembre 1761, en exécution de l'arrêt de la cour du 17 août précédent* (1762); Louis-René de Caradeuc de La Chalotais, *Second Compte rendu sur l'appel comme d'abus des Constitutions des Jésuites... les 21, 22, et 24 mai 1762* (1762).
43 La Chalotais, *Essai d'éducation nationale*, 20.
44 Palmer, *The Improvement of Humanity*, 59.
45 Guyton, *Mémoire sur l'éducation publique*, 273-275.
46 Ibid., 90-91.
47 Ibid., 82-85.
48 Ibid., 90-91.
49 Rolland, "Compte rendu," 34.
50 Ibid., 25.
51 Ibid., 42-43.
52 Ibid., xiii.
53 La Chalotais, *Essai d'éducation nationale*, 143.
54 On the return of the *collèges* to religious orders, see Bailey, *French Secondary*

Education, 15-17; Julia, "Les Professeurs, l'église et l'état après l'expulsion des Jésuites," 479-481.
55 Echeverria, *The Maupeou Revolution*, 24-34; also Hudson, "In defense of reform"; Baker, *Inventing the French Revolution*, 130-152; S. J. Barnett, *The Enlightenment and Religion: The Myths of Modernity* (New York, NY: Manchester University Press, 2003), 164; and Van Kley, *The Religious Origins of the French Revolution*, 250-252.
56 Pierre-Samuel Dupont de Nemours, "Mémoire au Roi, sur les municipalités, sur la hiérarchie qu'on pourrait établir entre elles, et sur les services que le gouvernement en pourrait tirer," in Anne-Robert Jacques Turgot, *Œuvres de Turgot*, T. II (Paris: Guillaumin, 1844), 502-550.
57 Manuela Albertone, "Du Pont de Nemours et l'instruction publique pendant la Révolution: de la science économique à la formation du citoyen," *Revue Francaise d'Histoire des Idées Politique - Les Physiocrates et la Révolution*, 20 (2004), 358.
58 Dupont de Nemours, "Mémoire sur les municipalités," 504.
59 Keith Michael Baker, "French political thought at the accession of Louis XVI," *Journal of Modern History*, 50:2 (1978), 295.
60 Dupont de Nemours, "Mémoire sur les municipalités," 505.
61 Albertone, "Du Pont de Nemours et l'instruction publique pendant la Révolution," 353-354; Manuela Albertone, "Physiocracy," in Alan Charles Kors (ed.), *Encyclopedia of The Enlightenment* (New York, NY: Oxford University Press, 2003), vol. 3, 283-284. For a brief overview of the Physiocrats' approach to education, see also Brunot, *Histoire de la langue Française*, T. VI, 139-144.
62 Albertone, "Dupont de Nemours et l'instruction publique pendant la Révolution," 358.
63 Ibid., 359.
64 Dupont de Nemours, "Mémoire sur les municipalités," 548. On the establishment of local, regional, and national political assembles, see Ibid., 510-523.
65 Ibid., 506. For the commitment to educate people from all levels of society, Ibid., 534.
66 Ibid., 506-507.
67 Ibid., 506-507, 549.
68 Ibid., 507.
69 Ibid., 549.
70 Ibid., 507.
71 Ibid., 508.
72 Louis Philipon de la Madelaine, *Vues Patriotiques sur l'éducation du peuple: Tant des villes que des campagnes* (Lyon: Chez P. Bruyset-Ponthus, 1783), 12-14.
73 Chisick, *The Limits of Reform in the Enlightenment*, 161.
74 Philipon de la Madelaine, *Vues Patriotiques sur l'éducation du peuple*, 8.

75 Chisick, *The Limits of Reform in the Enlightenment*, esp. 158–163.
76 Jeremy L. Caradonna, *The Enlightenment in Practice: Academic Prize Contests and Intellectual Culture in France, 1670–1794* (Ithaca, NY: Cornell University Press, 2012), Appendix F, 498 (available at www.jeremycaradonna.com/Appendix F.pdf [accessed April 2017]); Chisick, *The Limits of Reform in the Enlightenment*, 138–141.
77 Desgalois de la Tour, as quoted by Gontard, *L'Enseignement primaire en France*, 55–56.

3

Public instruction: a new pedagogy for a new politics

> For a young people to be able to relish sound principles of political theory and follow the fundamental rules of statecraft, the effect would have to become the cause; the social spirit, which should be created by ... institutions, would have to preside over their very foundation; and men would have to be before law what they should become by means of law.
>
> Jean-Jacques Rousseau, *The Social Contract*[1]

Before it was overthrown, the French monarchy collapsed.

Bankrupt, the government of Louis XVI was forced to convene the Assembly of Notables in February 1787. One year later, having been unable to convince the Notables to agree to new taxes and a plan for financial reform, the royal government had little choice but to call the Estates-General into session for the first time in 174 years. Unable to control the Estates-General, Louis XVI's government had, after June 1789, to contend with representatives of the Third Estate who had declared themselves the National Assembly and demanded a written constitution. The Bastille fell less than a month later, on 14 July 1789, and the day after that, Louis XVI appeared before the Assembly, describing himself as "one with the nation" and as having "complete trust" in the members of the Assembly, which he then recognized as a legitimate legislative body.[2]

The collapse of the Ancien Régime – both its government and its social order – conditioned the possibilities, expectations, and imaginations of those who sought to stabilize or reimagine French politics and society.[3] It also created a vast conceptual and institutional space in which calls for representative government flourished. During the financial and political crises of 1787–88, "a wide body of the French nation ... began to adopt, articulate, and act on ideas and aspirations for fundamental change in their monarchical government." Particularly prominent were "claims for consent to taxation and participation in government at both the national and provincial levels."[4] Ideas about how and under what circumstances political participation and political representation were legitimate and effective became central to the "revolution" that was taking shape and, as François Furet noted, the politics that ensued was often "a matter of establishing just *who* represented the people, or equality, or the nation."[5]

And yet, what "representative" and "participatory" governance meant remained deeply unclear in the early years of the Revolution. Their meaning took shape, was contested, and changed as the institutions, practices, and norms of revolutionary politics evolved and as citizens and deputies alike navigated the expectations and realities of the new politics.[6] This process was at once philosophical and practical, and citizens and deputies in Versailles, in Paris, and across France worked to design, improvise, and appropriate practices of collective debate and discussion, to harness or expand networks of communication, and to institutionalize forms of political participation that would make effective government both possible and workable.[7] With this, a rapidly evolving version of the "education question" presented itself to the deputies and citizens of revolutionary France.

Representative government and revolutionary pedagogy

The process of defining and establishing a system of representative government seemed to culminate in the review, approval, and presentation of the constitution in August and September 1791. Both the constitution and the process of its production were marked in important ways by tensions and disagreements within the Assembly and between the Assembly and Louis XVI. This remained true even in the months and weeks preceding the constitution's completion, when questions regarding the conditions necessary to serve as an elector, the relationship between the monarchy and the legislature, and even Louis XVI's suitability as king remained contentious and contested. And yet, what emerged was an affirmation of the "controlling principles and fundamental vision" that had shaped the deputies' work for more than two years, the vision of a polity that was "representative, broad-minded, pacific and tolerant."[8] That vision had taken shape between the convocation of the Estates-General and the late summer of 1789, though its translation into constitutional and legislative particulars continued up to (and beyond) the completion of the Constitution.

As the deputies settled the major procedural and constitutional disputes of these early years of the Revolution, the legitimacy and efficacy of their solutions seemed increasingly to rely on an educated populace engaged in active dialogue with the institutions of representative government. The populace would have to simultaneously learn about and navigate the new political institutions; this simultaneity of constitutional design, political education, and political engagement left the deputies to wrestle with the "legislator's dilemma" described by Rousseau (which serves as the epigraph for this chapter): the legitimacy and longevity of the new polity would depend upon the efficacy of institutions they were just then in the process of debating and designing.

In their efforts to preserve a substantive relationship with constituents after rejecting the binding mandate, in the encouragements and protections of political speech and publication presented in the *Declaration of the Rights of Man and Citizen*, and in the design of the suspensive veto, the deputies sought to secure the legitimacy of their representative institutions by creating channels for meaningful engagement with the populace beyond the Assembly's walls.[9] In so doing, they not only shaped expectations about the institutions of the French state, but also about the skills, habits, and behaviors that would be associated with political participation and engaged citizenship.[10] As Rogers Brubaker noted, the revolutionaries were trying to establish a traditionally restricted form of politically active citizenship (associated with Antiquity) as a "general" principle of modern national citizenship.[11] This model of political citizenship, and the system of representative government it was supposed to support and sustain, depended on the social, institutional, and habitual mobilization of learned skills under the protective influence of suitable civic sentiments and social dispositions. It depended on a process of social, political, and cultural "regeneration."[12]

With this, education assumed a central place in the revolutionary project and, like the reorganization of the judiciary and the state's administrative infrastructure, came to be seen as critical to "realizing the goals of the Assembly for the nation ... for ensuring the continuation of its ideals into the future after it had disbanded."[13] This, in turn, spurred new ways of thinking about education and its contribution to politics, giving rise to the idea of "public instruction," a pedagogical ideal in which the skills, habits, and dispositions necessary for participatory and contributive citizenship at once configured and conditioned one another, in which the schools would "participate in the construction of ... democracy."[14] This entailed a critical shift in how one thought about education's purpose and about the relationship between pedagogical and political practices. Education's anticipated role in the reinvention of social relations, cultivation of particular civic sentiments, and establishment of new political habits did not just build upon Ancien Régime precedents, it transcended them. The educational regime that the revolutionaries sought was one that would give citizens the skills needed for active engagement in the political life of the nation, the knowledge required to translate those skills into constructive and legitimate political participation, and the sentiments or dispositions necessary for that participation to sustain and strengthen the bonds of a national community despite the strains of political debate and discord. "Public Instruction" sought not just to train or educate people, but to create a political public.[15]

Imagined as an incubator of political community and an apprenticeship for political activity, the question of public instruction prodded revolutionary legislators to reflect upon the requirements, ambitions, and limitations of revolutionary citizenship. William Sewell, echoing Louis Althusser, notes that the label *citoyen* "'interpellated' Frenchmen as active participants in the sovereign will."[16] This was a social and institutional ambition as well as a rhetorical or ideological one, and it was under these auspices that the schools were supposed to give substance and structure to citizenship, the reform of education promising to institutionalize the new forms of *citoyenneté* emerging from revolutionary thought and practice. Proposals for new curricular emphases and institutional norms reflected views of what citizens might be expected to know or do. Debates over who should attend the schools served as a proxy of sorts for arguments about citizenship and its demographic or social limits. To be included in proposals for education was to be imagined as a potentially active member of the polity; to be excluded – as girls and women routinely were – was to be cast out of the political public. The debates in the National Assembly presented a relatively expansive but clearly circumscribed and conditional view of active citizenship, one that relied upon and reinforced the notion that "citizens" were male, independent, reasonable, patriotic, and social.[17]

At a minimum, participants in the revolutionary debates over education recognized that establishing a public composed of such citizens required the spread of literacy, and so increased attention to primary schools and elementary education.[18] The distinction between those who "could read and produce written matter" and those who could not was critically important to late-eighteenth-century ideas of politics, reinforcing the perceived break between "the people," on the one hand, and "the public," on the other.[19] Where "*le peuple*" was an illiterate, fickle, instinctual, and potentially dangerous mass, "*le public*" was the literate, rational, and legitimate tribunal before which political, cultural, and judicial disputes were to be brought. Malesherbes had described public opinion in the mid-1770s as "independent of all powers and respected by all powers ... the sovereign judge of all the judges of the earth"; it was, in the words of S.-N.-H. Linguet, "that supreme judge to which the most absolute tribunals are subordinated."[20] To create a political system founded on principles of equitable representation and relatively open participation, the revolutionaries had to turn the people into the public, a fundamentally pedagogical undertaking.

There was more than literacy to this undertaking though. There was also the crucial requirement that individuals engage in politics aiming "to promote the general or public good rather than ... their own self-interest and personal gain." As Marisa Linton has argued, the eighteenth century saw the ascendancy of a view "that the possession of virtue entitled people to participate in public life and eventually, by extension, to exercise political rights. By being those of 'virtuous citizens,' that is, moral public-spirited beings, people's voices were legitimised, the people became a moral force with a right to be heard, even before the Revolution of 1789 made them citizens with explicit political rights."[21] This went beyond questions of transparency, honesty, and interest, and included citizens' civic and social "sentiments" ("virtue" was itself considered a sort of sentiment).[22]

As in their views of economics, eighteenth-century political thinkers anticipated that political life would include competing interests and opinions (not least about economics), and they had long worried about how "a modern society based on commercial sociability could hope for a decent, stable community life and political order."[23] Amid the disputes that the revolutionaries recognized would characterize French social, political, and economic life, civic sentiments promised to "connect the individual to the larger relationships in which he or she lived (the society, or the family, or the state)" and so promote the values of a political "public."[24] Those sentiments and skills had, in turn, to be tethered to a set of social and interpersonal habits and customs. Membership in the political public required that citizens learn where and how politics happen (a problem with which the deputies were themselves wrestling), and that they embrace social and political habits conducive to civil and sometimes contestatory exchange. Given these varied but interrelated concerns, the establishment of a pedagogical regime that could cultivate socially ameliorative sentiments, give students specific skills, and prepare them for the social dynamics of a public politics became central to the pursuit of a political order that was at once participatory and representative.

This polyvalent pedagogical ambition transcended the Ancien Régime division between *éducation* and *instruction*, between moral improvement and the acquisition of technical skills or knowledge. While participants in these debates continued to employ the language of *éducation* and *instruction* (most famously Condorcet and, in criticizing Condorcet's proposal, Jean-Paul Rabaut Saint-Étienne, a dispute discussed below), the debates of the revolutionary years show the emergence of a pedagogy and a politics in which this division was less tenable than it had once seemed. Virtue and civic sentiment could not fulfill the demands of citizenship without being grounded in knowledge and mobilized through the public use of skills contributing to the general well-being; the acquisition of skills and knowledge was "monastic" unless oriented towards public utility; social and political engagement was dangerous unless inspired by civic sentiment and bound by constitutional and legislative structures. In short, what the revolutionaries called "public instruction" was an attempt to integrate students' acquisition of technical skills (especially reading, writing, and basic computation), their familiarization with social and political institutions and norms, and their development of politically ameliorative civic sentiments and social dispositions.[25] It was, as many of them remarked, an apprenticeship for political life.

The clearest articulation of this pedagogical ambition came in 1793 when Gilbert Romme, presenting a report on behalf of the National Convention's Committee of Public Instruction, described public instruction as a *"source de lumières & de vertus,"* one that would "include all things which might be said to pertain to instruction as well as all those which might pertain to education." He explained that

> education without instruction can do nothing more than form habits and create prejudices; its march is uncertain and slow, and even with pure intentions, it misunderstands truth ... [education] can be made to direct all of the individual's physical and intellectual forces in the name of error, so distracting him that he mistakes his ignorance for a virtue ... Public instruction is needed to enlighten opinion, and so aid the general will and, by that, improve all of the institutions of society.[26]

While particularly clear, Romme's was by no means the first attempt to synthesize and integrate the acquisition of skills, the development of habits, the cultivation of sentiments, and the establishment of a self-aware "public" that could sustain the new political order. Mirabeau had gestured towards this synthesis in his 1791 work on education (discussed below) when he called for a system of national education that would "found the people's well-being on their virtues, and their virtues on their enlightenment."[27] Others had sought to articulate this new ideal earlier still. Defining this new pedagogy, and then trying to give it institutional and practical expression, was the central problem of the revolutionary debates over education.

This led the deputies, as well as the instructors, administrators, and correspondents whose contributions we will look at in Chapters 5 and 6, to think in new ways about the relationship between pedagogical practices and the promotion of specific social and political dynamics. It led them to rethink the curricular emphases and the institutional infrastructure of the Ancien Régime schools, but also to appropriate and refashion educational tools such as catechisms, festivals, morality tales, theatrical productions, academic prizes, student competitions, songs, and more.[28] Generally associated with the cultural politics of the Convention and of the Year II, the integration of scholarly and civic education was part of the effort to "reconcil[e] civic virtue and individual effort" during the first years of the Revolution as deputies worked to "relieve anxieties about the social implications of the Revolution and … [to] shape the character of the emerging liberal society."[29] Festivals, prizes, competitions, and songs allowed students to demonstrate command of specific skills, familiarity with the documents, principles, and principal events of revolutionary history and politics, and membership in a larger community. Integrating these into a coherent pedagogy that included new curricular emphases and new institutional routines was critically important to how revolutionaries thought education might help to realize a new political order.[30]

Articulating a vision of "public instruction"

As early as July 1789, the constitutional committee had identified the organization of "national and public instruction" as one of its priorities, alongside the organization of the legislative branch of government, the establishment of new administrative structures, the reform of the judiciary, and the restructuring of the military.[31] A similar set of priorities was presented by Nicolas Bergasse on 22 September when he remarked that the deputies ought to focus on the reform of the courts, the creation of the municipalities, the establishment of the provincial assemblies, and the reform of education; these were all, as he put it, institutions with "the particular ability to modify the system of our habits in a direct and immediate manner."[32] What a system of national and public instruction entailed, and what it might aim to do, remained a point of contention though, and deputies' attempts to describe or define such a system offer important insights into how they thought about the new politics.

For some, education's importance stemmed from its power to compel obedience from the people. The Duc de Liancourt, for example, argued on 29 July 1789 that the Assembly should concern itself with popular education to secure from the people "respectful and blind submission to the law, obedience and fealty to the king."[33] This was particularly important in the uncertain circumstances of the Revolution, a point emphasized by the Chevalier de Ricard in his 23 September 1789 speech on the establishment of the National Guard, in which he described education as one among many instruments with which to prevent social discord or disharmony.[34] As Rolland d'Erceville had proposed a generation earlier, these deputies turned to education to create more loyal and obedient subjects.

Moving beyond the inculcation of obedience, Abbé Sieyès called on 12 August 1789 for the *collèges* and other educational institutions to offer instruction in the "elementary principles of legislation and of the constituent rights of the nation." These would be accompanied by lessons in civic morality, history, and the nation's laws, and by theatrical productions, festive celebrations, and the public recognition of "dignified" or "illustrious" citizens as models for others to emulate.[35] Drawing on a range of practices and institutions associated with Ancien Régime education, Sieyès's proposal gestured towards the synthesis of skills, knowledge, habits, and sentiments that would characterize "public instruction."

This approach to political pedagogy became more prominent over the course of 1789 and 1790, and the term "public instruction" was increasingly used to describe a system of education that would prepare students for their future as citizens, give them the knowledge and skills necessary to participate in their political communities, and cultivate the habits and sentiments that would translate the principles of the new political order into the animating spirit of people's social and civic lives.

The synthesis of political and pedagogical ambitions that underwrote Sieyès's proposal was picked up by Honoré de Mirabeau in October 1789, when he sought to incorporate a public festival celebrating "civic inscription" into a larger program of "civic education," one that would help to establish and to promote a dynamic of "civic emulation" among citizens. Marking individuals' admission into the political community, and reaffirming the equality of that community's members, the inscription ceremony was to be at once festive and functional, celebratory and educational. It was also supposed to encourage a spirit of civic emulation and to channel political instincts into constructive behaviors. Presented as part of the debate over the requirements to serve as an elector, Mirabeau's proposal rested on the idea that these festivals were not designed to inculcate blind obedience or docility, but to mark and maintain the conditions that made civic participation sustainable.[36]

Just a few days after Mirabeau presented his proposal for "civic education," Guy-Jean Baptiste Target returned to the intersection of public instruction and political publicity, this time addressing the relationship between education and the efficacy of revolutionary legislation. He described public instruction as "the legislation of [people's] souls," as "enlightening where the law commands," and as a bridge connecting the people and their representatives, a connection that would allow citizens to recognize themselves in the Assembly's work. He also promised that education would enable the people to resist the "seductions" of rumor and intrigue during periods of uncertainty, making the new political order more peaceful and more stable (and, perhaps, relieving some of the anxieties born of the October Days). Pressing the association between the publicness of the new politics and a new system of education, he proposed that the Assembly adopt two articles: the first establishing a committee to prepare, publish, and distribute explanatory pamphlets regarding important pieces of legislation; the second requiring that the members of that committee work with the constitutional committee to prepare and finalize a plan of "national education and public instruction." (The first article would prove contentious, and discussion on Target's proposal was suspended.)[37]

The tangle of political, practical, and pedagogical concerns that characterized "public instruction" was given fuller expression still in a September 1790 motion presented by Pierre-François Gossin, the deputy from Bar-le-Duc most often remembered for his work on the administrative and political reorganization of France and for his arguments supporting the legalization of divorce. Gossin, whose motion was later published as a seven-page pamphlet, stressed the need for a reformed system of education, criticized the institutions and traditions inherited from the Ancien Régime (while trying to draw upon their resources and experience), and emphasized the relationship between the reform of the schools and the success of the constitution. His proposal was shaped by the various ambitions that were coalescing in the ideal of public instruction: the desire to integrate the acquisition of knowledge and skills with the establishment of social dynamics conducive to a harmonious society; the need for schools to be accessible and responsive to the interests of a broader public; and the emphasis on cultivating moral and civic sentiments to animate social and political behaviors.[38]

Gossin criticized the educational institutions and practices of the Ancien Régime on grounds that were both political and pedagogical, but he also sought to preserve and build upon their institutional strengths and resources. He stressed the importance of offering instruction in French rather than Greek or Latin, remarking that people tend to "have more direct ties to the peoples of the present than to those of the distant past," and noting that advances in the sciences and in other fields had made engagement with contemporary works particularly important. At the same time, and like many of his contemporaries, he praised the Ancients as "closer to nature" and saw reasons that their works should "interest us now more than ever," particularly for their insights regarding the relationship between public and private morality and their ability to cultivate people's patriotic sentiments and passion for liberty.[39] A similar ambivalence was clear in his assessment of the University of Paris, which he called on the deputies to reform while taking care to conserve what was good in the institution; he hoped that a reformed university could benefit from its historical prestige, helping to establish the sorts of influence and "correspondence" between Parisian and provincial institutions that had been dreamt of since the establishment of the *agrégation* in the 1760s (he too gave voice to the familiar hope that the "schools of Paris would furnish instructors for all of the kingdom's schools").[40]

Gossin proposed reforming or retaining the existing institutions, but he stressed that the success of these reforms would require a new approach to education. As he put it, "we know well that new laws require new morals, and that it is through education that we can give people the morals that will lead them to respect and to cherish the new regime."[41] Of course, he clarified, the Assembly's work had already accomplished a lot on this front – "the dawn of a more perfect government, a government founded upon the law, has already done much to improve the people's morals" – but he warned that such a change would prove transient "as old habits reestablished their dominion … unless the change was made permanent with an educational system designed for the new constitution."[42] This meant more than a new curriculum and new books; it meant establishing a pedagogical regime in which students' experiences mirrored and prepared them for the sorts of active engagement required by a system of representative government.

Gossin saw this as the existing institutions' most critical shortcoming. He criticized the "beautiful sermons and magnificent lectures" alongside the "dull and ineffective lessons" of the old pedagogical regime, claiming that regardless of how enjoyable (or tiresome) the teaching, what was learned in schools was divorced from what was experienced in life and in political society. He saw the divorce as intentional and nefarious, complaining that "far from offering people the instruction they needed," the Ancien Régime and its schools had proscribed such an education: "to come together with others to discuss political affairs: that was a crime; it was illegal to speak, even to think."[43] The remedy, Gossin thought, was a system in which students learned the "true principles of good government" by practicing them: "if you want students to learn that all men are equal, allow them to live among one another in such a way that their lives preach the truth of that statement, so that everything around them demonstrates that the only real differences among men are those of talent and virtue."[44] Likewise, "one learns the meaning of justice far better through regular practice than through tiresome lectures."[45]

Emphasizing the public nature of public instruction, Gossin sought to incorporate social recognition, civic competition, and communal spaces into his curriculum. Public gatherings supervised by learned citizens would include games in which students competed for acclaim and recognition (from both their classmates and older citizens) as well as performances to reinforce and complement the lessons learned in schools. So too would the new society's laws, "customs, challenges, rewards, games, spectacles, images, public monuments, even the walls next to which people gather to unwind or to distract themselves from their work ... all of these will preach the new constitution."[46] Gossin's pedagogy was deeply grounded in sensationist principles and dependent on the social dynamics of emulation, and he argued that together these would "permanently engrave" the principles of the constitution on people's hearts. While language like this has led scholars to see such proposals as "authoritarian," Gossin saw these elementary lessons as enabling rather than pre-empting political debate, and he emphasized that learning to be a citizen was an active process of habituation and competitive emulation, one that taught students in practical terms what it was like "to live and to conduct themselves according to the principles" of the new constitution.[47] A system of "public instruction" had not only to adhere to those principles, but to reflect and reproduce them; the new educational regime was to be both an instrument and a result of a new political and social regime, and the success of each would depend on how successfully the new political principles could be translated into institutional norms and, ultimately, into the routines of everyday life.

That the new political and social order should be reflected and illustrated in a new system of education is particularly clear in the work of Honoré de Mirabeau, the charismatic and controversial deputy from Aix-en-Provence whose initial proposal for civic education was noted above. Since his death in April 1791, Mirabeau has been many things to many historians: he has been remembered as the *Tribun de l'Assemblée nationale*, as well as a traitor to the French Revolution, a staunch defender of liberty and the rights of man, and a covert collaborator with the forces of reaction, he was immortalized and pantheonized as a revolutionary and a patriot, and made infamous (and de-pantheonized) as a counter-revolutionary and villain. Ever since August 1792, when his secret correspondence with Louis XVI was discovered, the figure of Mirabeau has served as a flash point for polemics about the nature, course, and legitimacy of the French Revolution.[48] For the debates over education, however, he presents a more limited object of study: a posthumously published work that he never presented before the Assembly of which he was such a famous member.

For Mirabeau, the need for new political and pedagogical institutions to complement one another stemmed from the connection each had to public opinion and from their shared challenge: maintaining social cohesion amid interpersonal competition and contestation. This view of education and politics served as the premise for the *Travail sur l'éducation publique trouvé dans les papiers de Mirabeau l'aîné*, published a few months after Mirabeau's death.[49] This work has been overshadowed in histories of education and the Revolution, in part because it seems moderate when compared to proposals presented just one or two years later and in part because, unlike the proposals of Talleyrand, Condorcet, and others, it was never debated in the institutions that dominated revolutionary politics.[50] This is a pity, as Mirabeau's work illustrates well the reorientation of debates over education and their entanglement with revolutionary politics. It offers a clear sense of the interwoven nature of the political and pedagogical reform of France and reflects clearly the emerging paradigm of "public instruction." It is, in short, symptomatic of the concerns, uncertainties, and ambitions that shaped revolutionary politics in 1790 and 1791.

For Mirabeau, the power of education lay in its relationship to public opinion, which he described as both the source of the government's legitimacy and its greatest project; addressing his fellow deputies, he wrote: "after having been the organs of public opinion in establishing the great principles of liberty, [you] must hasten, by the active influence of new laws, to further develop that same opinion."[51] That public opinion could be at once relied upon and perfected was, for Mirabeau, due to the power of the printing press; where the printed word had previously been put to work on behalf of "tyrants and imposters," it would now spread and give force to the "philanthropic laws" emanating from the revolutionary government.[52] Of course, for this to work the people had to be literate, and so it would be the government's responsibility to ensure that every (male) French citizen had an opportunity to learn how to read and write. For Mirabeau, literacy and political legitimacy were inseparable, as were education and active citizenship (a point he reinforced with the proposal of a literacy requirement for active citizenship and upon which he relied in his exclusion of women from his proposed system of education, an exclusion he justified at considerable length and with invocations of natural difference, divine will, and the social division of labor).[53]

Literacy was not sufficient though, and Mirabeau warned his fellow deputies that "the science of liberty is not as simple as it might appear at first glance."[54] While the dissemination of revolutionary legislation and the force of public opinion were crucial to the revolutionary project, their efficacy was dependent on the establishment of social mores and habits that were conducive to liberty and participatory government. "Elevating the souls of the people to the level of [the] constitution" required the simultaneous spread of skills (like literacy), public access to the institutions of government (through the press), and the dynamic interaction of citizens who competed for one another's esteem as members of a national community. In pursuit of this multi-faceted ambition, Mirabeau offered five general principles for educational reform, focusing primarily on questions of political oversight, the need for curricular and institutional changes, and the beneficial effects of competition. While he did not provide the details of a future system of education, these principles offer us a sense of how Mirabeau thought about the new pedagogy and the new politics.

To Mirabeau, the most important of his principles (and the first in his presentation) was that the *collèges* and academies be supervised by departmental authorities, by representatives who were "elected and frequently renewed by [the people]." He warned that no other authority ought to have such a formidable "weapon" at its disposal, as "it is the pen that guides the sword ... and the instructors of children, the philosophers and the writers of all genres who lead nations to liberty, or who lead them into slavery." Legislative supervision promised to bind the members of the academies and the *collèges* to the people (or the representatives of the people), rather than to the executive authority of the monarch or his ministers. He warned that when academicians and professors relied upon the favor of the monarch or his ministers, they tended to serve their patrons' interests rather than those of the public, and so ceased to fulfill education's primary purpose.[55]

Looking beyond this legislative–academic bond, Mirabeau feared that what he considered one of the most desirable reforms was also one of the least likely to be pursued: rescinding the longstanding promise of free education in the *collèges*. While Mirabeau recognized that many people considered this one of the monarchy's kindest acts, he argued that free education undermined the instructor's interest in the quality of his work and the pupils' sense that the education they were receiving was worthwhile. By contrast, a system in which pupils selected and paid their instructors would give instructors a reason to constantly improve their methods and would prevent pupils from abandoning their studies frivolously (having already assumed a financial stake in their completion).[56]

To reinforce this competitive dynamic among instructors, Mirabeau argued against the maintenance of *corps enseignants*, secular or religious. Recognizing the potential utility of retaining the existing instructors, but also the danger that they would bring with them an *esprit de corps* contrary to the new order, Mirabeau argued that members of religious congregations ought not to be prohibited from teaching, but they should not be employed *as* members of those groups.[57] Instead, individual instructors would compete for students, winning public esteem (and attracting additional pupils) as they demonstrated their skill and their students' success or, alternately, revealing their incompetence and finding themselves without students and in search of a new profession. In keeping with a strain of eighteenth-century (and revolutionary) thought that stressed the virtues of unimpeded commercial activity, he called for the establishment of a national marketplace in instruction, a form of "*enseignement libre*" in which "everybody has the right to teach what they know, and even to teach what they do not know."[58] It was the job of the student-consumer to decide upon the value of what they purchased, and so to reward skilled instructors and weed out incompetents.

Building upon his distrust of free education and his faith in competition, Mirabeau argued that government funds and scholarships should be distributed as rewards for work already accomplished or as incentives to encourage continued success from those who had shown promise. He argued against the awarding of scholarships for the first stages of education, as there was no way to identify those who most deserved them at that point (this prohibition was qualified by a later argument that the state ought to pay for the early education of children from families too poor to send them to school; he recognized here that the meritocratic ambitions of his proposal required at least an initial intervention by the state).[59] As students performed well in their studies, scholarships would be awarded as both reward and encouragement.[60]

Mirabeau's competitive hierarchy culminated in his proposal for a *Lycée national*, an "*école encyclopédique*" bringing 100 students together in Paris as a "*jeunesse choisie*" to be trained as an intellectual elite and a source of public enlightenment.[61] Those students would be selected by departmental electors based upon lists of candidates provided by the communes.[62] As with the competition for scholarships, Mirabeau saw this as a goad to emulation and competition among students and, through that, a means by which to improve education all across France. He argued that being selected for the Lycée would win honor and esteem not only for the individual student, but also for that student's town, city, or department, and the resulting competition among aspirants would improve French education as a whole by inspiring communities to encourage more students to attend schools and to ensure that they were being educated as well as possible.[63] As a byproduct of the competition for places at the Lycée, the (male) population of France would be better educated – even those who were not included among this "*jeunesse choisie*."

While competition and social distinction would drive individual students and instructors, Mirabeau also sought to reform the "customs and morals of the nation," to create a national community bound together by a shared culture, a robust patriotism, and a sense of affection for the new political institutions.[64] To achieve this, he returned to his proposal for public festivals as a form of civic education (noted above). He argued that festivals would contribute to national regeneration and to the development of communal and fraternal bonds among the people. They would solidify the gains made by the Revolution by attaching the people to the government through "all of their senses," giving them a visceral and emotional attachment to the new political regime and to one another as fellow citizens.[65]

It was imperative that the revolutionary government mobilize public emotion because, according to Mirabeau, "man more often obeys his sentiments than his reason." He warned the legislators "not to ignore the extraordinary effects that festivals ... can produce among the people" and proposed a series of nine celebrations – four civic in theme, four military, and, finally, "*une grande fête nationale*" (the Fête de la Fédération).[66] For Mirabeau, who knew well the divisions and factions of revolutionary politics, festivals offered a means by which to cultivate citizens' kindest sentiments, nurture their goodwill towards one another, and deepen their love for the country; they would encourage citizens to take pleasure in one another's well-being and to celebrate the achievements of individuals and of the community. Confirming and extending the salutary effects of the new laws, and translating the spirit of those laws into new social customs and habits, Mirabeau's festivals were designed to combine the work of the legislator and the moralist, to establish a political corollary to the affective bonds of domestic life.[67]

Despite historians' claims that Mirabeau's proposal was "timid" and did not "express anything very unusual," the *Travail* is a valuable indication of how much the educational and pedagogical paradigm had shifted in the first years of the Revolution.[68] Mirabeau's work, like the emerging ideal of "public instruction," was not only supposed to prepare students for their future political, social, and civic lives (itself a relatively novel development), it was supposed to do so by reflecting the new order, by being of a kind with the new politics. In Mirabeau's case, this meant minimizing the distance between pedagogical institutions and the economic, social, and political dynamics that were taking shape across France. His pedagogy, like his politics, sought to capitalize on social competition and the emulative effects of meritocratic hierarchy, to harmonize the competitive dynamics of the "market" and the judgments of an informed populace, and to reconcile the interests of individuals, the state, and the national community.

As proposals like Mirabeau's and Gossin's suggest, "public instruction" would come to include a vast pedagogical, institutional, and social landscape.[69] As people came to know the new politics in the classroom and in public, legislators hoped that public instruction would help to preserve the legitimacy of representative institutions, encourage sustainable forms of political participation, and realize the promise of a public politics based upon the consent and will of the populace. These were tremendous ambitions, and the breadth and scope of the revolutionary proposals has no doubt contributed to the view that the deputies' approach to education was utopian, informed by myths and philosophical abstractions and indifferent to the peculiarities and personalities of individuals or groups.[70] And yet, as ambitious (and rhetorically grandiose) as the deputies' proposals were, their objectives were still practical and institutionally focused. Their pedagogical proposals were shaped by the need to articulate the social and political ideals of the Revolution and to translate those ideals into institutional norms and sustainable practices. As in so many arenas of revolutionary politics, the deputies' efforts were complicated by unforeseen developments and by tangentially related decisions or laws, and the conceptual evolution of "public instruction" was accompanied and conditioned by changes in what seemed possible, practicable, or necessary to reform education in revolutionary France.

Legislative developments and evolving expectations

Despite the novelty of their political and social ambitions, the revolutionaries' sense of how one actually went about reforming educational institutions was clearly shaped by the debates of the preceding generation, as were their expectations about how particular reforms would affect the educational system as a whole. The revolutionaries were inverting what had often been the premise of earlier debates – that is, they were attempting to give form and substance to a new social and political order, rather than reform or strengthen an existing one – but they nonetheless understood the institutional dynamics of educational reform in ways that are familiar from the pre-revolutionary debates. As in the earlier debates, the revolutionary "education question" focused on issues of teacher training and certification, political responsibility, authority, and oversight; like their Ancien Régime predecessors, revolutionaries debated who ought to have access to the schools and what they ought to be taught. They too had to consider the appropriate relationship between education and the political or social order, though this time with the latter explicitly in flux.

The familiar nature of these questions initially led some deputies to hope that educational reform would require relatively little, that they could refashion the Ancien Régime institutions without redesigning French education *in toto*. Dupont de Nemours, for example, claimed in September 1789 that the Assembly ought to focus on establishing educational institutions that would serve the poor, as the schools for children from wealthier families needed only "a new system and new books." This optimistic assessment was offered despite his description of the *collèges* as suffering from a "pedantic style of education, one driven by words but devoid of things, offering little that might prove useful to society."[71] By working with the existing institutions to reform themselves, drawing on the resources that those institutions possessed, and capitalizing on the experience and expertise of at least some of the faculty and administrators already in place (he was particularly complimentary of the Oratorians), a system of education appropriate to the new political and social order could be realized in relatively short order. He claimed that the gap between the existing and the necessary educational orders was smaller than some supposed, and that a new social and political climate might mobilize educational virtues that lay just beneath the Ancien Régime surface; indeed, anticipating the assessments of historians like Laurence Brockliss and Alan Kors, Dupont de Nemours argued that the existing institutions offered a more "modern" education than was generally recognized and claimed that "there are enlightened minds to be found even among people accustomed to the convents; enlightenment can penetrate anywhere, including the cloisters."[72]

This sense that the new pedagogical order would require little more than a "new system and new books" did not last long, as expectations regarding what seemed possible or likely were unsettled by laws being passed on other matters. These laws had material and political effects on existing institutions and on the contours of the debate over educational reform. Among the most important of these were the decrees of 4–11 August 1789, the November 1789 nationalization of the lands owned by the *collèges*, the Civil Constitution of the Clergy, and the abolition of corporations. These laws were particularly important because of their implications for two issues that would have to be central to any educational reform: finances and personnel.

On both fronts, laws passed by the National Assembly shaped expectations regarding what the deputies were likely to do in the future, but they brought as much uncertainty as they did clarity, and they complicated efforts to maintain the existing schools while the reform of education was being prepared. For example, the abolition of tithes on 4 August 1789 included the caveat that the abolition of certain tithes – namely those used to support the clergy, to help the poor, to maintain religious buildings, and to support "seminaries, schools, academies, [and] asylums" – was conditional upon the design of an alternate system by which those institutions would be funded. It stipulated that "until such provision shall be made and the former possessors shall enter upon the enjoyment of an income on the new system … the [existing] tithes shall continue to be collected according to law and in the customary manner."[73] But the "customary manner" was increasingly impossible, and even with the suspended execution for educational institutions, the abolition of the tithes made the old system of financing these institutions untenable.

The idea that a new and national system for financing the schools would soon be developed was further encouraged by the Assembly's decision to nationalize the *biens ecclésiastiques* in November 1789, including those lands associated with the schools and hospitals. The plan was to "sell these properties ... to private buyers, and use the funds thus received to pay off the debt and fill up the deficit under which the Bourbon monarchy had collapsed."[74] Such a sale commenced almost immediately. However, because the designation of their lands as *biens nationaux* deprived the *collèges* of one of their traditional forms of income – namely, the rental of those lands – and because the Assembly intended "that the existing colleges should continue to function as in the past, until the adoption of a sweeping educational reform," the sale of the lands associated with the *collèges* was suspended.[75] Control over those lands did not stay with the *collèges* though, but was instead transferred to the national government, to be administered by local authorities. Until a definitive system of education and educational financing could be established, those local authorities would continue to collect the rents and incomes associated with the lands and, from those funds, pay the expenses of the schools. This arrangement led many to expect (wrongly, as it turned out), that the lands formerly owned by the schools would be maintained so that they could serve as the foundation for a national educational endowment. The Assembly encouraged this view as late as 6 June 1792 when it indicated that the Minister of the Interior would provide funds from the national treasury to compensate the *collèges* and universities for revenues lost due to the abolition of tithes and nationalization of properties.[76]

If the abolition of tithes and the nationalization of the schools' lands shaped the debate over funding a new system of education, the Civil Constitution of the Clergy and the abolition of corporations shaped the more overtly political and ideological aspects of the debate, particularly those related to teaching and administrative personnel.

Deciding whether religious orders could be entrusted with schools and, if they could, under what conditions, was crucially important for any potential reform of French education. Because many of the ex-Jesuit *collèges* had been given to other religious orders after 1762 (and even more after 1771), maintaining Regulars as instructors offered institutional stability and access to a pool of experienced instructors. Moreover, as Nigel Aston has pointed out, the clergy represented a particularly well-educated segment of the population and were, by and large, dedicated in their efforts to fulfill the tasks and responsibilities assigned them.[77] Maintaining their place in French education was thus not only a convenient option; it was, for those who defended it, an attractive one. Despite these advantages, the abolition of privilege and the state's assumption of the schools' finances made entrusting education to religious authorities more difficult, as would escalating tensions about the relationship between Church and State.

The situation became more precarious still in February 1790, when the Assembly abolished religious orders and forbade the swearing of monastic vows, but exempted those religious orders or communities devoted to education.[78] As with the question of finances, the deputies found that their long-term hopes for reforming the institutional foundations of French society were complicated by more immediate and more practical pressures. As we will see in Chapter 6, the tension between these led to deep uncertainty among instructors and administrators across France, aggravating the deputies' practical problems and further complicating the design of a national system of public instruction.

Far more dramatic in its effects, the Civil Constitution of the Clergy of summer 1790, and the efforts to enforce the Civil Constitution through the Ecclesiastical Oath in winter and spring of 1790–91, represented a massive escalation in the tensions between the revolutionary state and the French clergy and, with that, in the debates over who would, and who could, teach in the post-reform schools. The requirement that each bishop and priest publicly swear an oath "to be loyal to the nation, the law, and the king, and to support with all his power the constitution decreed by the National Assembly and accepted by the king," divided even supporters of the Revolution, alienated many members of the clergy, and exacerbated a tremendously volatile fault line at the center of revolutionary politics.[79] The punitive requirement that non-juring priests be removed from their public functions – including their classrooms – created widespread uncertainty and then disruption regarding one of the fundamental issues of educational reform. Like the expulsion of the Jesuits almost thirty years earlier, the purge of non-juring priests left an overwhelming number of education-related vacancies and not nearly enough qualified and politically acceptable candidates with which to fill them.

At the same time that the Civil Constitution and clerical oath were upending expectations about who would teach in the schools, the abolition of guilds and of corporations (also in spring 1791) called into question the institutional infrastructure of French education. Inspired by an economic liberalism that viewed corporations as impediments to the functioning of the market, and by a view of political society that saw corporate identities as unnecessary and unwelcome vestiges of the

Ancien Régime's society of orders, the d'Allarde (2–17 March) and Le Chapelier (14–17 June) laws had several important consequences for the debate over education. In addition to their implications for the ongoing debates over the so-called *corps enseignants*, these laws challenged the organizational structure of the institutions inherited from the Ancien Régime, as the academies, universities, and *collèges* were unmistakably corporate entities.[80] Their corporate identities were clear in their histories, in their internal organizations and regulations, and in their distinctive dress, private festivals, and professional privileges, leading some to argue that the academies, universities, and *collèges* were outdated institutions antithetical to the purpose and politics of the Revolution.[81] And yet, the *collèges*, universities, and academies were again exempt from the Assembly's dissolutive works, spared and maintained as the starting point for conversations about public instruction's institutional future.

Dreams that a "new system and new books" might suffice to turn the inherited institutions into suitable instruments of public instruction, as Dupont de Nemours had initially hoped, did not survive long amid these changes to the political, ecclesiastical, economic, and social fabric of French life. Taken together, the abolition of tithes and dissolution of corporations, the nationalization of properties belonging to the schools and the Church, and the disputes surrounding the Civil Constitution and the clerical oath can seem to indicate that the deputies had "embarked on a scheme of destruction, in the hope of apparently being able to start afresh *ab initio*," as H. C. Barnard claimed.[82] Certainly, these laws transforming the legal, political, and religious landscape of France seemed to promise that a reformed system of education would differ considerably and in fundamental ways from its Ancien Régime predecessors. But recognizing this was a far cry from being able to anticipate what the reformed system would actually be like, a distinction made more problematic still by the decrees provisionally conserving the existing schools, instructors (if they had sworn the clerical oath), and curricula that were issued when the academic year was set to commence in October 1790 and, again, in October 1791.[83] Moreover, and more importantly, the "scheme of destruction" is one we have deciphered but not one the deputies consciously or intentionally pursued. They proclaimed a radical rupture in the history of French education, but they remained attuned to practical concerns and interested in preserving as many of the financial, institutional, architectural, and human resources as possible.

This tension between the promise (or threat) of radically different institutional and pedagogical structures, on the one hand, and the provisional maintenance and possible incorporation of the existing institutions and orders, on the other, complicated efforts to imagine the institutional form public instruction might take. But it did not fundamentally alter what public instruction had come to mean. Legislators and citizens across France continued to work towards a pedagogy that integrated the development of those skills, virtues, habits, and dispositions needed to prepare citizens for a participatory and representative brand of politics. Nor did the uncertainty regarding implementation prevent the goal of public instruction from taking hold of the revolutionary debates over education inside the Assembly and across France. By the time the constitution was presented to Louis XVI in September 1791, the establishment of a system of national and public instruction had been enshrined as a constitutional commitment, and recognized as a critical piece of unfinished business.

Notes

1 Jean-Jacques Rousseau, *The Social Contract, Or Principles of Political Right*, trans. G. D. H. Cole (New York, NY: Cosimo Press, 2008), 46–47.
2 J. Mavidal, E. Laurent, and E. Clavel (eds), *Archives parlementaires de 1787 à 1860: Recueil complet des débats législatifs et politiques des Chambres françaises. Première série, 1787 à 1799*. T. 8 (Paris: P. Dupont, 1875), 236, [hereafter *AP*, Tome: page].
3 Peter R. Campbell, "Introduction," in Peter R. Campbell (ed.), *The Origins of the French Revolution* (New York, NY: Palgrave MacMillan, 2006), 1–34; Ran Halévi, "The monarchy and the elections of 1789," *The Journal of Modern History*, 60 (1988), esp. S79-S80.
4 Vivian R. Gruder, *The Notables and the Nation: The Political Schooling of the French, 1787–1788* (Cambridge, MA: Harvard University Press, 2007), 365.
5 François Furet, *Penser la Révolution française* (Paris: Éditions Gallimard, 1978), 84.
6 Timothy Tackett, *Becoming a Revolutionary: The Deputies of the French National Assembly and the Emergence of a Revolutionary Culture (1789–1790)* (Princeton, NJ: Princeton University Press, 1996); Hunt, *Politics, Culture, and Class in the French Revolution*; Susan Maslan, *Revolutionary Acts: Theater, Democracy, and the French Revolution* (Baltimore, MD: Johns Hopkins University Press, 2005), 25–73.
7 Robert H. Blackman, "What does a deputy to the National Assembly owe his constituents? Coming to an agreement on the meaning of electoral mandates in July 1789," *French Historical Studies*, 34:2 (2011): 205–241.
8 Fitzsimmons, *The Remaking of France*, 33–68; 128–136. The quotes come from pp. 132 and 92, respectively.

9 On the binding mandate and efforts to maintain a relationship with constituents, see Tackett, *Becoming a Revolutionary*, 239; Blackman, "What does a deputy to the National Assembly owe his constituents?," 236. On the relationship between an educated populace and the *Declaration of the Rights of Man and Citizen*, see H. C. Barnard, *Education and the French Revolution* (Cambridge: Cambridge University Press, 1969), 57–58; Morange and Chassaing, *Le Mouvement de réforme de l'enseignement en France*, 107. On the suspensive veto as an "appel au peuple," see Marcel Gauchet, *La Révolution des pouvoirs: La Souveraineté, le peuple et la représentation, 1789–1799* (Paris: Gallimard, 1995), 61–79; also Baker, *Inventing the French Revolution*, 274. A far more critical view of this relationship is presented in Paul Friedland, *Political Actors: Representative Bodies and Theatricality in the Age of the French Revolution* (Ithaca, NY: Cornell University Press, 2002), 124–167; Baker, *Inventing the French Revolution*, 224–251.
10 James Livesey, *Making Democracy in the French Revolution* (Cambridge, MA: Harvard University Press, 2001), 179.
11 Brubaker, *Citizenship and Nationhood in France and Germany*, 40–43; William Rogers Brubaker, "The French Revolution and the invention of citizenship," *French Politics and Society*, 7:3 (1989), 36–39.
12 Antoine de Baecque, *Corps de l'histoire: Métaphores et politique (1770–1800)* (Paris: Calmann-Lévy, 1993); Alyssa Goldstein Sepinwall, *The Abbé Grégoire and the French Revolution: The Making of Modern Universalism* (Berkeley and Los Angeles, CA: University of California Press, 2005), 91.
13 Fitzsimmons, *The Remaking of France*, 69.
14 Philippe Poirrier, *Les Politiques culturelles en France* (Paris: La Documentation française, 2013), 13; see also Isser Woloch, *The New Regime: Transformations of the French Civic Order, 1789–1820s* (New York, NY: W. W. Norton & Co., 1994), 177.
15 Adrian O'Connor, "'Source de lumières & de vertus': Rethinking *éducation*, *instruction*, and the political pedagogy of the French Revolution," *Historical Reflections/Réflexions Historiques* 40:3 (2014): 20–43.
16 W. H. Sewell, Jr., "Le Citoyen/La Citoyenne: Activity, Passivity and the Revolutionary Conception of Citizenship," in Colin Lucas (ed.), *The French Revolution and the Creation of Modern Political Culture*, vol. 2: *The Political Culture of the French Revolution* (Oxford: Pergamon Press, 1988), 114.
17 Olwen H. Hufton, *Women and the Limits of Citizenship in the French Revolution* (Toronto: University of Toronto Press, 1992); Joan Landes, *Women and the Public Sphere in the Age of the French Revolution* (Ithaca, NY: Cornell University Press, 1988).
18 Woloch, *The New Regime*, 177.
19 Chartier, *The Cultural Origins of the French Revolution*, 37.
20 Chrétien-Guillaulme Lamoignon de Malesherbes, "Discours de réception à l'Académie française" (16 février 1775) in *Oeuvres inédites de ... Malesherbes*,

ed. N. L. Pissot (Paris, 1808), 151; S.-N.-H. Linguet, *Appel à la posterité, ou Recueil des mémoires et plaidoyers de M. Linguet pour lui-même* ... (1779), both as quoted by Baker, *Inventing the French Revolution*, 189.

21 Marisa Linton, *The Politics of Virtue in Enlightenment France* (New York, NY: Palgrave MacMillan, 2001), 2.

22 Ibid., 68–69.

23 István Hont, "Commercial Society and Political Theory in the Eighteenth Century: The Problem of Authority in David Hume and Adam Smith," in Melching and Velema, *Main Trends in Cultural History*, 54–94; these quotes appear on 57 and 71, respectively. Also Dennis C. Rasmussen, *The Problems and Promise of Commercial Society: Adam Smith's Response to Rousseau* (University Park, PA: The Pennsylvania State University Press, 2008).

24 Emma Rothschild, *Economic Sentiments: Adam Smith, Condorcet, and the Enlightenment* (Cambridge, MA: Harvard University Press, 2001), 9, 45.

25 Cf. Adrian Velicu, *Civic Catechisms and Reason in the French Revolution* (Burlington, VT: Ashgate, 2010); Catherine Kintzler, *Condorcet: L'Instruction publique et la naissance du citoyen* (Paris: Le Sycomore, 1984); Mona Ozouf, *Festivals and the French Revolution*, trans. Alan Sheridan (Cambridge, MA: Harvard University Press, 1988); Jean Bloch, *Rousseauism and Education in Eighteenth-century France* (Oxford: Voltaire Foundation, 1995), 97–104, 151; Colin Lucas, "The Crowd and Politics," in Lucas (ed.), *The French Revolution and the Creation of Modern Political Culture*, vol. 2, 281.

26 Gilbert Romme, *Rapport sur l'instruction publique, considérée dans son ensemble; suivi d'un Projet de décret sur les principales bases du plan général de l'instruction publique, présenté à la Convention nationale, au nom du Comité d'instruction publique* (Paris: Imprimerie nationale, 1793), 9–11.

27 Mirabeau, *Travail sur l'éducation publique*, 73.

28 Mona Ozouf has detailed the many ways in which Ancien Régime, and especially Catholic, practices were appropriated and imitated by the designers of the revolutionary festival, down to the costumes, altars, hymns, sermons, and rhetoric. Ozouf, *Festivals and the French Revolution*, 262–282.

29 Nira Kaplan, "Virtuous competition among citizens: emulation in politics and pedagogy during the French Revolution," *Eighteenth-Century Studies*, 36:2 (2003), 241.

30 Ibid.; Marie-Hélène Huet, *Rehearsing the Revolution: The Staging of Marat's Death 1793–1797* (Berkeley and Los Angeles, CA: University of California Press, 1982), 35–36.

31 This list was presented by Jérôme-Marie Champion de Cicé on 27 July 1789. *AP* 8: 282.

32 *AP* 9: 109.

33 *AP* 8: 303.

34 *AP* 9: 126.

35 Projet de Constitution soumis à l'Assemblée nationale par M. Abbé Sieyès, *AP* 8: 424-427.
36 *AP* 9: 596.
37 *AP* 9: 612.
38 AN, AD/VIII//21, no. 18, "Motion faite à l'Assemblée nationale, par M. Gossin, sur la nécessité d'établir les Ecoles nationales," 4 September 1790. Also *AP* 18: 574-576.
39 AN, AD/VIII//21, no. 18, Gossin, "Motion faite à l'Assemblée nationale," 4-5; Edelstein, *The Enlightenment*, 103.
40 AN, AD/VIII//21, no. 18, Gossin, "Motion faite à l'Assemblée nationale," 6.
41 Ibid., 1
42 Ibid., 2-3.
43 Ibid., 2.
44 Ibid., 4.
45 Ibid., 2.
46 Ibid., 3.
47 Ibid., 1. For the critique of "authoritarian" pedagogical programs, see Emma Rothschild, "Condorcet and Adam Smith on Education and Instruction," in Amélie Oksenberg Rorty (ed.), *Philosophers on Education: New Historical Perspectives* (London: Routledge, 1998), 217.
48 Jacques de Cock, *Mirabeau et la naissance du régime parlementaire* (Lyon: Fantasques éditions, 1999), 27.
49 Mirabeau, *Travail sur l'éducation publique*. Mirabeau's authorship has been questioned since the moment of the work's appearance, but there are good and generally agreed upon reasons to consider the work his, including Mirabeau's habit of presenting speeches in his own name that had been written by collaborators. I have followed custom and considered them "Mirabeau's discourses." Palmer, *The Improvement of Humanity*, 89; Gabriel Compayré, *Histoire critique des doctrines de l'éducation en France depuis le seizième siècle*, T. II (Paris: Hachette, 1880), 285-289.
50 For example, Gontard, *L'Enseignement primaire en France*, 84. Bronislaw Baczko, "Introduction," in Bronislaw Baczko (ed.), *Une éducation pour la démocratie: Textes et projets de l'époque révolutionnaire* (Genève: Librairie Droz S. A., 2000), 13-14; Palmer, *The Improvement of Humanity*, 88-89. Mirabeau's proposal was published as an annex to parliamentary debates of 10 September 1791, the day on which Talleyrand first presented his proposal for the reform of education: *AP* 30: 512-554.
51 Mirabeau, *Travail sur l'éducation publique*, 7-8.
52 Ibid., 7.
53 Ibid., 24; 37-38. A literacy requirement similar to the one proposed by Mirabeau would be included in the Constitution of Year III, intended to take effect in Year XII; the Assembly had earlier rejected a literacy requirement because to do so would have dramatically reduced the number of people who

could qualify as active citizens. See Fitzsimmons, *The Remaking of France*, 189.
54 Mirabeau, *Travail sur l'éducation publique*, 9.
55 Ibid., 15.
56 Ibid., 12, 18.
57 Ibid., 18–19.
58 Ibid., 17. On eighteenth-century views regarding economic liberalization, see Rebecca L. Spang, *Stuff and Money in the Time of the French Revolution* (Cambridge, MA: Harvard University Press, 2015), 40–44; John Shovlin, *Political Economy of Virtue: Luxury, Patriotism, and the Origins of the French Revolution* (Ithaca, NY: Cornell University Press, 2006), 103–104, 121–130, passim.
59 Mirabeau, *Travail sur l'éducation publique*, 19–20.
60 Ibid., 16.
61 Ibid., 138.
62 Ibid., 156.
63 Ibid., 134–135.
64 Ibid., 134.
65 Ibid., 81–82.
66 Ibid., 82–83.
67 Ibid., 77–78.
68 These critiques are presented in Gontard, *L'Enseignement primaire en France*, 84; Palmer, *The Improvement of Humanity*, 89.
69 This led at times to confusion and "territorial" disputes among legislators, as we see in an October 1790 speech by Talleyrand warning his colleagues that their work on projects like public gardens, libraries, and the like would be superseded by the constitutional committee's plan for public instruction. *AP* 19: 588–589.
70 For example, Figeac-Monthus, *Les Enfants de l'*Émile, 223–228; Mona Ozouf, *L'Homme régénéré: Essais sur la Révolution française* (Paris: Gallimard, 1989); Mona Ozouf, *L'École de la France: Essais sur la Révolution, l'utopie et l'enseignement* (Paris: Gallimard, 1984); Pierre Rosanvallon, *The Demands of Liberty: Civil Society in France since the Revolution*, trans. A. Goldhammer (Cambridge, MA: Harvard University Press, 2007), 6–34.
71 *AP* 9: 153.
72 Ibid. Also Brockliss, *French Higher Education*; Kors, *D'Hollbach's Coterie*, 180–182; Edelstein, *The Enlightenment*, 79–91.
73 *AP* 8: 397.
74 R. R. Palmer, "How five centuries of educational philanthropy disappeared in the French Revolution," *History of Education Quarterly*, 26:2 (1986), 182.
75 Ibid., 182, 186.
76 Archives Départemental de la Haute Garonne (hereafter ADHG), 1L 1004, no. 2, "Loi Qui accorde des secours provisoires aux différens Collèges qui ont

perdu leurs revenues par la suppression des Dîmes ou des Droits féodeaux. 6 juin 1792."

77 Nigel Aston, *Religion and Revolution in France, 1780–1804* (Washington DC: The Catholic University of America Press, 2000).

78 Ibid., 134.

79 Timothy Tackett, *Religion, Revolution and Regional Culture in Eighteenth-Century France: The Ecclesiastical Oath of 1791* (Princeton, NJ: Princeton University Press 1986); Aston, *Religion and Revolution in France*, 103–243.

80 Roger Hahn, *The Anatomy of a Scientific Institution: The Paris Academy of Sciences, 1666–1803* (Berkeley and Los Angeles, CA: University of California Press, 1971); Barnard, *Education and the French Revolution*.

81 Brockliss, *French Higher Education*, 52–53.

82 Barnard, *Education and the French Revolution*, 59.

83 AN, AD/VIII//21, no. 6, "Proclamation du Roi sur un Décret de l'Assemblée nationale, relative à l'Instruction & portant que les Rentrées dans les différentes écoles publiques, se seront cette année comme à l'ordinaire, 19 octobre 1790,"; AN, AD/VIII//21, no, 27, "Loi Relative à tous les Corps & Etablissemens d'Instruction & Éducation publiques, 12 octobre 1791."

4

Constitutional principles and concrete proposals: reconsidering Talleyrand and Condorcet on public instruction

– Il sera créé et organisé une Instruction publique commune à tous les citoyens, gratuite à l'égard des parties d'enseignement indispensables pour tous les hommes et dont les établissements seront distribués graduellement, dans un rapport combiné avec la division du royaume.

– Il sera établi des fêtes nationales pour conserver le souvenir de la Révolution française, entretenir la fraternité entre les citoyens, et les attacher à la Constitution, à la Patrie et aux lois.

French Constitution, 3 September 1791

When representatives of the National Constituent Assembly delivered the new constitution to Louis XVI on 3 September 1791, it signaled, they said, the "end of the Revolution."[1] Historians, of course, are quick to disagree, but so too were many of the deputies themselves, including members of the constitutional committee who pushed their colleagues to take up the reform of education before disbanding and handing the reins of government to the Legislative Assembly. They argued that the constitution not only promised a new and national system of education, it required one, and that the work of securing the Revolution's gains would continue until the benefits of such a system had taken root among the people.

As we saw in Chapter 3, the constitutional committee had identified the establishment of a national system of public instruction as one of its priorities as early as July 1789, when Jérôme-Marie Champion de Cicé included it in a list of legislative imperatives alongside settling the structure of the legislative branch, reforming the national system of political administration, and overhauling both the judiciary and the military. This ambition was reaffirmed in the constitution itself, which promised the establishment of a system "common to all" in which instruction would be free, at least at the levels "indispensable for all men." Translating that promise into institutional realities proved more difficult, and while the deputies accomplished a great many things between July 1789 and September 1791, settling upon a national system of public instruction was not among them. Despite the anxious pleas from political and pedagogical administrators across France (discussed in Chapter 6), and despite the complaints of their fellow deputies along the way, the constitutional committee did not present its proposal until after the constitution had been sent to Louis XVI for review and approval.[2] As late as 9 August 1791, deputies raised questions about the extent of the commitment being made in their constitutional clauses concerning education, and much remained uncertain even when the constitution left the halls of the Assembly.[3]

In this chapter we re-examine the two most important attempts to bridge the divide between constitutional promises and institutional realities: the proposals for national systems of education presented by Talleyrand and Condorcet in September 1791 and April 1792, respectively. Their proposals represented not only the fruits of work undertaken by the constitutional committee and then the committee of public instruction, but more generally the attempt by a particular strain of liberal deputies to translate the upheaval of revolutionary politics into a sustainable set of social, political, and institutional norms and practices. Having each been members of the Society of 1789, a group that "aimed to combine the qualities of a political club, an intellectual circle, and a vehicle of public instruction," Talleyrand and Condorcet approached the reform of education with ambitions that extended far beyond the classroom walls.[4]

Founded in April 1790, the Society of 1789 was at least in part a response to the October Days and its members' desire to reestablish "political order by applying the principles of [the moral and political sciences] to the development of a new constitution for France." The Society's members – many of them nobles – included some of the most influential figures of the early Revolution and of the debates over education, including not only Condorcet and Talleyrand but also Sieyès, Lafayette, Mirabeau, Dupont de Nemours, Isaac Le Chapelier, Rabaut Saint-Étienne, and Louis-Alexandre La Rochefoucauld.[5] It represented the sort of educated and "enlightened" elite that many liberals (including some of its members) had been hoping would emerge to lead France since the crises of 1788–89.[6]

The Society was modeled upon and sought to continue the work of Ancien Régime learned societies and academies and, in so doing, to contribute to the "development of the 'social art' and the application of [that art's] principles" to the new political order.[7] Its members sought to bridge the gap between abstract and practical work, between articulating the new political order's principles and giving those principles institutional and social force. That such a society would attract many deputies interested in the reform of education is unsurprising given the view of schools that had taken shape in the decades preceding 1789. A general consensus had emerged in those decades that the reform of education would not only contribute to, but was a necessary component of, reforming the social order; as Keith Baker puts it, "public education was to be geared towards the new patrie into which the historical reality was to be transformed, partly as a result of such education."[8] Re-examining these proposals, we are at the same time re-examining the sorts of patrie, and the sort of social reality, to which deputies aspired after 1789.

The proposals presented by Talleyrand and Condorcet on behalf of the constitutional committee and the committee of public instruction represent the fullest articulation of the National Assembly's approach to education and the culmination of a debate over political reform, social institutions, and representative government that dated back at least to Turgot and, in some sense, to the anxieties of the 1760s. They also demonstrate the interplay of political principle, social innovation, and practical calculation that characterized revolutionary state-building, in general, and the attempt to reform education, in particular.

Talleyrand and the workshop of social virtues

Where deputies like Champion de Cicé, Gossin, and Mirabeau had argued that their colleagues ought to view education as a constitutional concern, Charles-Maurice de Talleyrand-Périgord could present it as a constitutional promise already made. By the time he presented the *Rapport sur l'instruction publique* on behalf of the constitutional committee on 10, 11, and 19 September 1791, the guarantee of a national system of education, to be accompanied by educative festivals, had been enshrined in the recently completed constitution. Despite these constitutional commitments, the timing was inauspicious; having completed the constitution, Talleyrand's colleagues were preparing to hand over legislative responsibilities to the new Legislative Assembly.[9] As a result, and despite protests from Talleyrand and other members of the constitutional committee, the proposal was shelved and left for the incoming assembly to consider (or not).[10]

There were two reasons, in addition to the disruption and logistical inconvenience of handing the work off to their successors, that Talleyrand and the other members of the constitutional committee wanted the proposal taken up more quickly: the imminent start of the academic year (in October) and the role of education in "completing" the constitution being prepared for ratification. Talleyrand argued that the Assembly's work remained "incomplete" without a system of education and, moreover, that the constitution required such a system to give social and political force to its principles, to preserve its beneficial effects for future generations, and to prepare the citizenry for its role in the new politics.[11] Neither of these arguments swayed the deputies and so, as R. R. Palmer put it, Talleyrand's proposal arrived "stillborn" into the halls of revolutionary governance.[12]

Historians have paid more attention to the plan than did Talleyrand's colleagues, and their assessments have been generally positive. Gabriel Comparyré thought the plan "wise and moderate," and Maurice Gontard described it as "clear, precise, practical, and rigorously logical."[13] Palmer hailed it as "a great document in the history of education."[14] While these historians are right to highlight the proposal's exceptional qualities, their focus on its curricular and institutional practicality and philosophical coherence draws attention away from its more revolutionary attributes and from the points that make it an exemplary illustration of how public instruction was expected to shape the new political order. Despite its apparent moderation, the proposal staked out ambitious goals: to reform the schools so that they would reflect and reinforce the principles and practices of representative government; to develop individuals' moral, intellectual, and physical faculties while also cultivating the civic sentiments and forms of sociability conducive to collective self-governance; and to develop an educational infrastructure that would reconcile the interests of individuals or families, the variability of local experiences and expectations, and the needs and interests of the national community. If it is true that the "merit of the report lies not in its originality but in the sophistication and amplitude with which it expresses much prevailing opinion," that is a remarkable indication of how much the ambitions of "public instruction" had come to define the revolutionary debate over education.[15]

Talleyrand's proposal combined the Rousseauian view that an individual's development was shaped by a mix of innate, dormant, and acquired traits with a sense that society was a "vast workshop" in which it was "not enough that everybody be working, but ... that they be in their rightful place."[16] This left education with a tripartite assignment. First, to give each child the skills and knowledge that it was necessary for all citizens to have. Second, to help each person determine his or her "rightful place" in the social and economic order. Third, to give students at least an opportunity to acquire the skills and knowledge necessary to assume that place (which also meant not preventing individuals from acquiring such skills and knowledge elsewhere, that is, not keeping them in school when their time and effort would be better rewarded somewhere else). In accomplishing those three tasks, education would establish itself as not only a product of the society in which it was organized, but also "a source of good for that society, and a bountiful source of good for individuals."[17] Accomplishing this in practice was rather more complicated, and Talleyrand's proposal included a 123-page presentation of the principles and justifications underlying his system, a description of the institutions that should comprise such a system, and a *projet de loi* suggesting a course of legislative action; when these components were published together, the *Rapport* was 216 pages of revolutionary promise.

In the report, Talleyrand outlined a four-tier system of education, beginning with universally available (but non-compulsory[18]) elementary education in *écoles primaires*, continuing through *écoles de district* and *écoles de département*, and culminating in an *Institut national*, located in Paris but in communication with institutions around France. These four tiers of formal education would be supplemented with a program of festivals intended to cultivate a sense of *"amour de la Patrie"* through a varied repertoire of games, songs, and representations of great historical events.[19]

Talleyrand's proposal aimed to satisfy and surpass the Constitution's promises about education, to reinforce the spirit of liberty and equality upon which the Constitution was based, and to contribute to the expansion and perfection of scholarship and instruction in France. To do so, Talleyrand argued that reform needed to proceed from five principles: 1) education must be available to all, including the poorest and most humble; 2) there must be no privilege or monopoly over education, it being everybody's right not only to benefit from education, but to participate in its expansion; 3) any person so inclined must be allowed to open a school in his field of expertise, and every subject should be available for study somewhere, even if not necessarily all subjects everywhere; 4) education, at least at the elementary level, must be available to members of both sexes, its denial to females constituting a form of social disinheritance; 5) it should be available to people of all ages, serving to "conserve and perfect [among adults] what it had already accomplished" during the period of formal schooling.[20]

Talleyrand viewed the reform and expansion of education as part of the Assembly's constitutional work ("it is impossible to have understood the essence of the constitution without recognizing that all of its principles demand the support of a new system of education"),[21] and as central to the *practical* work of establishing liberty and equality among the French people. He saw in education a means by which to transform the letter of the new laws into the spirit of the new society and he worried that, without educational reform, the proclamations of liberty and equality would soon ring hollow, lifeless reminders of unfulfilled promises. His concerns were not only about the relationship between individuals and the state, but also about the social relationships that were supposed to reflect, maintain, and preserve the new political order:

> Men have been declared free, but isn't it clear that only instruction can constantly expand the reach of civil liberty, and only it can maintain political liberty against all species of despotism? Do we not know that, even under the freest constitution, the ignorant man is at the mercy of the Charlatan, and even more so is dependent upon the educated man ... He who cannot read, who cannot do basic computation, depends for everything on those around him.
>
> Men have been recognized as equals, but how little will this legal equality be felt, how unreal will it remain, in the face of such inequalities in fact, if instruction is not constantly employed to restore equilibrium among them, or at least to mitigate those harmful inequalities it cannot destroy![22]

In fulfilling the pedagogical promise issued in the Constitution, the new schools would pay the "debt that society owed each of its members"; they were also supposed to shape and, at least to a point, reflect the interpersonal, political, and economic dynamics of that society.

This began even in the first stages of education, as the *écoles primaires* were designed to offer students an introduction to society, to familiarize them with the "first elements of the nation," and to offer a course of instruction robust enough to fulfill the promise enshrined in the constitution.[23] Located in each canton (with multiple schools in those cantons where the population warranted them), the primary schools would offer free instruction in how to read and write, the principles of the French language, basic arithmetic, elementary land measurement, the new geographical and political organization of France, as well as the principles of religion (Catholicism), morality, the new Constitution, the responsibilities and obligations of citizenship, and the tales of virtuous citizens for the students to emulate. Through these "general" studies (and supplementary physical exercises), Talleyrand expected these schools to provide for and support the development of the students' "moral, intellectual, and physical faculties," each of which he addressed separately, and each of which he cast in terms of how best to engage students so that they would be independent in their affairs, devoted to the *patrie*, and useful to the society.[24] If they accomplished these goals, Talleyrand felt that the first level of his educational structure would have met the Assembly's constitutional obligations.

That the primary schools satisfy these requirements was important because Talleyrand thought this likely to be the only formal education most people would receive. In the case of young male students, Talleyrand had a largely economic rationale for this expectation; when it came to the question of female education, or rather, to its cessation after the first level of instruction, Talleyrand found himself in a more difficult position, one he himself recognized.

As noted above, Talleyrand's primary schools would be open to children of both sexes, and young boys and girls would be educated in common (at least until age 8, when it was expected that many girls would leave the schools, with many boys leaving a year later at age 9). Boys and girls were, after all, being educated into the same society, and so their introduction to the first principles of that society need not differ by sex. Once, however, the schools turned to preparing children for the places they would occupy within that society, Talleyrand's workshop metaphor trumped his universalism, revealing the limits of the social and political transformation he imagined. He explained that the number of boys entering the second level of schools – the *écoles de district* – would be limited by the "laws of necessity" that push young men towards more "promptly productive" ways of spending their time.[25] The well-run workshop of French society would require that only some boys continue beyond the first level of school; it would not require that any girls do so, a point that led Talleyrand to discuss more generally where women fitted into the new social and political orders and why. As he recognized, "one cannot separate questions relative to women's education from an examination of their political rights."[26]

"If we are to recognize for women the same [political] rights as for men, we must give to them the same ability to make use of them. If we think women's place ought to be restricted to the management and maintenance of the home, then we must give to them the disposition to fulfill that role." The question having been put directly, Talleyrand proceeded to give two answers, the first recognizing the impossibility of any abstract defense of the latter position, and the second defending it. On the first point, he claimed that it was "impossible to explain, from any abstract principle, why one half of humanity would be excluded by the other half from any participation in government, how they could be natives in fact but foreigners by law in the very land in which they were born, and how they could own land but be denied any direct influence in governance or even representation within government." Abstract political principles were, however, only one way of approaching the issue and, he claimed, not the best one. Instead, presenting the utilitarian principle that "the goal of all institutions ought to be the happiness of the greatest number," he argued that women's continued exclusion from public life served the interests of most members of society, male and female alike.[27]

This argument relied not just upon a notion of "natural" difference between the sexes, but also a "natural" division of social and familial labor. Talleyrand paired his utilitarian argument with a description of women's "delicate constitution ... [and] peaceful disposition," and of the numerous responsibilities of motherhood. He claimed that women were called to "gentle occupations and domestic cares," and that the division of labor between the sexes had secured for women the "*beau partage dans la vie.*"[28] He did permit an exception for female orphans and for the daughters of the poorest families, for whom the state might act as a "tender and vigilant mother" and provide continued education. While not ideal, he claimed that such an arrangement was necessary to "protect the innocence" of these unfortunate girls and to offer them the preparations for domestic life that they were not receiving from their families.[29] The purpose of female education in the new politics was, then, to teach girls "not to aspire to those things they were refused by the new Constitution, but to recognize and appreciate the things they were given by it" and, beyond that, to permit them to learn the sorts of things that would actually be useful to them. On this second front, Talleyrand argued that such lessons were better learned in the home than in the schools.[30]

Those (male) students who did continue their formal education would do so at *écoles de district*, where they would pay at least part of the expenses associated with their education, the state having fulfilled its obligations with the primary schools. Like Mirabeau, Talleyrand made an exception for students who had demonstrated exceptional talent but lacked the funds for further instruction.[31] In order to pay for these scholarships, he proposed that the foundations associated with the *bourses* of the Ancien Régime *collèges* be consolidated into a national fund, one that would be divided among the departments and then awarded by the departmental authorities to deserving children from their department.[32] This need- and merit-based subsidy would extend through all levels of post-primary education, ensuring that all schools, including the Institut National, reflected a meritocratic hierarchy and that the state did not "lose or neglect" the talents and skills of its citizenry due to differences in socio-economic background.

The district schools were intended as a sort of intermediary between primary instruction and more specialized study in theology, law, medicine, or the military sciences, each of which was to receive a specifically designated institution. They were essentially "the regenerated *collèges* of the Old Regime," and were designed to "serve the same purpose [as had the *collèges*], to produce the educated class of French society."[33] The curriculum itself was relatively familiar, if somewhat more practical than its Ancien Régime predecessors, with a seven-year course of studies in grammar (in both French and Latin), humanities (or belles-lettres), rhetoric and logic, and mathematics and physics, as well as courses in living languages and in Greek.[34] Talleyrand did, however, propose two important and related changes: first, in how the curriculum was organized; and second, in the recruitment, selection, and oversight of instructors.

The first of these consisted of a shift from a pedagogical routine based on "classes" to one arranged by "courses." The difference, in essence, was that instructors would now specialize in a particular subject rather than teaching all subjects to the students in his "class." Talleyrand claimed that the existing arrangement created confusion among the students as to what they were to be learning at any given moment. He argued that a program of "courses" was not only better suited to the natural development of the pupils' faculties, but would help to ensure that instructors were well-qualified to teach the subjects for which they were hired.[35] This last point was to be reinforced by the second significant change, which focused on the recruitment and certification of instructors.

Given the upheaval caused by the Civil Constitution of the Clergy, and the broader changes in the relationship between the state and the religious orders, a change in the recruitment, certification, and oversight of the personnel at the district schools seemed unavoidable. Talleyrand, seeking instructors who were "both enlightened and virtuous," designed a multi-stage examination and nomination system. As a first step, would-be instructors had to pass a public and subject-specific examination held in the principal city of the department and refereed by a panel of five judges (at least two of whom were themselves instructors). Those who passed would be included in a list of eligible instructors compiled from all of the departments of France, and that list would serve as a pool of candidates for local political authorities whenever a position became available in their local schools. The nomination of a candidate would then be submitted to the national government for review by the Assembly and approval by the king, after which the candidate would swear the civic oath and assume his position as *maître*. A similar system was proposed for the primary schools, although the examinations to be taken by those candidates would not be subject specific because the primary schools would not be divided into courses, and the examinations would take place at the district level rather than in the principal city of the department. Instructors in both the primary and district schools would then be overseen and paid by local authorities (although instructors at the district schools would also receive fees from their students, and so their state salary would not be as generous as it might have been in a fully state-funded system).[36]

Vetted in a public *concours*, selected by local authorities, approved by national representatives (including royal administrators), and loyal to the constitution, Talleyrand's instructors represented an ideal distillation of the competing concerns and imperatives that shaped the debate over teaching personnel during the early Revolution. Like all such plans for recruiting and installing instructors, however, Talleyrand's had to offer some indication of where these instructors might come from. Here, as at many points in his proposal, Talleyrand recognized that the successful establishment of a new system would depend on the incorporation of much that had been inherited from the Ancien Régime institutions. He even included an article stipulating that preference be shown to instructors who had experience in the schools being replaced. Those who were not selected to continue in the reformed incarnations of their previous positions would be included on the list of "eligible candidates" being made available to local authorities. Those who did not receive positions – or who chose not to continue in the profession after its reorganization – would be offered pensions by the state, even if their non-participation stemmed from a refusal to swear the civic oath.[37]

This "translation" of Old Régime institutions into the new regime of public instruction continued at the higher levels of Talleyrand's plan, where he recreated (or regenerated) the university faculties and the elite institutions of Ancien Régime scholarly life. The department schools proposed by Talleyrand were essentially reorganized versions of the higher faculties of the French universities, offering courses of study in religion, law, medicine (including pharmacology and surgery), and – here he added to the university faculties – the military sciences. Each of these schools would exist independently of the others (rather than under the combined auspices of a university), and their curricula would be largely vocational.[38]

Atop Talleyrand's system would be an Institut National. Located in Paris, the Institut was to serve the interests of all of France, bring together the accumulated intellectual wealth of the nation, and put the savants of France in cooperative dialogue with their colleagues and institutional counterparts in other European nations.[39] The Institut was in many ways a reorganization of the elite intellectual institutions of the Ancien Régime, almost all of which Talleyrand proposed be suppressed (and the resources of which he would use to pay the Institut's expenses).[40] Thus, the chairs at the Collège de France, the various learned academies, the Jardin du Roi, and similar institutions were to be "suppressed," but their functions were to be recreated within the Institut, thereby establishing an intellectual Olympus for France.[41]

To oversee this vast system (what he called "*cette immense machine*"),[42] Talleyrand proposed a permanent General Commission of Public Instruction, located in Paris but responsible for educational institutions and education-related legislation across France.[43] Nominated by the king (who would also have the power to remove members, but only with a judgment of the legislature), the six members of this Commission would oversee a team of inspectors who could be sent "on mission" to inspect schools across the country, as well as a member of each department's Directory, who would offer more consistent and local oversight of education. The Commission would also administer the lands and finances associated with education and would provide an annual account of the system's finances to the legislature. In a note on the penultimate page of his monumental proposal, Talleyrand claimed that it might be best for the oversight of education to be in the hands of the legislature, rather than a royally appointed commission, but as a recent decree had placed education under the supervision of the executive, his proposal would follow suit.[44] In this, as in the Report overall, Talleyrand outlined what he thought legally and constitutionally required while also gesturing towards a more ambitious vision of education's role in revolutionary society.

In dividing his proposal between what the state was obliged to offer its citizens – the education necessary to "complete" and fulfill the promises of the Constitution – and that which the state had an interest but not an obligation in providing, Talleyrand's proposal reflected the practical imperatives and limitations that were shaping the Assembly's debates. Presented with two deadlines looming – the dissolution of the Constituent Assembly and the start of the academic year – Talleyrand presented a rather restrained vision; the state's obligation would be fulfilled by two years of elementary education, and a non-compulsory two years at that. His proposal also reflected the more ambitious and creative attempt to translate the principles of a new political regime into the pedagogical and practical norms of national institutions. Less frequently remarked upon by historians, this part of Talleyrand's proposal gives a clearer sense of how public instruction sought to transform education in France. Its ambitions were most clearly articulated in the section devoted to cultivating citizens' moral sensibilities and civic attachments.

Near the conclusion of his report, just prior to the appended discussion of female education and women's role in the new polity, Talleyrand devoted fifteen pages to moral education, the socialization of student-citizens, and the relationship between the institutional norms learned in school and the habits needed for active citizenship.[45] He offered three principles upon which to found a system of "instruction for the whole of one's life": to make childhood an apprenticeship in the arts and virtues of society; to cultivate among students the affective bonds that would lead them to do good; and to present citizens with the sorts of moral examples and illustrations that could help to turn abstract principles into a sort of civic sensibility, one that could be developed into civic sentiments and social habits.[46] By establishing civic associations for the young that mirrored the nation's "grand social organization," and by organizing institutions (like schools) as models of participatory engagement and representative self-government, Talleyrand aimed to reproduce the revolution that had taken place in French politics, to transform "a tyrannical regime" into one in which a separation of powers and a just constitution led students toward "respect for the laws, morality, and order, to nurture in their souls a spirit of equality and of liberty."[47]

This meant thinking anew not only about the pace and order of courses and the training of instructors, but about the respective role of instructors and students in the internal administration (or governance) of the schools. Talleyrand recognized that schools were not ideal places for the establishment of perfect equality – after all, students had to submit to the authority of their instructors.[48] But this did not preclude the schools from offering lessons in social equality, nor did it excuse them from their role in familiarizing students with the habits, practices, and interpersonal dynamics of collective and representative self-governance. Quite to the contrary, Talleyrand thought that if the schools were reformed appropriately, the tension between freedom and submission characteristic of a student's life could provide a valuable microcosm of civic life.

Such a reform would start, as had the political revolution, with a separation of powers. By distinguishing between those arenas where authority was reserved for the instructors and those where it was held by the "social body" of the students, Talleyrand hoped that the schools could simultaneously protect the rigor and quality of instruction while giving students the liberty and responsibilities of collective governance. Entrusting students with most elements of school administration and with the maintenance of discipline (under only the "most general" supervision of instructors) would teach them to balance principles with personalities, justice with understanding, the pursuit of honor and the assignation of blame.[49] These were lessons that had to be learned in both practice and principle, through observation of oneself, of others, and of "society"; they required a pedagogy that appealed to students' sense of honor, conscience, and reason, and their lessons had to be reinforced through historical examples, artistic productions, public festivals, and pedagogical spectacles.[50]

Even as he sought to integrate these many pedagogical instruments into a national system of public instruction, Talleyrand also sought to preserve the familial, local, and regional variations that gave meaning to people's social and political lives. In his call for festivals, for example, he explained that while it was important for there to be at least one celebration that was uniform and national, the others should vary according to local circumstances. Festivals should be designed to accommodate the "irregularity that suits the human spirit," and the deputies should resist the temptation to plan too much, to interject themselves in the preparations for festive occasions and civic celebrations. As he put it: "monotony destroys [a celebration's] charm," and "joy, like pain, is no more orderly than are people."[51] Instead, Talleyrand imagined that the affective bonds of the new social and political order would be forged and reinforced through a mix of national, departmental, local, and even private celebrations as citizens found their place in the political, economic, and social "workshop" of the new regime.

As Talleyrand and many of his colleagues repeatedly noted, a plan for education was, at the same time, a plan for society and for the new politics, and this plan reveals much about how Talleyrand and, by extension, the constitutional committee imagined the social and political future of revolutionary France.⁵² It suggests a polity in which social, professional, and political hierarchy remained, in which the "natural" inequalities among men were mitigated but not erased (and in which the "natural" division between the sexes remained), in which merit and talent were rewarded, in which individuals found purpose in the common good and submitted willingly to the rule of law. It was, in short, a politics in which everybody "found their place." To occupy one's place was not, however, to become passive; given the ability to read, write, and sustain oneself independently, each person would be capable of political self-representation and participation in the establishment of the "general will," that newly codified source of law and sovereignty. Their participation would be informed by "social virtues" and the bonds of patriotism, shaped by moral sentiments and the newly reconciled mandates of honor and conscience, and manifest in political and personal habits that would sustain the body politic during times of discord and dispute. This description was supposed to apply as aptly to the new pedagogy as it did to the new politics, a point on which Talleyrand's proposal embodies well the concept of "public instruction" and reminds us that the work of "regeneration" was as much institutional as it was ideological.

As reasonable and logical as Talleyrand's plan has appeared to historians, his was not an uncontested view of the political or educational system appropriate to the new regime. Moderates expressed approval of the proposal, and the *Ami des patriotes* in particular "lavished praise" on it. But the *Rapport* was criticized from both the Left and the Right (sometimes directly and sometimes through neglect and silence).⁵³ It was also criticized by correspondents who wrote to the Assembly, sometimes on political grounds, and sometimes on more logistical or practical issues. To take just three examples, a group of *maîtres de pension* in Paris wrote to the Assembly complaining that Talleyrand's proposal was inadequate in its arrangements for primary education, the *Appel à l'opinion publique sur l'éducation nationale* sent to the Assembly in late 1791 (and discussed in Chapter 5) included a complaint that the plan was "too complicated, too vague, too expensive to implement, and too prone to the establishment of distinctions," and the professors at the University of Strasbourg condemned his proposal to suppress the universities.⁵⁴

In the end, the Constituent Assembly decided to leave the problem of educational reform to its successor, the Legislative Assembly, which met for the first time less than a fortnight later.⁵⁵ With that, the constitutional promise of public instruction passed to new hands, most notably those of the philosopher-statesman Marie-Jean-Antoine-Nicholas de

Caritat, marquis de Condorcet, and his colleagues on the newly formed Committee of Public Instruction.

Condorcet and the "social art"

When the deputies of the Legislative Assembly turned to the question of educational reform, they began not by returning to Talleyrand's report but by creating a new committee, the Committee of Public Instruction, to which they assigned the task of drafting an entirely new proposal. This committee, established during the evening session of 28 October 1791, had twenty-four full members (with thirteen auxiliaries), and met for the first time two days later, on 30 October 1791.[56] The committee, and the proposal it produced, are most closely associated with Condorcet, the *philosophe* and perpetual secretary of the Academy of Sciences, but the other members of the committee were also "men of standing and experience suited to their task," several of whom had experience in the scholarly and educational institutions of the Ancien Régime.[57] In addition to Condorcet, there were the professors, Louis-François-Antoine Arbogast (who taught mathematics, artillery and physics, and was the Rector of the University of Strasbourg), Yves-Marie Audrein (who was a member of the Faculty of Arts at the University of Paris and had submitted proposals for reform in 1789 and 1790), and Gilbert Romme (a professor of mathematics and physics), as well as Bernard-Germain-Étienne de Lacépède, the Parisian naturalist who had worked at the Cabinet d'histoire naturelle, the archaeologist Antoine-Chrysostôme Quatremère-Quincy and, among the auxiliaries, Guyton Morveau, whose proposals for educational reform were discussed above in Chapter 2.[58]

Equally striking is the inclusion of many deputies who had positions in the Church. Among the twenty-four regular members of the committee, six were clerics, with two vicars (Audrein and Gaudin), two priests (Gilbergues and Vayron), and two bishops (Fauchet and Torné). There was also a bishop among the *suppléants* (Lamourette). After a year marked by disputes over the Civil Constitution and the clerical oath, the Assembly was aware that it would have to be able to marshal support from what remained of the loyal clergy.

In its first meeting, on Sunday, 30 October 1791, the Committee members elected Condorcet as their president, Pastoret as vice-president, and Lacépède and Arbogast as secretaries, and decided that they would meet at six o'clock in the evening, three times a week, after which they adjourned until that Tuesday, 1 November.[59] From the outset, the work was practical. It was also largely driven by Condorcet who provided the Committee with the "*Mémoires sur l'instruction publique*" he had published in the *Bibliothèque de l'homme public* over the course of that year.[60] Five months later, when the Committee presented its proposal on 20 and 21 April 1792, it was Condorcet who spoke as its representative, and the proposal brought before the Legislative Assembly was largely his work.[61]

The proposal called for a five-tier system of education, beginning with *écoles primaires*, followed by *écoles secondaires, instituts, lycées*, and finally the *Société nationale des sciences et des arts*, a research institution intended to oversee the instruction offered in the other institutions and to contribute to the "general perfection of human reason."[62] In presenting the plan, Condorcet argued that all four levels of instruction ought to be free (the *Société nationale* would not have pupils or offer "instruction" in the way the others did), not only because this would permit students from poor families to pursue their studies as far as their talent and disposition allowed, but also because the expansion of education served the interests of the state and of society as a whole. An expanded system of free education would help the new regime satisfy the demands of "equality" by establishing a more fluid society, one in which being born into a family with limited means did not mean being destined for a life of poverty and ignorance. The economic and social benefits conferred upon a child by a lucky birth would be balanced by a system that encouraged and rewarded the talent, merit, and work of those born into less advantageous circumstances.

Condorcet also thought that a state-funded system of instruction promised pedagogical benefits. Instructors who were dependent on fees paid by students – that is, on the number of students they "attracted" – would have a financial incentive to "dazzle" their students rather than instruct them, and so Condorcet worried they would shy away from dispelling or disputing students' prejudices or false beliefs.[63] Unlike the Physiocrats and unlike Mirabeau, Condorcet did not see education as a form of commerce, to be guided by the logic and dynamics of the market, but rather as a preparatory institution, one responsible for giving students the knowledge, skills, and independence of mind needed to become good and capable citizens as adults.

In the primary schools, which both boys and girls would enter no earlier than age 6 and in which they would stay for four years, students would be taught how to read and write (in French), would learn basic arithmetic, and would study the moral precepts and social principles upon which the new order was founded. This curriculum would continue into the secondary schools, though Condorcet expected that many boys – and all girls – would cease to attend after primary instruction concluded (around age 10). In rural areas, this curriculum would be supplemented with instruction in the agricultural sciences and economics, whereas in towns and cities there would be instruction in the arts and in the principles of commerce.[64] Thus the primary schools would concentrate on subjects "absolute necessary to all citizens"; those who continued into the *écoles secondaires* would find a curriculum that covered much of the same material but sought to incorporate some degree of vocational or professional training. As Condorcet conceived these first degrees of education, the primary schools would prepare each person to fulfill the basic functions and responsibilities of citizenship and secondary schools would prepare them to occupy a legitimate place in civil and political society.[65]

The third level of Condorcet's proposed system – which he considered the final level of "general education" – would include 109 institutes distributed throughout France (one per department, with twenty-six more distributed according to regional needs and resources).[66] These schools would be divided into four classes, with a certain preference accorded to the first: 1) mathematics and the physical sciences; 2) the moral and political sciences; 3) the application of the sciences to the arts; and 4) literature and the beaux-arts.[67] The institutes would offer instruction – again, in French – not only in those things that all citizens needed to know regardless of their profession, but also in subjects which, if made available to a broader public, could contribute to the improvement or perfection of the professions. They would also train instructors for the primary and secondary schools.[68]

Together, these three levels comprised Condorcet's system of "general" instruction. They were designed to fulfill the constitution's promise of national education and to prepare the citizenry for the new social and political regimes. They were essentially preparatory and preservative; by contrast, Condorcet's fourth and fifth levels of education aimed to improve human society through the production of knowledge, the development of the sciences, and the perfection of human reason. Their inclusion within a system of national public instruction rested upon the claim that what was good for science was good for France, and that what was good for French scholarship was good for the French people.[69]

Condorcet designed the fourth level in his system, the *lycées*, to train savants, professors, and a learned elite. Each of the nine *lycées* would offer students the opportunity to study the sciences "in all of their fullness." They would be arranged in the same fashion as the institutes, with the same four topical divisions, but with a greater number of professors and a greater degree of specialization in the courses they offered.[70] Moreover, and perhaps more importantly, the *lycées* were intended to serve as institutions through which "each generation can transmit to the next that [knowledge] they have received from their predecessors, as well as that knowledge they have added" to the common store.[71]

Finally, atop Condorcet's proposed system was the *Société nationale des Sciences et des Arts*, an institution devoted to research and to overseeing the rest of the educational system. Divided into the same four classes as were the institutes and *lycées* (again with a greater number of professors per class and a greater degree of specialization within each field),[72] this was nonetheless an institution apart from and above the others. In administrative terms, the *Société* would oversee a vast pyramid of institutional supervision, one in which each educational institution created a directory of members to oversee the institution below it. Unlike the other institutions of Condorcet's system, however, this institution was not intended "for the instruction of children, nor even that of men, but rather for the instruction of the entire generation, the perfection of human reason; it is not intended to increase the knowledge of any individual in particular, but rather to increase the amount of knowledge itself." Building upon the legacy of the Ancien Régime academies (the critiques of which were, he claimed, "often exaggerated, if sometimes warranted"),[73] the *Société* would serve as a capital for the Republic of Letters and would allow France to draw on the fruits of international science while also allowing the international community to remain abreast of advances being made in France.

Condorcet's inclusion of such elite institutions, and his repeated denunciation of programs for moral, political, or religious "education," provoked criticism from his fellow deputies, most famously from Jean-Paul Rabaut Saint-Étienne. Rabaut argued against Condorcet's plan by emphasizing the Ancien Régime distinction between *éducation* and *instruction*, calling for a program of "national education" (rather than "public instruction"), one the people of France would find "enjoyable, seductive, and enchanting."[74] The argument that Condorcet's plan was excessively "philosophical" and insufficiently political resonated in the Convention (where it was ultimately debated), and the proposal is often still described as the work of a "cold rationalist," a passionless embodiment of Enlightenment ambitions. It is, on such a reading, symptomatic of what Nicola Peter Todorov described (in a different context) as the "ideal of abstract rationality generally ascribed to revolutionaries inspired by the Enlightenment."[75] In more recent works, however, Condorcet has emerged as a more humane, nuanced, and pragmatic philosopher-statesman.[76] Emma Rothschild and David Williams have each sought to understand Condorcet's work across the many philosophical, political, and intellectual fields in which he was active; in so doing they have recalled our attention to the importance of civic sentiment, moral regeneration, and discursive sociability in his thinking about how societies did and should function. This has suggested important ways in which we might reconsider Condorcet's philosophy and his politics and, with that, his engagement with the ideal of "public instruction."

Condorcet's approach to education has generally been understood through his work in social mathematics, his jury theorem, and his analysis of the conditions under which collective decision making is likely to lead to advantageous (or disadvantageous) outcomes. Emphasizing the role of people's "independence" and "competence" in determining their collective capacity to make good decisions, he seemed primarily concerned with giving people knowledge and skills, less with the cultivation of civic sentiment or political virtues.[77] R. R. Palmer summed up this view:

> [Condorcet] emphasized the cognitive rather than the moral side of education, which must above all else impart the 'truth'; hence he gave great weight to the scientific, technical, and vocational subjects on which future progress must depend ... He distinguished between *l'instruction*, which developed knowledge and skills, and *l'éducation*, which was designed to form character and commitments. He expected that with right knowledge the desired virtues would naturally emerge. Sheer enlightenment would be enough.[78]

This view can be supported by many of Condorcet's own arguments, including his condemnation of efforts to teach the constitution as an object of veneration, his arguments against a system of public "education" that sought to establish people's "political, moral, or religious opinions," his opposition to calls for a national catechism, and his reduction of political education to "matters of fact" rather than "articles of faith."[79] In his *mémoire* on the "nature and purpose of public instruction" he argued that "the more men are prepared by education to reason correctly, to understand the truths presented to them and to reject the errors intended to victimize them – the more a nation sees its enlightenment increasing and extending over a greater number of individuals – the greater hope must there be of obtaining and maintaining good laws, a wise administration, and a truly free constitution."[80]

Despite having embraced a pedagogical language of "*instruction*" rather than "*éducation*," Condorcet's sense of what it meant to be "instructed" was far more engaged, civic-minded, sympathetic, and socially oriented than the reductive binary of those categories would seem to permit; indeed, it was built upon the idea that the pursuit of a more perfect society required attention to the political, social, economic, and emotional condition of man, and especially to the interactions and tensions that arose across those arenas.[81] His opposition to plans that would enshrine particular moral or political "truths" was rooted in a "somber" skepticism regarding one's own principles, his recognition of the uncertainty that plagues all political and legislative ambitions, and an optimistic sense of what might be born of "endless and judicious public discussion."[82] He feared that imposing "truths" through catechisms or political sermons would move the people further from freedom and from the possibility of enlightened self-governance, from the "*disposition des esprits*" that characterized the enlightened mind.[83] Recognizing this skeptical underpinning, and noting Condorcet's anxieties about the workings of commercial and industrial society, we can look past Condorcet's proscriptions and recognize the role of sentiment, emotion, and social interactions in his view of pedagogy, political society, and the "social art" upon which regeneration would depend.[84]

Despite his concern that the state would seek to impose moral, political, or religious opinions on the people, Condorcet recognized the influence of people's moral and political education on the well-being of the body politic and the state's interest in the moral character of its citizens. He saw that people's decisions would be shaped not only by their reason, but by their sense of justice, by their sympathy for other people, and by their sentimental attachments to broader communities.[85] Cultivating such sentiments, sympathies, and sensibilities was very much a part of Condorcet's political and pedagogical agenda, and he called in his "*Mémoire de l'instruction commune pour les enfants*" for instruction to include short moral tales to animate and to focus pupils' attention on their moral sentiments. Here too he warned against establishing any "maxims" or imposing "principles of conduct," but this did not mean ignoring or neglecting a moral education; he explicitly called for these lessons to develop students' sense of sympathy for other people and for animals. These, after all, were the sensibilities and sentiments that prevented human interactions from devolving into a series of "cold" and "calculated interests" and that allowed for the diversity of interests and opinions characteristic of political and economic intercourse to produce "civilized conflict" rather than destructive passions.[86]

In addition to moral tales and novels, Condorcet sought to establish the sorts of public ceremonies that had come to characterize the new pedagogical ideal and that are familiar from proposals discussed above. Calling for public lectures to be held each Sunday, Condorcet sought to integrate the lessons of the classroom and the social dynamics of the new public. He described ceremonies in which the instructor was assisted by "citizens of all ages," but especially by children too young to have sworn the civic oath, and in which the instructor publicly reviewed the materials being taught in the schools, discussed the useful arts, inventions, and agricultural techniques, lectured on the constitution and the laws that every citizen needed to know – especially those most useful to members of juries, justices of the peace, and municipal administrators – and, finally, offered instruction in the principles of morality and natural law.[87] These public conferences were to serve as a bridge between civil society and the classroom, between sentiment and science.

Teaching citizens and students to reflect on their sentiments and the relationship between those sentiments and possible courses of action was one of the conditions for people to become truly "free": "Every being is free who is able to have two contradictory sentiments relating to the same action, and who can decide either to wish, or not wish, to take that action in complete awareness that his will is conforming to one of the two sentiments."[88] Proscribing the teaching of moral or political certainties was important because such certainties precluded independent thought, political freedom, and a reflective relationship with one's own moral and political opinions. An independent and educated citizen had to be able to cope with uncertainty, even on issues of fundamental moral and political importance (perhaps especially on such issues), and so Condorcet's proscriptions were of a kind with his view of education as a "civic necessity," one that "followed on naturally as an essential extension of civic virtue and patriotic obligation."[89] From the outset, then, Condorcet's vision of deliberative democracy required and relied upon a form of sentimental citizenship and civic education. This was clear in his arguments regarding the nature of political independence and social equality, his curricular emphases and expectations, and in his sense of how educational institutions might serve the new political and social orders.

At the heart of Condorcet's thinking about both politics and public instruction were the demands of individual independence and social equality. The interwoven nature of these demands was evident in his explanation of why public instruction was central to the realization of the political promise articulated in the *Declaration of the Rights of Man and Citizen* and in the Constitution of 1791:

> Public Instruction is an obligation of society towards its citizens. It would be vain to declare that all men enjoy equal rights, vain for the laws to respect the first principle of eternal justice, if the inequality in men's mental faculties were to prevent the greatest number from enjoying these rights to their fullest extent.[90]

Condorcet thought education necessary for the establishment of "equality" because it offered the means by which to abolish relationships of "dependence" between individuals. He wrote in the first of his *mémoires*:

> The man who does not know how to read, write, and do arithmetic really depends upon the more literate man to whom he must constantly have recourse. He is not the equal of those to whom education has given this knowledge; he cannot exercise the same rights to the same extent and with the same independence. Similarly, the man who has not been instructed in the basic laws governing the rights of property does not enjoy these rights in the same way as the one who has: in discussions arising between them, they do not engage on equal terms.[91]

This description of dependence and inequality calls to mind the "coldly rational" Condorcet who saw in public instruction a means by which to increase the pool of competent participants in his political "jury," and that is certainly an important part of his proposal. It is not, however, the entirety of it.

In his defense of "curiosity" in the second *mémoire*, Condorcet describes a similar encounter between educated and uneducated citizens, this time revealing the deeply interpersonal and emotional nature of the threat posed by ignorance. There he writes of instruction as a guard against "that painful disquiet which is associated with being aware of one's own ignorance, and which produces the vague fear of not really being in a position to defend oneself against the ills by which one is threatened."[92] These sorts of "vague fears" threatened to incite destructive social passions, to undermine the social order, and to deprive individuals of their sense of security and of independence. As he warned in the first *mémoire*:

> A truly free constitution, in which all classes of society enjoy the same rights, cannot subsist if the ignorance of some of its citizens prevents them from understanding the nature and limits of these rights, and obliges them to pronounce on what they do not know, choosing when they cannot judge.

Such a constitution would destroy itself after a few convulsions, degenerating into one of those forms of government that can preserve peace in the midst of an ignorant and corrupt people.[93]

Having warned of the dangers of anarchy and "political convulsions" since before 1789, and especially since the October Days, Condorcet sought to protect against such dangers by cultivating public confidence in the new political order and by nurturing the sorts of civic sentiments that would turn subjects into citizens.[94] This meant ensuring that "each individual [was] sufficiently instructed to exercise for himself the rights guaranteed him under the law, without subjecting himself blindly to the reason of another."[95] But it also required that people learn to "be good," which they do "not by learning the rules of how to be good, but by a long, recursive process of feeling sympathy, and disliking cruelty, and thinking about one's feelings."[96] This sort of instruction was not designed to preempt political disputes or to eradicate social hierarchy and inequality (though it might narrow some of the differences in opinion, taste, and sentiment that followed from and exacerbated social stratification),[97] but Condorcet did hope that it would prevent political disputes and social inequalities from becoming injurious to individuals or to the constitutional order.

Because Condorcet's proposal was never put into practice, and because its attention to learned and elite institutions seems to confirm the caricature of its author as a cold rationalist devoted to abstract political principles, it has been too often read in isolation from revolutionary politics, regarded as a brilliant but anomalous call for an enlightened politics. Read in this way, Condorcet's proposal can be divorced from other attempts to design and establish a system of "public instruction." But Condorcet was not a *philosophe* apart, and his proposal offers us a good sense of what public instruction was (and what it was not) under the Constituent and Legislative assemblies. His attempt to translate the "social art" into an educational infrastructure aimed to encourage the sciences and the scientists, but also to counter the influence of "vague fears" that corrode social relations and spoil civic sentiments. Criticism from colleagues like Rabaut notwithstanding, Condorcet recognized clearly that the importance of "public instruction" stemmed from its power to transform social relations and from its contribution to the establishment of a sentimental foundation for the new politics. If he was opposed to prescriptive moral and political education, it is because citizens needed to develop moral and political sensibilities rather than memorize maxims and slogans. The new political and social orders promised not just liberty and equality, but also "different [and] disconcerting lives," lives that Condorcet knew would require more than "reason" and "right knowledge."[98] Public instruction would have to prepare citizens to be independent and free; its most important work was focused not on what people knew, but on how they would communicate and interact with one another, how they entered into the "intersubjective game that is politics."[99]

Condorcet's plan was presented to the Legislative Assembly on 20 and 21 April 1792, just as France declared war on Austria and as the nation (and Condorcet) turned its attention to foreign affairs and counter-revolutionary plots, as questions of loyalty, patriotism, and revolutionary devotion (rather than educational reform and other such "civic improvements") came to dominate the political landscape.[100] By the time his proposal was properly debated, the Legislative Assembly and the constitutional monarchy had fallen and the National Convention had begun work on a very different constitutional order amid very different political, diplomatic, and social circumstances. By December 1792, when the Convention finally took up Condorcet's plan, it had come to seem anachronistic, and criticisms like those leveled by Rabaut resonated among the *conventionnels*.[101]

And yet, at the time of its presentation in spring 1792, Condorcet's hope that the French people might engage in political debates by "examin[ing], discuss[ing], and com[ing] to slow and reflective judgments about political projects" was neither utopian nor outlandish.[102] They were engaged in just such a debate on the question of public instruction, as people across France wrote to their representatives with exhortations, suggestions, criticisms and requests and, in so doing, both emphasized and illustrated the importance of education in the new politics. In the next two chapters we turn to their letters and to the national debate over public instruction that those letters reveal.

Notes

1 François Furet, *Revolutionary France, 1770–1880*, trans. A. Nevill (Oxford: Oxford University Press, 1992), 97.
2 For examples of deputy complaints, see *AP* 24: 281, 690–691; 25: 105–109.
3 For example, Emmanuel Fréteau-Saint-Just argued that the constitutional articles ought to include the promise of state support for students beyond the primary levels of education, but his colleagues decided that this was a point that warranted legislative rather than constitutional consideration. *AP* 29: 301.

4 William Doyle, *Aristocracy and its Enemies in the Age of Revolution* (New York, NY: Oxford University Press, 2009), 232. See also Keith Michael Baker, *Condorcet: From Natural Philosophy to Social Mathematics* (Chicago, IL: University of Chicago Press, 1974), 272-285; Tackett, *Becoming a Revolutionary*, 280-282.
5 Baker, *Condorcet*, 272; Tackett, *Becoming a Revolutionary*, 280. On the social composition of the Society, see especially Daniel L. Wick, *A Conspiracy of Well-intentioned Men: The Society of Thirty and the French Revolution* (New York, NY: Garland Publishers, 1987).
6 Tackett, *Becoming a Revolutionary*, 89-95.
7 Baker, *Condorcet*, 273-274.
8 Ibid., 287.
9 Palmer, *The Improvement of Humanity*, 101.
10 The project was formally adjourned to the next legislature on 25 September 1791. *AP* 31: 324-325. Jean Le Chapelier also expressed "regret" that the Assembly was leaving the reform of education to its successor, and Jean-Louis Emmery described the proposed delay as a "dishonor" to the Assembly. See *AP* 31: 340.
11 Charles-Maurice de Talleyrand-Périgord, *Rapport sur l'instruction publique, fait au nom du Comité de Constitution à l'Assemblée nationale, les 10, 11 et 19 septembre 1791* (Paris: Imprimerie nationale, 1791), 1.
12 Palmer, *The Improvement of Humanity*, 101.
13 Compayré, *Histoire critique des doctrines de l'éducation en France*, T. II, 307; Gontard, *L'Enseignement primaire en France*, 85.
14 Palmer, *The Improvement of Humanity*, 95.
15 Ibid., 95.
16 Talleyrand, *Rapport sur l'instruction publique*, 7-8. On the attempt to "synthesize" sensationism and Cartesianism in Rousseau's work, see Bloch, "Rousseau and Helvétius on innate and acquired traits." Talleyrand states clearly the relationship between his view of "dormant" attributes and his pedagogy; see Talleyrand, *Rapport sur l'instruction publique*, 90-92.
17 Talleyrand, *Rapport sur l'instruction publique*, 8.
18 Ibid., 25-26.
19 Ibid., 110-113.
20 Ibid., 8-10.
21 Ibid., 3.
22 Ibid., 4.
23 Ibid., 15.
24 Ibid., 15-16, 28-29, 95-96, *passim*.
25 Ibid., 16.
26 Ibid., 118.
27 Ibid., 118.
28 Ibid., 118-119.

29 Ibid., 121; 210-212. Palmer, *The Improvement of Humanity*, 98.
30 Talleyrand, *Rapport sur l'instruction publique*, 120.
31 Ibid., 22-23.
32 Ibid., 84-86.
33 Palmer, *The Improvement of Humanity*, 96; Compayré, *Histoire critique des doctrines de l'éducation en France*, 303.
34 There were to be ten *maîtres* in all: a principal or *"Inspecteur d'études,"* two professors of grammar, two of the humanities, two for rhetoric and logic, one for mathematics and physics, one for living languages, and one for Greek; the professors of those courses for which there were two would each teach their two-year course through completely.
35 Talleyrand, *Rapport sur l'instruction publique*, 32.
36 Ibid., 145-147.
37 Ibid., 144; 147-149.
38 Ibid., 17. On the *écoles de département*, see Palmer, *The Improvement of Humanity*, 98.
39 Talleyrand, *Rapport sur l'instruction publique*, 66-67.
40 Ibid., 173, 181-184.
41 Palmer, *The Improvement of Humanity*, 98; Compayré, *Histoire critique des doctrines de l'éducation en France*, T. II, 305.
42 Talleyrand, *Rapport sur l'instruction publique*, 76.
43 Ibid., 212-215.
44 Ibid., 215. He was criticized on this point by the deputy Camus, who claimed that granting oversight to the royal administration "separated" these institutions from the nation. See Compayré, *Histoire critique des doctrines de l'éducation en France*, T. II, 306.
45 Talleyrand, *Rapport sur l'instruction publique*, 102-117.
46 Ibid., 103.
47 Ibid., 104-105, 107.
48 Ibid., 105.
49 Ibid., 107.
50 Ibid., 107-109.
51 Ibid., 112.
52 Talleyrand stated explicitly that his aim was to "reproduce an image of [representative government] within the walls" of the new schools. Ibid., 105.
53 On the reception of Talleyrand's report, see Palmer, *The Improvement of Humanity*, 99-101.
54 AN, AD/VIII//21, no. 25, "Observations sur le rapport que M. de Talleyrand-Périgord, ancien évêque d'Autun, a fait à l'Assemblée nationale ... suivies d'un plan d'instruction primaire, nationale, par les maîtres de pension de Paris," (Paris, 1791); AN, F/17//1309, dossier 1, no. 9, "Appel à l'opinion publique sur l'éducation nationale"; Institut national de recherche pédagogique, Mont Saint-Aignan, no. 2002-2092, Isaac Haffner, *De l'Éducation*

littéraire ou, Éssai sur l'organisation d'un Établissement pour les hautes sciences (Strasbourg: La Librairie Académique, 1792).

55 In addition to ordering that Talleyrand's proposal be printed and presented to the Legislative Assembly for consideration, the Constituent Assembly did pass one piece of education-related legislation before disbanding, ordering on 26 September 1791 that the Faculty of Law in each university designate one of its members to offer instruction in the new constitution. *AP* 31: 340.

56 *AP* 34: 498.

57 Palmer, *The Improvement of Humanity*, 104.

58 *AP* 34: 1–25; also Palmer, *The Improvement of Humanity*, 104.

59 James Guillaume (ed.), *Procès-verbaux du Comité d'Instruction publique de l'Assemblée législative* (Paris: Imprimerie nationale, 1889), 1–2.

60 Ibid., 12. The first of these *mémoires*, "*Nature et objet de l'instruction publique*," is translated and reprinted in Jean-Antoine-Nicolas de Caritat, Marquis de Condorcet, *Selected Writings*, ed. Keith Michael Baker (Indianapolis, IN: Bobbs-Merrill Co., 1976): 105–142 [hereafter (*SW*)]. This first *mémoire* was followed by four others: "*De l'instruction commune pour les enfants*," "*Sur l'instruction commune pour les hommes*," "*Sur l'instruction relative aux professions*," and "*Sur l'instruction relative aux sciences*." Jean-Antoine-Nicolas de Caritat, marquis de Condorcet, *Écrits sur l'instruction publique*, ed. Charles Coutel and Catherine Kintzler, vol. 1 (Paris: Edilig, 1989), 35–241; also, and with his essay "*Sur la nécessité de l'instruction publique*," in Jean-Antoine-Nicolas de Caritat marquis de Condorcet, *Œuvres de Condorcet*, ed. A. Condorcet O'Connor and M. F. Arago, T. VII (Paris: Firmin Didot frères, 1847–1849): 169–573 [hereafter (*OC*)].

61 Palmer, *The Improvement of Humanity*, 124–125.

62 Guillaume, *Procès-verbaux du Comité d'Instruction publique de l'Assemblée législative*, 208–209, and a lengthy footnote on 210–213.

63 Ibid., 209.

64 For the curricula, see Ibid., 190–193, 226–228 as well as the second of Condorcet's mémoires, "*De l'instruction commune des enfants*" in Condorcet, *OC*, 7: 229–324.

65 Guillaume, *Procès-verbaux du Comité d'Instruction publique de l'Assemblée législative*, 194–196, 229; also Condorcet, *Écrits sur l'instruction publique*, vol. 1, 104–114.

66 Guillaume, *Procès-verbaux du Comité d'Instruction ublique de l'Assemblée législative*, 231. The total number of *instituts* proposed seems to have been a matter of some debate, the original copy stipulating 114 (as did Condorcet's *Rapport*), and the definitive copy settled upon by the Committee giving 110. Similarly, for the number of *instituts* to be created beyond the eighty-three departmental ones, the original copy called for thirty-one, but the definitive copy settled on twenty-seven. The proposal recreated in the *procès-verbaux* calls for 109 *instituts*. See Ibid., 196, 231–232, n. 1–2.

67 Ibid., 230–232.
68 Ibid., 196.
69 Condorcet, *Écrits sur l'instruction publique*, vol. 2, 253.
70 Guillaume, *Procès-verbaux du Comité d'Instruction publique de l'Assemblée législative*, 206–207.
71 Ibid., 206.
72 Condorcet called for forty-eight members in the Parisian *sciences mathématiques et physiques* class, with an equal number in the other departments, as well as eight foreign members; sixty-eight members of the *sciences morales et politiques* class (thirty in Paris, thirty in the departments, and eight abroad); 144 members of the *application des sciences aux arts* class within France (seventy-two each in Paris and in the departments), and twelve foreign members; and 100 members of the *littérature et beaux-arts* class (forty-four members in Paris, an equal number in the departments, and twelve abroad). Ibid., 237–241.
73 Ibid., 221–222.
74 J-P. Rabaut Saint-Étienne, *Projet d'éducation nationale* (Paris: Imprimerie nationale, n.d.), 1–4.
75 Nicola Peter Todorov, "Le Transfert du canton dans l'Allemagne napoléonienne," in Yann Lagadec, Jean Le Bihan and Jean-François Tanguy (eds), *Le Canton: Un territoire du quotidien?: Actes du colloque organisé à l'université Rennes 2 Haute Bretagne, 21–23 septembre 2006* (Rennes: Presses universitaires de Rennes, 2009), 62.
76 Rothschild, *Economic Sentiments*; Emma Rothschild, "Condorcet and Adam Smith on Education and Instruction"; David Williams, *Condorcet and Modernity* (New York, NY: Cambridge University Press, 2004).
77 Baker, *Condorcet*, 294–297.
78 Palmer, *The Improvement of Humanity*, 125.
79 Condorcet, "*Nature et objet de l'instruction publique*," SW, 124–133.
80 Ibid., 108.
81 Emma Rothschild makes a similar point regarding Condorcet's view of political society and political conflict, claiming that Condorcet's views were "subversive" of the "dichotomy of uniformity versus diversity, or of universal connectedness versus the endlessness of conflict." Rothschild, *Economic Sentiments*, 197.
82 Ibid., 190–192; Rothschild, "Condorcet and Adam Smith on Education and Instruction," 218.
83 Rothschild, *Economic Sentiments*, 15.
84 On the "social art," see J. J. Chambliss, "Condorcet," in J. J. Chambliss (ed.), *Philosophy of Education: An Encyclopedia* (New York, NY: Routledge, 1996), 105–107; Baker, *Condorcet*, 273–274.
85 Rothschild, *Economic Sentiments*, 210–211.
86 Condorcet, *OC*, 7: 234–235; Rothschild, *Economic Sentiments*, 10–11; 204–206.

87 Condorcet, *OC*, 7: 532.
88 Condorcet, "On Freedom. On the Meaning of the Words 'Freedom,' 'Free,' 'a Free Man,' 'a Free People'" (1793–1794) in *Condorcet: Political Writings*, ed. Steven Lukes and Nadia Urbinati (New York, NY: Cambridge University Press, 2012), 31.
89 Williams, *Condorcet and Modernity*, 103.
90 Condorcet, "*Nature et objet de l'instruction publique*" (*SW*), 105.
91 Ibid., 106.
92 Condorcet, *OC*, 7, 259.
93 Condorcet, "*Nature et objet de l'instruction publique*," *SW*, 120–121.
94 Baker, *Condorcet*, 270.
95 Condorcet, "*Nature et objet de l'instruction publique*," *SW*, 106.
96 Rothschild, "Condorcet and Adam Smith on Education and Instruction," 222.
97 Condorcet, "*Nature et objet de l'instruction publique*," *SW*, 107.
98 Rothschild, "Condorcet and Adam Smith on Education and Instruction," 219.
99 This description of politics is from Sophia Rosenfeld, "On being heard: a case for paying attention to the historical ear," *American Historical Review*, 116:2 (2011), 328.
100 Timothy Tackett, *The Coming of the Terror in the French Revolution* (Cambridge, MA: Harvard University Press, 2015), 165–171.
101 Palmer, *Improvement of Humanity*, 129–134; Baker, *Condorcet*, 292–320.
102 Rothschild, "Condorcet and Adam Smith on Education and Instruction," 216.

5

Revolutionary politics *à la plume*: the public on education and politics

Jules Michelet described the spring of 1789 as the "true era of the birth of the people. It called the whole nation to the exercise of its rights. They could at least write their complaints, their wishes, and choose the electors."[1] While historians have been quick to note the distance that separated the representatives in Versailles and the people who had elected them, Michelet's point is worth remembering. The citizens could write.

And write they did. They built upon the precedent of the *cahiers de doléances*, embraced the promise of article 6 of the *Declaration of the Rights of Man and of the Citizen*, and aimed to contribute to the formation of the General Will and of the law, not only through their representatives, but themselves, in person or with their pens. They wrote to the Assembly in droves, and their letters helped to establish a degree of legitimacy for the representative institutions taking shape in Versailles, and then Paris, while offering citizens a way to act at a distance, to reject the divide between "absolute" and "participatory" political representation.[2] Like the printing press, the correspondents' pen allowed citizens to position themselves as members of a public "that was unreliant on proximity."[3] Their letters wed participatory and representative government, and they help us to recall an avenue of political participation and a mode of political representation that was central to the promise of the Revolution, was embraced by a great many citizens, and was among the reasons that so many people thought education was essential to the success of revolutionary politics.

Habermas famously described the eighteenth century as the "century of the letter," but the letters sent to the Assembly and to other political authorities were not contributions to the "public sphere" in the customary sense.⁴ While some were read aloud on the Assembly floor and others were "read" into the Assembly's minutes or into those of its committees, the vast majority were both designed and destined to go no further than a deputy's (or a clerk's) desk. Nonetheless, these letters gave citizens a chance to be present before their representatives, even when they could not be there in person. As noted in a pamphlet submitted by the colonial adventurer Pierre Wouves d'Argès, whose *Appel à l'opinion publique* was noted briefly above and will be discussed in greater detail below, reading and writing were the "source of [one's] moral existence [under a system of representative government], and so truly indispensable."⁵ Historians and philosophers have echoed Wouves's sentiment, noting the role of writing in the emergence (and enculturation) of the modern subject, in the development of "an autonomous but relational subjectivity."⁶ These letters also helped to maintain the Assembly's claim to representative legitimacy after the rejection of the binding mandate by allowing the deputies to present themselves, in Honoré de Mirabeau's description, as giving "public existence to all of those individual existences which have freely developed, and form[ing] the general will out of all of those private wills."⁷ While Mirabeau's description may sound more like divination than devoted representation, the expectation that one could write to deputies in the Assembly and lay claim to their time and attention was a remarkable development and was an important moment in the navigation and negotiation of what representative government might mean (even if citizens' letters did not always receive such attention in practice).

This expectation began to take shape even before the Revolution became revolutionary, as the drafting and submission of the *cahiers de doléances* had helped to establish the principle that some form of popular participation would be crucial to the new politics (the *cahiers* were, in fact, the immediate reference for the Michelet quote with which this chapter began). The *cahiers* were embraced as venues for the public airing of ideas or grievances open to people traditionally excluded from the institutions and avenues of public debate or decision making, and they helped to shape expectations about how the people might engage with the new government. As Gilbert Shapiro and John Markoff noted, the *cahiers* were important at least in part because of the contrast between the 'openness' they represented and the generally "constrained" quality of political discourse under the Ancien Régime:

> This first convocation of the Estates-General in 175 years provided an opportunity that was unique for almost all of those who took part, and, if

only for this reason, was generally prized. The government not only permitted ordinary people to express their views on matters of public policy for the first time in their lives, it was even expected to be responsive to their views, as these were recorded in the *cahiers*, and advocated by their elected deputies.[8]

In response to this opening up of the political process, or at least to the perception that a space had been opened within the political process, approximately 40,000 *cahiers* were submitted for the Estates-General's consideration.[9] Those *cahiers* offer us an opportunity to assess where the "education question" stood at the start of the Revolution and a reminder that the process of reading, writing, and circulating political views was central to the dynamics of revolutionary politics from their very start.

According to Shapiro and Markoff, who tracked the frequency with which specific issues appeared in the *cahiers* (with 1 designating the issue which appeared most frequently in the *cahiers* of each group, and 1088 those that appeared least), the issue of public education tied as the 74th most frequently raised issue in *cahiers* from the nobility and was 87th in the *cahiers* of the Third Estate. Secondary education was the 77th most frequently raised issue among the submissions from the Third Estate (174th among those of the nobility), and the category "Education – Miscellaneous," ranked 300th among the issues of the parish *cahiers*, 140th among those of the Third, and 201st among those of the nobility. "Primary Education" ranked 315th among parish *cahiers*, issues related to the universities were tied for 167th among the *cahiers* of the Third, and those related to military schools were 156th among the nobility. As a point of reference, the terms of eligibility for deputies was 225th among the *cahiers* of the parishes, 394th among those of the Third, and 288th among those of the nobility, the purchase of noble titles was 407th among the parishes, 307th among the Third, and 105th for the nobility. If education was not the most pressing of issues in the France of 1789 (unsurprisingly, taxation was the issue most frequently raised in the *cahiers*), it was a subject that received considerable attention and in which citizens expressed clear interest.[10]

The *cahiers* reveal a general consensus that education ought to be more widely available and that the schools should serve public as well as private or individual interests. The clergy in Boulounnais, for example, argued that the costs of education should be borne by the community because the communal "benefits of education are well worth the sacrifice."[11] Clerics from Auxerre (Burgundy) and Dourdan (Île-de-France) argued for the establishment of schools in "every parish of the kingdom," and members of the Third Estate in Villiers-le-Bel (also in the Île-de-France) called for education to be made available to children of both sexes in every village across France.[12] Many of the *cahiers* calling for greater educational access for "the people" did so in the name of improving civic education. The nobles of Paris, for example, called for the creation of an elementary-level textbook which would provide a "summary of the principal points of the Constitution," and would "serve above all to educate the young."[13] Similar demands were made by nobles of Blois, Lyon, Saintes, Arras, Dourdan, Nantes, Guyenne, and Touraine.[14] Even some members of the clergy included calls for expanded civic education alongside demands for greater religious instruction, suggesting that instruction be expanded in fields such as civil law and, in some cases (as in the submission from the *sénéchaussée* d'Albret), that a "national catechism" be drafted and widely distributed.[15] In general, the *cahiers* show that while "nobody was entirely satisfied" with the state of French education in 1788–89, the proposals for reform were relatively moderate.[16]

The emergence of revolutionary politics and the explicit pursuit of a constitution led to a dramatic shift in the debate over education and politics. The need to "teach the Constitution" was not a pressing concern for those who wrote the *cahiers*; it ranked 1088th (that is, among the least frequent) among issues in the *cahiers* of the parishes, tied for 824th among those of the Third Estate, and was 689th among those of the nobility.[17] Over the course of 1789, however, as revolutionary politics took shape and as the ambitions of the National Assembly came to focus on what Michael Fitzsimmons has called a new "ideal of the polity," the relationship between educational reform and constitutional politics became a leitmotif among deputies and citizens alike. "Teaching the constitution" became a nearly omnipresent theme in the debates over education and politics.

While the *cahiers* were quickly overtaken by the revolutionary events of summer 1789, the precedent and the expectations that they had helped to establish bore fruit throughout the period of the constitutional monarchy and beyond. This is evident in the registers of letters received by the Constituent and Legislative assemblies, which include more than 50,000 entries for the period between September 1789 and the proclamation of the Republic in September 1792 (putting the traffic in correspondence under the assemblies in the same ballpark as the *cahiers de doléances* in terms of size, if not intensity).[18] The actual number of pieces received is surely much higher, not only because these records are incomplete in their coverage of the period (the registers for 21–30 June 1790 and for the months from September to December 1791 are missing from the archives; if the patterns from surrounding months held steady, the total would be approximately 55,000 entries), but also because the notaries or scribes would sometimes consolidate multiple submissions into one entry. For example, the Assembly's nationalization of church lands in November 1789 led to a vast survey of these properties and their value. This meant hundreds upon hundreds of pieces of correspondence for the Assembly and, for the scribe, hundreds upon hundreds of virtually identical entries.[19] By early February 1790, it was not unusual for 40 percent or more of the correspondence received on a given day to be related to church lands and nationalization. By the end of that month, the scribes had stopped recording these receipts individually, instead recording them in a single entry, often without indicating the number of pieces thereby "recorded." It seems safe to say that the Assembly received many more letters than there are entries, that is, many more than the approximately 55,000 entries that I've estimated we would find if we had complete registers for these years.

Unsurprisingly, many of these letters were from local political agents or representatives, political institutions, and other correspondents engaged in the "official" business of the state. The solicitation and transmission of information, opinions, and new laws required a great deal of paperwork and was critically important to the work and legitimacy of both the government and the state. As Ben Kafka has noted, "paperwork had become a technology of political representation."[20] It also became an instrument of political participation, and there were many letters from individuals and institutions unaffiliated with the offices of government. There were letters from political clubs and groups, *sociétés*, institutions, and other such corporate, quasi-corporate, or socio-collective bodies.[21] There were also letters from groups of citizens writing together as co-signatories to a common piece of correspondence (sometimes including a note attesting to the presence and endorsement of those who were present but could not sign their names). Then there were letters – many letters – from individual men and women who sought a letter writer's audience with the National Assembly.

The notes included in the Assembly's registers suggest at least four, sometimes-overlapping, sorts of letters. First, there were pieces of correspondence between government agencies or representatives. Again, many were part of the day-to-day workings of the government, including the transmission of information, registration of laws, execution of responsibilities, responses to inquiries, and the like. Many others among these were descriptive, aiming to help the deputies govern a territory too vast for them to maintain immediate knowledge of its workings. Second, there were attempts to persuade, to argue, to acclaim or to protest actions taken or proposed by the Assembly. While some of these were negative (the proposed *marc d'argent*, for example, led to an avalanche of disapproving correspondence), many were supportive, or at least constructive, offering suggestions rather than blanket condemnations. The third sort were abstract commentaries on the nature of government, on the idea of self-governance, on the role of religion in politics, on constitutional matters, and on the world being ushered in by the Revolution. These letters reveal a public wrestling with the conceptual underpinnings of the new social and political order and they are, perhaps, a less structured and more immediately political afterword to the sort of "participatory Enlightenment" that Jeremy Caradonna traced in his study of pre-Revolutionary *concours academiques*.[22] Finally, there were letters from people who sought the support of the state, whether in the form of a job, a pension, a promotion, a release from military service, or some other such thing.

Even this last sort, the directly "interested" appeals to the Assembly, offers us insight into how the Revolution was being received and engaged with by the citizenry. As Greg Downs has argued regarding the politics of dependency in the United States after the Civil War, these sorts of "interested" appeals were often employed by citizens as "a strategy, a tool to mediate politics for their own benefit" during a period of social tumult, personal hardship, or professional uncertainty, and to do so amid a shifting landscape of political institutions and expectations.[23] The same is true of correspondents in revolutionary France. Moreover, these letters suggest a transfer from the king to the Assembly not (or not just) of sacrality, but of anticipated or supposed efficacy and responsibility. If people were writing to the National Assembly, it is because that had become the place to write.[24] Also, and more to the point here, if people were *writing* to the National Assembly, it is because that was how they could be present before the political authorities even when they could not be there in person.

We do not, and perhaps cannot, know precisely how many letters were sent to the Assembly about education during these years. This is particularly true for the period prior to October 1791 (when the Committee of Public Instruction was established), as debates related to education lacked a clear administrative home prior to that point, taking place across at least four separate committees: the *Comité ecclésiastique*, *Comité d'aliénation*, *Comité de Constitution*, and the *Comité des finances*.[25] Many of the letters or proposals regarding education were sent to the Constitutional Committee (reinforcing the sense that the two were interwoven). Others, however, wound up elsewhere, and many made appearances before several committees, being shuffled from committee to committee as their contents became known.[26] That many elude us in the archives is certain.

What follows, in this chapter and the next, is based upon a review of hundreds of letters, reports, and pieces of correspondence sent to the National Assembly, the departmental authorities in the Haute Garonne, and the municipal authorities in Toulouse. These letters were part of a debate over political change and educational reform that extended far beyond the halls of the Assembly, was not dominated by the figures and celebrities of national revolutionary politics, and was shaped at one and the same time by political ambitions, practical concerns, and provisional expectations of a revolution in flux.[27] It builds upon a suggestion offered by Jean-François Chassaing's study of *livres élémentaires* submitted for the *concours* of year II, which he drew upon to explore the "*mentalité révolutionnaire* ... not just of its leaders, but of people who simply looked favorably upon the Revolution."[28] Read in this light, these letters reveal political and pedagogical authorities, teachers, students, and members of a broader public trying to understand, navigate, and contribute to the Revolution, trying to articulate and foster a collective "*mentalité révolutionnaire.*"

The public weighs in on "instruction publique"

Between the start of the Revolution and the collapse of the constitutional monarchy, citizens across France wrote to the Assembly urging their representatives to take up the issue of educational reform and fulfill one of the Revolution's most fundamental promises and obligations. They argued that educational reform should be among the legislators' highest priorities as it was central to the broader work of making a new political order take root and flourish in France (botanical metaphors were common). They agreed with Mirabeau's sentiment that "liberty is not as simple as it might appear at first glance," and that the people had to be prepared for their role in the new political system.[29] As a Monsieur de LaFontaine of Paris wrote in June 1791, "Please take up the cause of instruction; honor it and protect it. Then the Constitution, planted in a soil that has been well cleared and well cultivated, will be assured to produce superb branches, and give us all shelter from the scourges of tyranny from which other nations suffer."[30]

Most of the letters were unsolicited, and they show citizens embracing an epistolary form of participatory politics and public debate. They vary widely in terms of length and level of detail (the *Plan d'éducation nationale* submitted by a M. Hidince of Lyon, for example, lays out 237 proposed articles of reform in fifteen tightly packed handwritten pages, whereas a one-page handwritten letter from M. Sudrand, a priest and prison chaplain from Angoulême, asks simply that the legislators create a *"Comité de mœurs,"* without detailing how such a committee might work or what it might do).[31] They also differ dramatically in style, in rhetorical and intellectual sophistication, in the areas on which they focus their attention, and in their estimate of how much education "the people" of France required in order to become "the public" upon which a new politics could be built. Most of these letters were handwritten, but most were also of fairly considerable length, generally at least three or four pages, often ten pages or more and, in some cases, quite a bit longer still. They came, according to the correspondents' self-identifications, from individuals and institutions with a variety of professional or political associations.

These letters reveal a populace, or at least a portion of the educated and politically engaged populace, that remained informed about the political debates over education, thought education and educational reform important to the political project headlined by the Constitution, and felt it within their rights – and often among their civic duties – to participate in that debate by submitting their letters, proposals, criticisms, and suggestions. These correspondents saw education as crucial to the fate of the new political regime and saw the debate over educational reform as an arena in which they could contribute to the work of the new politics.

These points were often expressed in anxious terms, as correspondents noted the "futility" of attempting to implement "even the wisest laws" or constitution in a country inhabited by ignorant or uneducated citizens. As the Conseil Général de la Commune de Soissons put it in a November 1790 address to the National Assembly, "in vain will the Constitution give us the finest laws, if its reign has not been prepared by a system of public education."[32] These correspondents did not ignore the need for education to promote economically useful skills and publicly useful knowledge, nor did they reject the idea that the schools ought to work towards the improvement of the sciences and professions, but more important than either of these was education's role in promoting and protecting the principles of the new Constitution. Again and again they stressed that what was at stake in the debates over education was the character and identity of the new political society.

These correspondents were concerned not only about anti-revolutionary forces, but also that the members of the National Assembly would not go far enough in their constitutional efforts, that they might design a new political infrastructure without establishing the social conditions within which that infrastructure could be given practical force, or that they might institute a participatory system of representative government without giving the French people the knowledge and skills necessary for political participation.[33] Others expressed exasperation that the reform of education was taking so long, that the legislators allowed themselves to be distracted from such an important task.[34] Their worry was not (or at least not only) protecting the Constitution from foreign enemies or counter-revolutionary conspirators, but safeguarding it against political timidity and legislative inertia.

This theme was emphasized in correspondence sent to the Assembly even after the Constitution of September 1791 was presented to and accepted by Louis XVI, albeit with a shift in emphasis from education's role in helping to establish a constitutional regime to its role in perfecting or protecting that regime. A M. Gadolle, for example, explained to the deputies in October 1791 that it was "through the enlightened zeal of instructors that our Constitution will arrive little by little at that level of stability and perfection that good sense leads us to anticipate, and it is through them that [the Constitution] will receive its majestic and sonorous voice."[35] While their appeals were not always so lyrical, many of the correspondents stressed the need for an educational system that would solidify, support, and reflect the principles of the new constitutional regime. Others stressed the fragility of the gains made by the Revolution and the fear that they might be lost, whether to "enemies of Liberty" or to the hands of time, if they were not re-enforced and protected through education.

Like Mirabeau and his proposal for politically ameliorative festivals, many of the correspondents argued that the government needed to cultivate sentiments that would attach the populace to the new regime. Here, ideas about education, human sentimentality and sensibility, and civic or social interaction became entangled with one another, leading correspondents to explain how new ways of organizing and approaching education might remake how citizens perceived and thought about one another (as individuals and as a collective), and how this in turn might strengthen the "social chain" that turned people into a polity. Like the Physiocrats a generation earlier, these correspondents believed that part of education's purpose was to make people aware of their social, political, and economic relations with one another, their dependence upon one another, and their prospects for mutual benefit when social institutions functioned properly.[36] They also anticipated public debate and, at least implicitly, disagreement, proposing measures to inform the populace about the new political institutions and norms and to promote the sort of civic sentiments that would make political society sustainable. A correspondent from Verneuil listed the sentiments he deemed necessary for the new society, including "love for God and for men, *bienfaisance*, kindness, patience, equality, liberty, a willingness to ignore injury and pardon offense," attributes he thought should be developed in the schools alongside instruction in Latin and French, history, geography, mathematics, morals, music, and dance.[37]

Others stressed the need for such sentiments to be cultivated among non-student populations as well, designating both public and private spaces as sites for educational events, including public squares, churches, private homes and, after the regular school day had concluded, the schools themselves.[38] In November 1791, for instance, a M. Lespomarede from the Haut-Rhin proposed that all laws and decrees be published and distributed among the nation's *pères de familles*, along with whatever explanations might be needed to make those laws fully understood, that public festivals be used to bring the people together and attach them to the new regime, and that public lectures be held in churches during inclement weather and in public squares when the weather permitted. These sessions would include the reading aloud of public laws (either laws recently passed by the National Assembly or the "fundamental" laws that underwrote the new order) and would contribute to the formation of a rejuvenated "*esprit public*." This would, he promised, help to guard against the "enemies of the *Patrie*" who sought to "uproot the tree of Liberty" and keep the people in ignorance.[39]

In their efforts to integrate or synthesize models of civic education and more technical instruction, these letters reveal a public complement to the idea of public instruction taking shape among the legislators in the Assembly (described in Chapter 3). These correspondents saw public instruction as encompassing a vast array of subjects and as contributing to many of the revolution's ambitions. The synthesis of academic and political ambitions was sometimes explicit, as in the proposal from a M. Codel, *homme de loi* in Rennes, which was sent to the Assembly by the administrators of the Departement de l'Isle et Vilaine as a model for a "complete and truly national system of education," one that incorporated the sciences of nature and those of political society into a single pedagogical plan.⁴⁰ In other cases "public instruction" meant offering lectures and lessons in new environments, as in the proposal for a "theater of national education" submitted by Laurent-Gaspard Gérard of Paris. Gérard described his theater as offering not "amusement or distraction, but instruction," a form of instruction that could complement and reinforce what was learned in books or in more traditional venues such as the *collèges* (the anticipated reform of which Gèrard cited as the contextual background to his own proposal). The performances would be preceded by a public lecture outlining the production's central concepts and principles; together, the lecture and the dramatic performance would offer a practical synthesis of political instruction and morally improving entertainment.⁴¹

The desire to coordinate the principles and practices of "public instruction" was particularly evident in the proposals of Léonard Bourdon, the later Jacobin, regicide *conventionnel*, and particularly "rabid [member] of the Mountain."⁴² Bourdon, who would establish the *Société des jeunes françaises* in 1792, had already taken up the question of educational reform in the years prior to 1789.⁴³ In 1788, he had proposed the formation of a model school, called the *Société Royale d'Émulation*.⁴⁴ Bourdon's proposed school, which resembled closely the Swiss model described approvingly by Rousseau in his *Considerations on the Government of Poland* (discussed in Chapter 1), was designed for those whom "birth and fortune call to high position," and was priced accordingly (he proposed an annual fee of 3,000 *livres* per student, compared to 700 *livres* paid by the king for each cadet at the *écoles militaires*).⁴⁵ While predicated upon the social hierarchy of the Ancien Régime, Bourdon's proposal reflected the emphasis on participatory self-governance that was gaining momentum amid the crises of the 1780s and offered a template that he would translate into a more democratic language after 1789.

Bourdon proposed a school that was overseen and administered by a series of committees staffed by professors, *maîtres* and, most importantly, students. Students would be responsible for maintaining order among themselves, for disciplining and rewarding one another, and for electing student-representatives to participate in the governance and administration of the school. Bourdon believed that this arrangement would serve two important purposes: first, by freeing the instructors from their role as disciplinarians, it would bring an end to the "habitual state of war" between students and instructors, which he saw as poisonous to the bonds of affection and *émulation* that motivate pupils to learn; second, it would give students experience in an orderly form of self-governance, one that would serve as a sort of "social apprenticeship" and prepare them for the important functions they would later assume in French society and politics.[46] The scheme was not realized, though Bourdon claimed to have received the government's promise of financial "encouragements" (those "encouragements" were in fact non-pecuniary, and any promise of future financial support depended upon Bourdon's ability to establish the school himself and show that his model worked).[47] It did, however, serve to legitimize Bourdon as an authority on education just as French politics was about to focus intently on the subject once again. It also established the primary theme of Bourdon's work on education: that schools ought to both reflect and provide an "apprenticeship" for one's social, political, and professional life.

In May 1790, Bourdon sent a number of pieces to the Assembly's constitutional committee, including his proposal for the "regeneration of public education" and a copy of the "*Idées sur l'éducation nationale*" that he had sent to the Estates-General. In October of that same year, he submitted copies of two ministerial letters expressing approval of his earlier work.[48] In his prefatory letter, Bourdon again wrote of education as a form of social and political apprenticeship, writing that the schools ought to be "an apprenticeship for life, and for liberty."[49] Returning to and adapting his earlier theme of ending the "habitual state of war" between students and instructors, Bourdon argued that the schools ought to be administered under a "constitution" that was analogous to, and preparatory for, the national constitution, one that included a "separation of powers" between the students and their instructors, thus "re-establishing harmony among them" and serving as the "base for a solid and durable accord."[50]

Bourdon dismissed the existing institutions as beyond repair, being "too opposed to the new order of things ... and to the natural development of man's faculties." He indicted the education offered in the pre-revolutionary schools as suffering from an "*esprit de système*" that was both capricious and arbitrary. The result, he claimed, was an educational regime in which instructors became "oppressive" and "despotic" while the students were crushed under a "spirit of insubordination, aversion, and indifference."[51] Linking pedagogy and politics, he called for a "positive revolution" in French education and proposed schools in which students were led, by both perception and practice, towards the principles, ideas, and habits that would "inscribe in their hearts notions of justice, of order, and of virtue." This would "put [students] in a state of society, one that is an accurate model of the society in which they will one day live."[52]

In his *Projet de Décret sur l'Éducation Publique*, Bourdon outlined a three-tier system of education, starting with *petites écoles* in each canton offering free instruction in reading, writing, basic mathematics, and the principles of morality and of the constitution.[53] Next were *écoles de district*, located in the chief city of each district and replacing the Ancien Régime *collèges*. Making use of Ancien Régime resources, Bourdon proposed that the schools take over the buildings of their predecessors (or of religious houses where there was not a *collège* to be replaced) and that they be funded with the endowments and lands formerly associated with the *collèges*. The *écoles de district* would offer instruction, again free, in design, mathematics, the French and Latin languages, physics, rhetoric, logic and law (the last including moral, political, and civil law). Finally, Bourdon proposed a series of *écoles de département* in which, in addition to the subjects taught in the district schools, courses would be offered in public law, Greek, and modern European languages. Bourdon acknowledged that his curriculum mirrored those of the Ancien Régime *collèges*, but argued that the efficacy of lessons depended upon context as well as content and, in the case of the *collèges*, an inappropriate and poorly designed institution had spoiled even well-selected content.

Bourdon's real focus was not on curricular matters, but on the social and political lessons offered by life in the schools, particularly in the administration and "governance" of the schools. Here he sought to balance the need for a national system of education with the schools' mission to prepare students for life as autonomous members of a democratic society. To do so, he called for a uniform system of regulations that would apply in all of the nation's schools, but also for the maintenance and execution of those regulations to be entrusted to the students, a point with which Bourdon returned to the central theme of his educational philosophy. Presenting arguments very similar to those in his 1788 proposal for a *Société Royale d'Émulation*, he stipulated in articles 25 and 29 of the *Projet de Décret* that "the students form among themselves a council of discipline, on which two professors would serve as assistants, and this council will be responsible for meting out punishments as well as rewards." More generally, he proposed that "all school functions that do not relate to instruction will be conferred upon the students."[54] This would create, he claimed:

> a new order of things, in which the *maître* would be replaced by the law, and instructors would be freed from any appearance of having to fulfill functions other than those of instructing and teaching. This will assure

them the confidence of their students, and give to them the liberty to draw upon and deploy all of their forces, to steer their students in ways unseen, but necessary to have them apply themselves, to give them experiences and a sense of good order, and to attach them through the two bonds of sentiment and reason to the accomplishment of their responsibilities; thus public consideration, that almighty domain, will rediscover its energy: the young will become moral instructors, one to the other, and thus their good actions as well as their faults, their rewards and their punishments, will be put to the benefit of all.[55]

In the schools as in the Assembly, a system within which authority stemmed from personality would be replaced by the authority of the law, a fair and impartial system of justice would both create and permit social spaces for people to organize and (informally) police themselves, and the system would be maintained by a social environment in which the pursuit of honor and esteem would goad people into loving and protecting the new regime. In its explicit mirroring of political and pedagogical reforms, Bourdon's program highlights what was novel about public instruction, a point that the Jacobin club of Paris, including Alexandre Beauharnois, Alexandre Lameth, and Collot d'Herbois, seized upon when it voted in March 1791 to endorse Bourdon's plan and to encourage Rabaut Saint-Étienne to promote it in the constitutional committee and to the Assembly at large.[56]

Even as correspondents gave voice to these new pedagogical emphases and ambitions, more familiar concerns remained, a point that was particularly clear in the many letters encouraging the Assembly to ensure that all citizens were taught to read and to write. As noted in the preceding chapters, and as we will see again below, establishing widespread literacy was recognized as central to preparing the people for participation in politics. Without a national system of education and, with that, an educated and literate populace, correspondents feared that the promise of the *Declaration of the Rights of Man and Citizen* would remain unfulfilled and equality before the law would exist only on paper.[57] The nation would be divided, a Jacobin club in Brignoles warned, between "one part, enlightened by the thought of a philosophical century which has seen the dawn of liberty," and another, "less well-instructed, but no less courageous, left to make do with only that general desire [for freedom] that nature engraved in the hearts of all men."[58] Others worried that the ill-informed views of illiterate citizens would lead to adverse political outcomes, endangering the public well-being and jeopardizing the new political institutions.[59] These concerns are evident in the near consensus among correspondents that the state ought to require all students to remain in school at least to the point of literacy. Reading and writing were among the skills considered, as the Constitution of 1791 would put it, "*indispensables pour tous les hommes*." Just a few months after the promulgation of that constitution, the point was made more forcefully still in Pierre Wouves's *Appel à l'opinion publique sur l'éducation nationale*, noted above and discussed in greater detail below, in which it was argued that the ability to read and write was the very foundation of representative government.[60]

The anticipated role of a literate populace in the new politics, and ideas about education's role in securing and preserving the constitution, gave rise to concerns about the accessibility – or inaccessibility – of schools in rural areas. Correspondents worried that the peasantry was "trapped in a vile ignorance of the principles of the Constitution."[61] They worried that there would not be enough qualified instructors in rural areas.[62] They worried about the political sympathies and influence of those instructors who could be found.[63] Others framed their arguments in terms of political participation, representation, and legitimacy, raising concerns that the illiteracy of the rural population would lead to the corruption or degradation of the political process. The Jacobin Society on rue Saint Honoré in Paris proposed a series of weekly "news campaigns" to ensure that citizens in rural areas were kept up-to-date on developments shaping the Revolution.[64] A correspondent from the Department des Deux-Sèvres, who identified himself only as "le bon patriote," wrote to the Assembly in July 1790 concerned that the shortage of literate citizens in rural areas would leave communities with no real choice in electing municipal officials, and that those who could read and write would hold a virtual monopoly on power in these areas.[65] Others worried that the votes of illiterate citizens would be misreported or misrepresented by self-interested scribes or notaries.[66] These correspondents saw both the efficacy and the legitimacy of representative government as dependent upon the literacy of the populace, and they saw the countryside as a source of concern on both fronts.

These anxieties were symptomatic of the larger tension between the process of realizing education's promise, which would take time, and the Revolution's need for people to demonstrate promptly the skills, habits, and dispositions necessary for participatory and representative government to survive. As a correspondent from Bayeux wrote to the deputies, "the first fruits of your labors will not be realized until the next generation. To ensure that that happens, you will have to support the constitution with your leadership and with force" in the present.[67] As this correspondent and others like him recognized, the revolutionary process was generational, but its success depended upon its benefits being available at its conception. They invoked this version of the "Legislator's Dilemma" described by Rousseau (and discussed in Chapter 3) to urge the Assembly to act promptly on educational reform and to begin the work of "eternalizing" the constitution.[68]

Given the relative consensus that education was crucial to the success of the new political order, and perhaps unsurprisingly given that these correspondents chose to write the Assembly about education, most seemed to assume that the costs associated with the new system would be paid by the government. This was not universally true, as some continued to argue that education ought not to be free, that the improvement of education required that both students and teachers be driven by the incentives, interests, and consequences of commercial exchange. Nonetheless, as we saw in Chapter 3, the expectation that the state would be responsible for funding the new system was encouraged by many of the laws coming from the National Assembly, starting with the nationalization but non-sale of the lands associated with educational institutions in November 1789.

There were also positive political reasons for education to be state funded though, including some that bound the question of finance to education's role in preventing social inequality from undermining equality before the law. Echoing arguments like Rolland d'Erceville's in the 1760s, an anonymous correspondent from the Departement d'Indre argued in October 1790 that a free education would foster a more meritocratic social order and allow the state and the society to take advantage of "rare" and extraordinary talents that might not otherwise be recognized.[69] State funding for education was embraced by some as a means by which to further integrate educational institutions into the national political infrastructure (and so students and teachers into the national community). The argument worked in reverse too, as those who argued against state funding were subject to condemnation as counter-revolutionaries who sought to defend privilege and undermine the new constitutional order.[70]

Just as the design of educational institutions evolved in dialogue with proposals for the reform of other revolutionary institutions – such as the judiciary – it was also shaped by ideas about how educational institutions had functioned in the past. Unsurprisingly, what correspondents thought of the schools inherited from the Ancien Régime influenced what they thought schools should or could do in the future. On this, the letters reveal a deeply ambivalent populace. Many of the correspondents were critical of the *écoles*, *collèges*, universities, and academies of the Ancien Régime, leading some to follow Rousseau in despairing of public institutions and calling for the educational system to be pared down as far as was politically feasible (the citizens of Ecully les Lions, for instance, decried the government's expenses on *collèges* as wasteful, "ambitious," and contrary to nature, demanding instead that children be educated at home by their parents).[71] Most, however, agreed that public education was valuable and that the government needed to create additional institutions, leading to requests that the institutions inherited from the Ancien Régime be preserved (at least until the Assembly settled upon a reformed system of national education), or for reformed versions of the Ancien Régime's schools to be re-established and made more widely accessible.[72] Occasionally, correspondents would argue that the schools ought to remain as they were, including a demand that the University of Douai be preserved "in all of its privileges."[73]

While such wholesale defenses of Ancien Régime institutions were rare, most correspondents seemed to envision a series of reforms after which educational institutions would differ from, but would be recognizably related to, their pre-revolutionary predecessors. Many called for a state-run (and state-funded) system that extended beyond the primary level, and the most frequently described system was one in which there were primary, secondary, tertiary, and research institutions that improved upon the Ancien Régime model. The continuity was functional as well as curricular, as correspondents asked that the existing institutions be preserved at least provisionally and, in some cases, that they be incorporated into, rather than dismantled and replaced by, a new system of national education.

These requests came not only from the schools themselves (which will be discussed in the next chapter), but also from local political administrators, from political clubs, and from groups of citizens petitioning collectively. They praised the schools they had, and some worried that the schools' valuable work was being unnecessarily (or at least prematurely) upset by attempts to anticipate what the Assembly might do. They noted the benefits that the schools offered current students, local communities, and the French nation. Some noted the economic benefits that came with a *collège*, both in giving parents an opportunity to educate their sons inexpensively and in generating business for local enterprises.[74] The Jacobin club in Rennes drew upon both practical and political arguments when they wrote to the Assembly in November 1790 asking that the schools offering free instruction in surgery, mathematics, and design be maintained and supported in their work, arguing that these schools contributed to the "public good" and promoted "political and moral virtues." The Jacobins worried that disruptions would "slow students' progress, cut short the development of useful knowledge, and abandon these students to a period of idleness" that would undermine their health and their later usefulness to the country.[75] They proposed that these schools be kept open until a new system of education was in place and, more ambitiously, proposed that the existing schools be built upon to turn Rennes into a regional center of public instruction.

At the same time, many correspondents were wary of trying to integrate Ancien Régime schools into revolutionary society. They saw these institutions as unprepared or ill-designed to serve the needs of a democratic society and, often, as too tainted by historical association to be embraced by the revolutionary public. Their criticisms mixed grievances familiar from the years before 1789 with new concerns, though the two often overlapped. For example, the *collèges*, universities, and academies were criticized in the decades prior to the Revolution for being antiquated and trapped in a curricular tradition that made them incapable of serving the interests of either the people or of the state. With the coming of the Revolution and the expectation that France, and France's interests, would change dramatically, those critiques became all the more intense. Critics described the *collèges* as "moribund" and antiquated and noted their historical and administrative associations with the monarchy and the Church, making them targets as those two institutions fell increasingly out of favor.[76] A correspondent named M. Bienvenue from St Briene, whose proposal for training instructors will be discussed in greater detail below, described the *collèges* of the Ancien Régime as "gothic institutions" in which students traditionally spent nine or ten years being poorly instructed in obscure lessons, learning nothing of any use to society, acquiring instead a set of absurd and dangerous prejudices that they would do well to forget once they left the schools.[77] Sentiments such as these bode ill for the schools' continued existence.

More fundamental still were criticisms that the principles and practices of the Ancien Régime schools were antithetical to the animating principles of the new social and political order. For example, as we have already seen in Mirabeau's work, critics influenced by laissez-faire economic thought found the *collèges* and institutions like them to be incompatible with the idea that competition would produce the most effective and efficient system of education. Some correspondents argued for what they called "*enseignement libre*," a system in which instructors would compete for students and, in its purer or more radical iterations, in which instructors would not have to be sanctioned or certified by a professional authority or by the state before offering their services to pupils and parents. These proposals synthesized faith in an academic "market" and anti-clerical or anti-institutional impulses. The former built upon the growing visibility of "*cours public*" in the last decades of the Ancien Régime. These courses were offered outside (though often in close proximity to) the universities and *collèges*, focused primarily on "useful" subjects, and required that students pay (generally modest) fees. By the end of the Ancien Régime, these courses were sufficiently popular to indicate a shift in how people thought about education and, perhaps, to suggest new possibilities for funding, publicizing, administering, and maintaining educational institutions.[78]

The anti-clerical, or at least anti-monastic, strain of this argument was made explicit in the September 1790 letter sent to the Assembly by a Frère Jérôme of Amiens, who claimed that entrusting schools to religious orders was "contrary to the principles of political liberty and of individualism, the foundations of the new Constitution."[79] To others, particularly those who considered the establishment of social equality an important part of the revolutionary project, the *collèges* were criticized as instruments of social differentiation that enabled elites to enjoy and protect their social status and privileges. For others still, the schools were simply corrupt instruments of elite self-promotion and preservation, as in the case of an anonymous correspondent who charged that the universities were selling law degrees to wealthy but unqualified candidates who had not studied and who knew little of the law.[80] A Monsieur Maubauch, distilling these critiques to their social essence, complained that "there [was] no national education [in France], only an education for the privileged, or, if you will, an aristocratic education."[81]

Finally, the *collèges*, universities, and other Ancien Régime institutions were criticized because they were corporations in a society that was increasingly anti-corporatist and in which, after summer 1791, corporations were legally non-existent (with the aforementioned exception for *collèges*, universities, and academies). This left defenders of the academies, *collèges*, and universities to answer for their institutional structure and to explain why they warranted special treatment. They attempted to do so by emphasizing the utility of these institutions, by highlighting their role in disseminating knowledge and skills – a point that was supposed to answer the criticism that guilds and corporations were exclusive institutions designed to deny opportunities or resources to those who sought them – and, for the schools, by arguing that their institutional shortcomings would be addressed by more public forms of recruiting and certifying instructors.

Anti-corporatist attacks on the *collèges*, universities, and academies were not new in, and after, 1789. But they were given new energy and force by the upheaval of revolutionary politics, the attacks on privilege, the dismantling of the society of orders, and the promise of a regenerative egalitarianism.[82] These forces were evident in the *Palladium de la constitution politique, ou régénération morale de la France* submitted to the Assembly by Lambert Rivière in 1790; Rivière wrote that "every corporation that is not necessary to the working of the state is necessarily harmful." He thought universities particularly loathsome, and he described them as "privileged corporations that exercise an aristocratic position that ought to be odious in the Republic of the Sciences and Letters, and is incompatible with a free constitution. Vicious by their nature, essentially useless and radically harmful, they foment ignorance and pride, inspire Charlatanism, and favor ineptitude and prejudice over merit." His assessment of the *collèges* was no kinder: "The *collèges* are not only useless, but are morally and physically harmful to children and they pose an insurmountable obstacle to a good education; they will never be able to change their nature, no matter what new form and organization they are given … they are contrary to the [national] goal of a salutary regeneration, and they should be suppressed."[83] As Rivière's indictment made clear, revolutionary anti-corporatism blended critiques familiar from the pre-revolutionary decades with a language of moral and political regeneration; this mix would prove particularly potent regarding debates over how to best recruit, train, and retain desirable teachers.[84]

The embrace of sensationist philosophy and emphasis on the emulative dynamics at work in the classroom had led, in the decades preceding the Revolution, to a new and expanded sense of what made for a good instructor. Looking beyond the instructor's role in getting students to study, correspondents noted that teachers would exert tremendous influence upon the sentiments, allegiances, and aspirations of the young. For example, in a June 1791 letter in which they complained that priests who had not taken the ecclesiastical oath continued to teach, and in which they implored the government to replace those refractory priests with "patriotic instructors who are friends of the new laws," the members of the Directoire du Département du Nord claimed that the "first impressions made upon the young are always the strongest, and for that reason, the most dangerous as well."[85] Given the importance of education to the preservation of the new order, the Assembly could not permit the schools to be inhabited by instructors who were anything less than zealous in their support of the new politics.

For those who anticipated a relatively limited reform of the institutions and practices associated with education, the requirement that all priests (and so all priest-teachers) publicly accept the Civil Constitution of the Clergy and swear an oath of fealty to the French state was supposed to have addressed the issue of how to vet instructors.[86] Others thought this insufficient, arguing that instructors needed to be fully invested in the society they were helping to form, and so should be drawn from among the most engaged and active of citizens, and especially among *pères de famille*, who they thought would bring an immediate and unshakable sense of purpose to their work in the classroom. While those who wrote to the Assembly proposed a variety of measures intended to integrate instructors and instruction into the new social order, they almost all agreed that the recruitment and selection of instructors was an issue that would have to be addressed.

The problem of recruiting, training, and installing appropriate instructors into the classroom was at the heart of proposals presented by M. Bienvenue of St Briene (noted above) and by a M. Beaurien in St Quentin (Picardy).[87] Their proposals were similar in many ways. Each described a three-tier system of schools organized at the level of the canton, the district, and the department. Each called for the government to bear most of the cost of the system, though Bienvenue extended that support further than did Beaurien. The former called for state funds, drawn from the revenue generated by nationalized lands, to pay for all three levels of schooling; the latter limited completely free education to the *écoles de canton*, with fees introduced incrementally after that and offset by scholarships for students "*privés de fortune.*" Beaurien's curriculum was more ambitious than was Bienvenue's, though each was clearly working from pre-revolutionary models while aiming to incorporate more "useful" fields alongside the classical curriculum. Where they differed, and where each developed his most forceful and passionate arguments, was on the recruitment, selection, training, and certification of instructors.

Bienvenue presented something akin to the Physiocratic proposals of the pre-revolutionary period and to Mirabeau's almost contemporaneous work. He described teaching as the "important and noble job of raising and forming citizens," one that required the convergence of good morals, patriotism, and talent in "*un homme tout entier.*"[88] He was optimistic that the legislature could attract such exceptional men if it employed the right means: namely, to appeal to people's vanity and their desire for profit. To attract learned and talented men, Bienvenue proposed a seemingly straightforward solution: pay them well. This would not only appeal to their financial interests, it would also demonstrate the esteem in which they were held by society, and so appeal to their sense of pride.[89] Having attracted desirable candidates, the question remained how to select them, as Bienvenue stopped short of the more radical forms of *enseignement libre* in which teachers were largely unregulated. Instead, he called for a public concours open to all interested candidates. The proposed concours reflected the multi-faceted expectations being placed upon instructors, as candidates would be required to submit two dossiers: the first containing certificates of morality, probity, and civic standing signed by the relevant political authorities; the second with the candidates' professional and scholarly credentials and demonstrations of their aptitude as an instructor. The concours would then be judged by academic authorities (professors) and political administrators, demonstrating again the overlapping interests and concerns at work in the selection of suitable instructors from among even the most desirable candidate pools.

Where Bienvenue turned to social competition, financial interests, and a mix of political and professorial oversight, Beaurien turned to a model that was familiar from pre-revolutionary guilds and teaching orders, one that drew upon institutional mentoring and memory to ensure consistently well-trained instructors. To create a public version of this pre-revolutionary dynamic, he called upon the state to design and implement a lengthy process of examination and apprenticeship for prospective teachers, one that would give them the expertise and experience needed to teach effectively. During their training, apprentice instructors would supervise younger students and be supervised in turn by an Inspector General, a more experienced teacher who was at least 45 years old. The Inspector General would serve as both model and tutor, shaping the candidates' experiences and ensuring the sort of institutional stability that religious orders had offered before the Revolution. To maintain standards and prevent favoritism, Beaurien would require that a candidate be endorsed by a majority of the inspectors under whom he had trained. Acknowledging that this was a reformed version of an Ancien Régime model, Beaurien argued that this would "abolish the abuses of the old system" while enabling the state to find instructors who were both learned and attached to their profession.[90]

A model synthesizing the approaches of correspondents like

Bienvenue and Beaurien was presented by the philosopher and theologian Antoine-Joseph Dorsch of Strasbourg, who called for the establishment of *collèges des maîtres d'école* in a March 1792 letter outlining his *Projet d'établissement de collèges pour l'instruction d'école*.[91] Dorsch claimed that the schools he proposed were "unlike any other institution of public education," though many elements of his proposal are familiar from proposals discussed above.[92] He sought to combine the kinds of competitive principles embraced by Bienvenue and Mirabeau, the institutional regularity of proposals like Beaurien's, and the national standardization of training that had been debated since the 1760s and had been gestured towards but left undeveloped and incomplete by the creation of the *agrégation* in 1766. Wary of proposals that relied upon the enthusiasm and initiative of instructors, and perhaps mindful of the tension between national plans and local circumstances, he implored the Assembly to take responsibility for reform, to design a regular curriculum and uniform institutions, but at the same time to promote competition among candidates and allow local populations some control over who would run their schools.[93] For Dorsch, the combination of these three elements was crucial to the success of educational reform, which required not only a new system for training instructors (and administrators), but also the coordination of national and local interests and supervision as that new system was implemented.

Dorsch described schools in which future *maîtres d'écoles* would be offered instruction in religion, morality, and the French Constitution, as well as reading and writing, arithmetic, natural history, the physical sciences, agricultural theory, history, and pedagogical method. The merit of such institutions was, he thought, obvious, and so he did not bother describing their utility beyond pointing out that they served the public good and would "spread true enlightenment, and the spirit of the Constitution, among the people." These schools would provide a set of uniform standards for France while also protecting the right of local communities to control their schools. To strike this balance, Dorsch proposed that attendance at one of these *collèges* be a necessary condition for employment as a *maître*, but not a guarantee of such employment; hiring decisions would be made through local elections, enabling citizens to decide who would run their schools just as they could decide who administered their government.[94]

In his systems of training, certifying, and selecting instructors, Dorsch sought to reconcile the imperatives of regeneration, nationalization, and popular sovereignty, illustrating again the complementary dynamics of political and pedagogical reforms. Each would depend upon and reflect the other, a mirroring process that made the work of reform both important and unstable. Dorsch, like the many correspondents who sent letters, pleas, or plans to the National Assembly, found that a proposal for the schools was a proposal also for the polity. So too was their epistolary engagement.

Politics à la plume

Across the range of issues discussed in this and the preceding chapters – the relationship between education and representative government, between literacy and political participation; the funding of educational institutions; the viability of Ancien Régime institutions as a point of departure for designing revolutionary schools; and finally the recruitment, training, and certification of instructors and administrators – the correspondence is remarkable in its demonstration of a letter-writing public that kept itself informed of ongoing legislative debates and decisions, weighed in with both critical and contributive commentary, and engaged actively and often directly with the debates, proposals, and laws of the National Assembly. Something like an ideal form of this epistolary politics is revealed in the trajectory of Pierre Wouves's *Appel à l'opinion publique sur l'éducation nationale*, received by the Assembly on 1 November 1791 and noted several times above.

In the *Appel*, the perceived role of education in securing and perpetuating the new political system was made explicit:

> Every nation or society that has a reasonable, well-ordered, and functional system of government ... or which awaits the consequences and perfection of such a system, naturally desires to perpetuate it; in that vein, education is nothing but the art of preparing individuals to replace, within that same society, the functions of those individuals who become absent, whether by choice or by the force of nature.[95]

The tension between education's conservative and creative aspects, evident in the distinction between societies or nations with an established and functional government and those that await the consequences or perfection of such a system (such as the France for which M. Wouves wrote), is an important reminder of how the Constitution of 1791 both did and did not change the expectations and ambitions of those who sought to reform French society, culture, and education. What the new constitution meant in political terms, and what it meant for French society, remained open questions, susceptible to multiple and contradictory responses even after it had been promulgated and publicized. What the constitutional promise of free education in those areas "indispensable for all men" meant was similarly unsettled, and while Talleyrand's September 1791 proposal was supposed to clarify things, it too became the subject of debate and disputation rather than consensus. Indeed, it was Talleyrand's proposal that prompted Wouves to write.

Arguing against the proposal put forward by Talleyrand – which he described as "too complicated, too vague, too expensive to implement, and too prone to the establishment of distinctions, which are directly contrary to the true principles of the Constitution" – Wouves outlined an ambitious plan of elementary and adult education in sixteen relatively detailed pages (including twenty-one proposed articles for decree).[96] He followed the constitution and Talleyrand in distinguishing elementary education, or "*éducation nationale*," from secondary education (which was to include the arts, sciences, and all other branches of knowledge, and ought to be both "encouraged" and "protected" by the government so that no citizen was unfamiliar with such subjects), and each of those from the education of adults. While the *Appel* would include discussions of, and proposals for, all three types of education, particular emphasis was placed on *éducation nationale*, which was described as "essential" to the preservation of the new constitution and necessary throughout all of France, even down to the "*moindres villages*."[97] Education in these schools would be free (supported by revenues from the nationalized properties of Ancien Régime schools and seminaries), and the classes would be divided into two groups, the first for students between ages 9 and 12, the second for those aged 12 to 15. They would also be reserved for male students, as Wouves thought female education a separate matter, one that the Assembly should take up with an eye towards girls' futures as mothers and household managers.

Instruction in these schools would take place only in the morning, so that the schools would be available for adult education in the afternoons and evenings and so that the system of public instruction did not run afoul of the realities of economic necessity and economic freedom: necessity because of the many families who could not afford to give up their children's labor for the entire day; freedom because the purpose of education was not only to impart knowledge, but also to help students decide upon a future profession and acquire the skills necessary for whichever profession they chose. During the afternoon, once free from school, students would be able to explore potential careers and gain experience and expertise in their chosen profession.[98]

These schools, called *maisons d'éducation nationale*, would be overseen jointly by the National Assembly (through a permanent *comite d'éducation*) and local authorities, and would be financed by the national treasury. They would offer a uniform course of study, one that included reading, writing, and basic arithmetic, as well as knowledge of the laws and of the new constitution.[99] These skills and types of knowledge were, Wouves argued, the foundation upon which representative government could be built, and ensuring that every citizen had them was the principal challenge for those who would govern a society based upon equality before the law and individuals' right to autonomous self-determination.

To see that challenge met, Wouves proposed a number of measures, taking up questions of finance and the selection of personnel as well as the daily schedule of instruction and the cultivation of patriotic sentiments. Throughout the proposal, he sought to establish institutional norms and practices that reflected and were responsive to the principles of social equality, communal attachments, and collective decision-making. To make the schools responsive to the local community he proposed that instructors and administrators be chosen in elections modeled on those for municipal offices. To encourage a sense of equality among students, which he described as "the foundation of national education," he banned tutors, domestics, servants, and other luxuries that would bring society's inequalities into students' relationships with one another.[100] To turn equality into sociability he promoted festivals and the daily recitation of a "hymn that would evoke to students the idea of the *patrie* ... remind them of their responsibilities to the country," and inculcate among them the sorts of social and fraternal sentiments that would prepare them to some day enter a society of citizens.[101] These mutually reinforcing reforms would integrate the social and academic ambitions of public instruction and were, he argued, "essential" to the establishment of a "reasonable, well-ordered, and functional system of government."[102]

This pamphlet represents a model of political participation that was critically important to the ambitions and expectations which underlay the work of the Constituent and Legislative assemblies in the early years of the Revolution. It was born of a citizen's attention to, and engagement with, the debates of the National Assembly. That citizen then drew upon his ability to read and write and his perceived rights as a citizen to draft and, in this case, print a response containing both feedback on the deputies' work and suggestions for future legislation. That text was then transmitted to the Assembly where it made its way to the appropriate committee for more careful consideration. It apparently received at least some degree of attention at the committee level, for it was noted by the Committee of Public Instruction as containing "important objections to the plan presented by M. Talleyrand."[103]

This pamphlet may present an ideal rather than a representative case, but it is not an unrecognizable outlier. Like the *Appel*, the letters sent to the Assembly from across France illustrate an important facet of how people believed the new politics might work. These correspondents not only stressed the importance of education and an educated citizenry as the foundation of a participatory form of politics, they also gave practical force to that politics through their letters, *mémoires*, proposals, pleas, and exhortations. As Michelet said: they could write and, in so doing, they could help to realize the promise of a new politics in eighteenth-century France.

At the same time, and as many of these correspondents noted, sowing this sort of politics on a national scale was going to require not just letter-writing and debates over education, but the actual reform and rejuvenation of institutions across France. Attempts to realize this, or at least to initiate the process, were already underway in schools across France where administrators, faculties, instructors, and students struggled to anticipate what reforms might come from the Assembly and worked to find a place for Ancien Régime institutions in a new political order. We turn to them in Chapter 6.

Notes

1. Jules Michelet, *History of the French Revolution*, ed. Gordon Wright (Chicago, IL: University of Chicago Press, 1967), 83.
2. Gauchet, *La Révolution des pouvoirs*, 61–79. The role of correspondence in helping to bridge the distance between representatives and constituents has been noted by Timothy Tackett, who discusses such exchanges as part of the larger attempt to maintain "close deputy-constituent relations as part and parcel of the new phenomenon of representative democracy." Tackett, *Becoming a Revolutionary*, 239. See also Robert H. Blackman, "What does a deputy to the National Assembly owe his constituents?"
3. Chartier, *The Cultural Origins of the French Revolution*, 32. For a similar argument focused on the newspaper press as an instrument of "virtual presence," see Jeremy D. Popkin, *Revolutionary News: The Press in France, 1789–1799* (Durham, NC: Duke University Press, 1990), 3. A pre-revolutionary form of this community-by-correspondence dynamic, one that bridges the public-press divide, is discussed in Elizabeth Andrews Bond, "Circuits of practical knowledge: the network of letters to the editor

in the French provincial press, 1770–1788," *French Historical Studies*, 39:3 (2016): 535–565.
4   Habermas, *The Structural Transformation of the Public Sphere*, 48.
5   AN, F/17//1309, dossier 1, no. 9, "Appel à l'opinion publique sur l'éducation nationale," 2–3. This letter is included in Guillaume, *Procès-verbaux du Comité d'Instruction publique de l'Assemblée législative*, 3–7. On the colonial exploits of Wouves d'Argès in North America, see David Narrett, *Adventurism and Empire: The Struggle for Mastery in the Louisiana-Florida Borderlands, 1762–1803* (Chapel Hill, NC: University of North Carolina Press, 2015), 142–144.
6   Dena Goodman, *Becoming a Woman in the Age of Letters* (Ithaca, NY: Cornell University Press, 2009), 3. See also Michel de Certeau, *The Practice of Everyday Life*, trans. S. Rendall (Berkeley and Los Angeles, CA: University of California Press, 1984): 131–153; Walter J. Ong, *Orality and Literacy: The Technologization of the Word* (London: Methuen, 1982): 77–102.
7   Mirabeau, *Travail sur l'éducation publique*, 10. The uses and abuses of such claims to speak for the "public" are discussed by Jon Cowans, *To Speak for the People: Public Opinion and the Problem of Legitimacy in the French Revolution* (New York, NY: Routledge, 2001).
8   Gilbert Shapiro and John Markoff, *Revolutionary Demands: A Content Analysis of the Cahiers de Doléances of 1789* (Stanford, CA: Stanford University Press, 1998), 128.
9   An estimate of roughly 40,000 *cahiers* is most common, although others range from 25,000 to 60,000. Shapiro and Markoff, *Revolutionary Demands*, 114. For the lower end of the spectrum, see Beatrice Fry Hyslop, *A Guide to the General Cahiers of 1789: With the Texts of Unedited Cahiers* (New York, NY: Octagon Books, 1936); for the higher end, see Michel Vovelle, *La Chute de la monarchie, 1787–1792* (Paris: Édition du Seuil, 1972), 111.
10 Shapiro and Markoff, *Revolutionary Demands*, Appendix I-I, pp. 438–474, especially 438–439.
11 Gontard, *L'Enseignement primaire en France*, 75.
12 Ibid., 66-67. For additional analyses of education's place in the *cahiers*, see Ernest Allain, *La Question d'Enseignement en 1789 d'après les cahiers* (Paris: Librairie Renouard, 1886); Philippe Grateau, "Les Français et l'instruction d'après les cahiers de doléances de 1789," in Alain Croix, André Lespagnol, and Georges Provost (eds), *Église, éducation, lumières: Histoires culturelles de la France, 1500–1830* (Rennes: Presses universitaires de Rennes, 1999), 139–145; Pierre Goubert and Michel Denis, *1789: Les Français ont la parole… Cahiers de doléances des états généraux* (Paris: Julliard, 1964).
13 Morange and Chassaing, *Le Mouvement de réforme de l'enseignement en France*, 108.
14 Ibid., 108, n. 4.
15 Ibid., 108–109.

16 Gontard, *L'Enseignement primaire en France*, 69–77.
17 Shapiro and Markoff, *Revolutionary Demands*, Appendix I-I, 439.
18 AN, C/II//8 – C/II//16, *Adresses et pétitions reçues par les Assemblées constituante et législative*.
19 The work process of these clerks is described in Ben Kafka, *The Demon of Writing: Powers and Failures of Paperwork* (New York, NY: Zone Books, 2012), 44–45.
20 Ibid., 44.
21 Michael L. Kennedy, *The Jacobin Clubs in the French Revolution: The Middle Years* (Princeton, NJ: Princeton University Press, 1988), 101–103.
22 Caradonna, *The Enlightenment in Practice*.
23 Gregory P. Downs, *Declarations of Dependence: The Long Reconstruction of Popular Politics* (Chapel Hill, NC: University of North Carolina Press, 2011), 2.
24 That these letters indicated public confidence in the government was a view expressed by the president of the Reports Committee in 1791, when he explained that "the French people's confidence in the National Assembly will attract to it a mass of petitions of all genres, both from the administrative corps and individuals." Quoted in Kafka, *The Demon of Writing*, 46.
25 Gontard, *L'Enseignement primaire en France*, 84.
26 To note just one such example, a June 1791 letter from the Département du Nord was submitted initially to the Comité de Mendicité, though its contents dealt primarily with the department's efforts to improvise a functional system of education while awaiting word from the Assembly on how to reform existing institutions. See AN, F/17//1310, dossier 6, no. 57. For an illustrative list of documents sent from one committee – in this case, the Comité de Constitution – to others, including other committees likely to have business related to education, see AN, D/IV//67, dossier 2006, no. 2.
27 Gontard, *L'Enseignement primaire en France*, 84–85; Palmer, *The Improvement of Humanity*, 89–94.
28 Morange and Chassaing, *Le Mouvement de réforme de l'enseignement en France*, 98–99.
29 They did not, apparently, share the faith in a natural "common sense" that Sophia Rosenfeld has highlighted as one of the conceptual underpinnings of modern democracy. They clearly did, however, embrace the idea that democracy relied upon the establishment of a shared sensibility, a "common sense," among the people. Sophia Rosenfeld, *Common Sense: A Political History* (Cambridge, MA: Harvard University Press, 2011), 3–5.
30 AN, F/17//1309, dossier 1, no.1, M. de LaFontaine, "Plan d'Instruction Publique," 14 June 1791.
31 AN, F/17//1309, dossier 4, no. 10, M Hidince (Lyon), "Plan d'éducation nationale," 1791; F/17//1309, dossier 4, no. 2, letter from M. Sudrand, 24 October 1791.

32 AN, F/17//1310, dossier 6, no. 52, Address from the Conseil Général de la Commune de Soissons, to the National Assembly, November 1790.
33 For example, AN, D/IV//13, dossier 194, no. 4, Request for the establishment of a public library, submitted to the National Assembly by the Société des Amis de la Constitution in Cherbourg, 8 August 1791, 1-2.
34 AN, D/IV//13, dossier 194, no. 14, letter submitted to the National Assembly by a M. Arnault, 5 May 1790; D/IV//21, dossier 430, nos 1-3, letters from the Société des Amis de la Constitution in Moyaux, and from municipal officials in Bayeux, writing to urge the National Assembly to establish schools, April-May 1791; AD/VIII//21, no. 2, Abbé Auger, *Projet d'éducation pour tout le royaume, précédé de quelques réflexions sur l'Assemblée nationale* (Paris, 1789), iii. Others sought to prompt the Assembly into action by criticizing the false starts of the Ancien Régime's attention to educational reform. For example, AN, AD/VIII//21, no. 16, Anon., *Mémoire sur les principaux objets de l'Education publique* (Paris, 1790), 5-6.
35 AN, F/17//1309, dossier 1, no. 3, M. Gadolle, "Avis sur l'éducation de la jeunesse," October 1791, 29.
36 For example, AN, AD/VIII//21, no. 1, M. Leclerc, *Abrégé des études de l'homme fait, en faveur de l'homme à former...* (Paris, 1789), 74-75, 82-83.
37 AN, D/IV//27, dossier 652, no. 1, "Plan d'établissement de collège nationale dans la ville de Verneuil," submitted to the National Assembly by Louis Protrou, September 1790, 2-3.
38 For example, AN, F/17//1309, dossier 1, no. 9 "Appel à l'opinion publique sur l'éducation nationale," 1 November 1791, 11.
39 AN, F/17//1309, dossier 2, no. 4, Letter from M. Lespomarede to the National Assembly, 2 November 1791.
40 AN, F/17//1310, dossier 7, no 79, Letter from the Département de l'Isle et Vilaine regarding the plan proposed by M. Codel, April 1791.
41 AN, F/17//1310, dossier 7, nos 85-87, Letters from M. L.-G. Gaspard about theater and national education, 23 August 1791.
42 M. J. Sydenham, *Léonard Bourdon: The Career of a Revolutionary, 1754-1807* (Waterloo, Ontario: Wilfrid Laurier University Press, 1999), 53, 112; Palmer, *The Improvement of Humanity*, 142.
43 Sydenham, *Léonard Bourdon*, 9-11; 229-236. For the correspondence between Bourdon and the government related to the *Société des jeunes françaises*, see AN, F/17//1012, dossier 6, folders 4-5.
44 Léonard Bourdon de la Crosnière, *Plan d'un Établissement d'Éducation Nationale, autorisée par Arrêt du Conseil du 5 Octobre 1788, sous le titre de Société Royale d'Émulation* (Orléans, 1788), 11-12.
45 Palmer, *The Improvement of Humanity*, 142.
46 Bourdon, *Plan d'un Établissement d'Éducation Nationale*, 17-24, 32-35, 16.
47 Sydenham, *Léonard Bourdon*, 44.

48 AN, F/17//1310, dossier 7, nos 64-75, Memoranda submitted by Léonard Bourdon, October 1790.
49 AN, F/17//1310, dossier 7, no. 65, Letter from Léonard Bourdon to National Assembly, October 1790, 1.
50 Ibid.
51 Ibid.
52 Ibid., 1, 2.
53 AN, F/17//1310, dossier 7, nos 69-71, Léonard Bourdon, *Projet de Décret sur l'Éducation Publique*, 1790.
54 Ibid.
55 Ibid.
56 AN, D/VIII//21, no. 22, *Rapport fait à la Société des Amis de la Constitution de Paris, le 11 mars 1791, au nom des commissaires nommés pour l'examen du mémoire de Léonard Bourdon, sur l'instruction et sur l'éducation nationale, par Alexandre Beauharnois* (Paris, 1791). Jacobin clubs across France showed interest in education and its reform, often weighing in for or against particular candidates or religious orders as instructors, helping to recruit candidates, and seeking to integrate the political and pedagogical agendas of the Revolution. Kennedy, *The Jacobin Clubs in the French Revolution*, 102-108 (the approval expressed for Bourdon's proposal is noted on 103).
57 AN, D/IV//45, dossier 1317, no. 2, Letter from the Société des Amis de la Constitution de Bergues St Winox, April 1791.
58 AN, F/17//1310, dossier 6, no. 59, Letter from the Société des Amis de la Constitution in Brignoles, March 1791.
59 AN, D/IV//11, dossier 157, nos 22-24, Letter and petitions submitted by municipal officials and citizens in Die, February 1790.
60 AN, F/17//1309, dossier 1, no. 9, *Appel à l'opinion publique sur l'éducation nationale*, 2-3.
61 AN, D/IV//36, dossier 950, no. 2, Petition from Jean Vidal, curé and mayor in Langeac, 29 May 1790, 2-3.
62 AN, D/IV//20, dossier 398, no. 1 Letter from M. Brenard, undated (received 5 August 1790), 1-2.
63 AN, D/IV//13, dossier 192, no. 2, Anonymous letter to the National Assembly, received 30 December 1790, 1-2.
64 AN, D/IV//21, no. 26, Letter from the Société des Amis de la Constitution, Paris, undated, 1-2.
65 AN, D/IV//70, dossier 2122, no. 84, Anonymous letter, signed "le bon patriote," from the Département des Deux-Sèvres, 5 July 1790, 2.
66 AN, D/IV//10, dossier 140, no. 11, Letter from municipal officials in Nogent-sur-Seine to the National Assembly, 9 January 1790, 1-2; D/IV//70, dossier 2122, no. 85, Letter from M. d'Estey to the National Assembly, 4 February 1790.

67 AN, D/IV//21, dossier 424, no. 2, Anonymous letter to the National Assembly, signed "un citoyen de Bayeux," 7 July 1790, 1-2.

68 AN, F/17//1310, dossier 6, no. 59, Address submitted by the Société des Amis de la Constitution in Brignoles, March 1791.

69 AN, D/IV//34, dossier 829, no. 1, Anonymous letter regarding public and communal education, submitted to the National Assembly, October 1790.

70 For example, AN, F/17//1310, dossier 3, no. 22, C. Maubauch, "Réflexions sur l'importance de l'instruction publique," May 1792.

71 AN, F/17//1309, dossier 6, no. 4, Letter from the citizens of Ecully, 26 February 1792.

72 For example, AN, F/17//1309, dossier 1, no. 3, M. Gadolle, *Avis sur l'éducation de la jeunesse*, October 1791, 16.

73 AN, D/IV//45, dossier 1313, Address from the municipality of St Amand requesting the conservation of the University of Douai, September 1790, 4.

74 AN, D/IV//34, dossier 823, no. 5, Petition to the National Assembly from the city of St Gontier, January 1791, 7.

75 AN, D/IV//37, dossier 962, no. 3 Address from the Société des Amis de la Constitution in Rennes, November 1790, 2-3.

76 For example, AN, F/17//1309, dossier 1, no. 13, Letter from the Doctrinaires-non-prêtres du Collège de Narbonne, 19 November 1791; F/17//1310, dossier 3, no. 22, C. Maubauch, "Réflexions sur l'importance de l'instruction publique," May 1792; F/17//1309, dossier 5, no. 14, Letter from M. Delmasse, homme de loi à Dijon, undated, 1.

77 AN, F/17//1310, dossier 7, no. 62, S. Bienvenue, de St Briene, "Projet d'Institution publique et Nationale," January 1791. A similar claim is made in AN, F/17//1309, dossier 6, no. 4, Citizens of Ecully, 26 February 1792, 2, where pre-revolutionary education is described as *"une institution gothique"* and as *"une plante parasite qui s'entrelace à l'arbre constitutionnel pour l'empêcher de se développer et l'étouffer dans son germe."*

78 Belhoste, "Un espace public d'enseignement aux marges de l'université," 220-227.

79 AN, D/IV//64, dossier 1923, no. 9, Letter from "Frère Jérôme" condemning the Frères des Écoles Chrétiennes, 9 September 1790.

80 AN, D/IV//13, dossier 232, no. 1, Anonymous letter condemning the universities, January 1790; D/IV//4, dossier 27, no. 18, Anonymous letter condemning abuses in the Faculty of Law at Reims, undated.

81 AN, F/17//1310, dossier 3, no. 22, C. Maubauch, "Réflexions sur l'importance de l'instruction publique," May 1792.

82 Hahn, *The Anatomy of a Scientific Institution*, 135-136, 226-240.

83 AN, AD/VIII//21, no. 11, M. L[ambert] Rivière, *Palladium de la Constitution Politique, ou Régénération Morale de la France* (Paris, 1790), 30-32.

84 For examples of these intersecting concerns, see AN, F/17//1309, dossier 5, no. 17, *Projet d'établissement de Collèges pour l'Instruction des Maîtres d'école*

... *présenté à l'Assemblée Nationale par Antoine-Joseph Dorsch*, 7 mars 1792 [reproduced in Guillaume, *Procès-verbaux du Comité d'Instruction publique de l'Assemblée législative*,148–151]; as well as AN, F/17//1309, dossier 4, no. 10, *Plan d'éducation nationale* submitted by a M. Hidince, de Lyon, 1791; F/17//1309, dossier 2, no. 20, Address to the National Assembly from the Doctrinaires professeurs au Collège de Lavaur, 22 January 1792; F/17//1309, dossier 1, no. 3, M. Gadolle, "Avis sur l'éducation de la jeunesse," 30–31; F/17//1309, dossier 1, no. 9, "Appel à l'opinion publique sur l'éducation nationale," 7–8.
85 AN, F/17//1310, dossier 6, no. 57, Letter from the Directory of the Département du Nord to the Comité de Mendicité of the National Assembly, 19 June 1791.
86 This supposition was shared, or at least encouraged, by the National Assembly and government of Louis XVI. In the law of 28 October 1791, the professors and members of ecclesiastical orders who were teaching provisionally in the *collèges* were ordered to remain in place, *if and only if* they had sworn the clerical oath. See ADHG, 1L 1004, no. 1, *Loi Relative à l'Enseignement public dans les différens Collèges du Royaume*.
87 AN, F/17//1310, dossier 7, no. 62, S. Bienvenue, de St Briene, "Projet d'Institution publique et Nationale," January 1791; AN, F/17//1309, dossier 3, no. 2, "Projet d'Education publique à exécuter à St Quentin," 4 January 1792.
88 AN, F/17//1310, dossier 7, no. 62, S. Bienvenue, de St Briene, "Projet d'Institution publique et Nationale," January 1791.
89 This argument, like the proposal that instructors be elected, mirrored steps taken during the reform of the judiciary, when the National Assembly "established generous salaries" so that qualified candidates would view judicial careers as desirable. Fitzsimmons, *The Remaking of France*, 105.
90 AN F/17//1309, dossier 3, no. 2, "Projet d'Education publique à exécuter à St Quentin," 4 January 1792.
91 AN, F/17//1309, dossier 5, no. 17, Antoine-Joseph Dorsch, "Projet d'établissement de Collèges pour l'Instruction des Maîtres d'école," 7 March 1792, 1–2.
92 Ibid., 1.
93 Ibid., 1.
94 Ibid., 3.
95 AN, F/17//1309, dossier 1, no. 9, "Appel à l'opinion publique sur l'éducation nationale," 1 November 1791, 2.
96 Ibid., 1.
97 Ibid., 5–6.
98 Ibid., 11–13.
99 Ibid., 5.

100 Ibid., 8-9.
101 Ibid., 9.
102 Ibid., 2.
103 AN, F/17//1309, dossier 1, Feuille d'Extraits, section du Plan général, 2.

6

New wine in old bottles?
Ancien Régime schools imagine the future

Efforts to design new political institutions in the early years of the Revolution were accompanied by attempts to reform or reimagine existing ones so that they might contribute to the emerging social, political, and economic orders. The interplay of invention and reinvention, reform and regeneration was characteristic of revolutionaries' work across a range of concerns, from reforming the judiciary to redrawing the administrative map of France, from reimagining poor relief to liberalizing the press, from fashioning legislative and parliamentary procedures to refashioning the relationship between Church and State. A similar dynamic shaped the debates over education, and while the Assembly and the public debated, the administrators, instructors, students, and others affiliated with the schools were left navigating the uncertain terrain between reform and reinvention.

Those who worked and studied in the schools and scholarly institutions inherited from the Ancien Régime participated actively in the debate over educational reform, proposing their own answers to questions about whether the *petites écoles*, *collèges*, universities, academies, and other such institutions could be integrated into the new society, whether they could be turned into instruments of "public instruction." They also worked to keep these institutions running, to demonstrate the schools' value to society, to improvise and experiment with new curricula and regulations, and to accommodate sometimes suddenly changing circumstances.[1] The routines of educational planning – setting academic calendars, securing and allocating resources, designing and implementing curricula, training and hiring personnel, and all sorts of other practical activities – took on increased significance (and brought increased scrutiny) because of the central position schools had come to occupy in the political imagination of eighteenth-century France. As theoretically "national institutions," the schools seemed to offer a glimpse into possible futures for the Revolution and the nation. Teachers, administrators, students, and local authorities were well aware of this, making their proposals for reform, pleas for resources, justifications of existing practices, and condemnations of alternatives or abuses valuable sources for understanding how people thought about, and engaged with, a revolution in motion.

Like the letters and proposals discussed in Chapter 5, those examined here offer insight into how citizens sought to understand, articulate, and navigate the changing currents of revolutionary politics. At the same time, because these letters and proposals came from people with direct interests in, experience of, or responsibilities to the schools, they offer specific insight into the "assumptions of the acceptable and the ideal" that shaped the debate over education during these years.[2] Despite this, they have received relatively little attention from historians.[3] When they have been drawn upon, it is customarily to illustrate the abstraction and irrelevance of deputies' proposals for reform or to illustrate the disarray into which the schools fell while the deputies debated. The sense that there was a fundamental divorce between legislative proposals and local circumstances is affirmed by these customary uses; it is belied by the correspondence examined below. While local authorities (political and pedagogical alike) often found themselves scrambling to translate the Assembly's laws into institutional practices, or to mediate the impact of specific laws on the schools, it is no less true that many teachers, professors, school administrators, local political authorities, and students across France sought to contribute substantively to the design and establishment of a system of public instruction. Their efforts (and dilemmas) conditioned what it meant to pursue "public instruction" in revolutionary France, and their letters, proposals, and pleas allow us to recognize the interplay of political discourse and positional logic in the revolutionary debates over education.[4]

This correspondence does not reveal a uniform political inclination or ideology that we might trace to the writers' professional interests or experience. But it does reveal a shared set of practical and particular concerns, some of which are familiar from the debates in the Assembly and the popular correspondence, some of which are more unique. More broadly, these letters are suggestive of how people tried to understand revolutionary change in professionally, institutionally, and geographically specific terms. These were written by "people acting politically and locatedly (that is, from the vista of their own location)." Those people were, as Sarah Knott describes the "situational" historical agent, "pragmatic and strategic ... tak[ing] action based on what is in view."⁵ Their view was from the classroom out, locating them and their letters at the conceptual break between institutions and ideas inherited from the Ancien Régime, on the one hand, and the ambitions and expectations of revolutionary politics, on the other.

Building upon almost thirty years of unrealized designs, and embracing the system-building spirit of the early Revolution, most of these correspondents argued for a uniform, national, and inclusive approach to educational reform.⁶ The deputy, Yves-Marie Audrein, who was also a vice-regent of the Collège des Grassins in Paris and, later, a member of the Legislative Assembly's Committee of Public Instruction, stressed this point to his colleagues in the Assembly, imploring them: "You must reject any partial system: national education cannot exist in piecemeal; you must reject any plan that isolates students: you must promote the public spirit and realize the Constitution!"⁷ *Agrégés* in the Var and in Aix similarly declared that "any partial program of regeneration is but a chimerical enterprise."⁸ Like the constitution it was supposed to complete and conserve, educational reform had to embrace at once every corner of France.⁹ And yet, as we will see, these correspondents balanced their desire for systemic remedies to structural dilemmas with the need to improvise solutions to pressing problems and local concerns. Their letters illustrate the entanglement of institutional, ideological, political, and material imperatives, and they give us insight into how administrators, instructors, and students worked to find their bearings amid a "horizon of prognosis ... [that was] first extended, then finally broken" by the Revolution.¹⁰

These efforts began even before the political dynamics turned explicitly revolutionary. Like the *cahiers de doléances*, the first letters and memoranda from people associated with Ancien Régime schools were shaped by the intersection of pre-revolutionary ambitions and unfamiliar circumstances. This was apparent in the April 1789 *mémoire* sent to the Estates-General by representatives of the University of Poitiers.¹¹ Written by the rector and former rector of the university (both members of the Faculty of Theology), this proposal sought to reanimate the idea of a national and uniform system of education by resurrecting proposals familiar from the debates of the 1760s, especially those presented by Rolland d'Erceville (discussed in Chapter 2).¹²

Like Rolland, the rectors in Poitiers imagined a system in which France was divided into educational districts, with each of the French universities serving as both the administrative and intellectual center of a district. They proposed that a series of *maisons d'institution pour les maîtres* be established in the major city of each district, helping to produce a reserve of instructors who would be "always on hand and prepared to assume whatever vacancies might become available."[13] The universities' role as administrative and intellectual hubs would be reinforced through inter-institutional relationships which the rectors, echoing Rolland, described as a system of "*correspondence.*"[14] They hoped that this would establish a uniform set of practices, standards, and expectations for the nation. It would also, and here the proposal re-presents the most characteristic feature of Rolland's plan, do so without establishing any meaningful system or mechanism for political authorities to intervene in the schools. Undertaken with the consent – and under the authority – of the monarchy and other political bodies, this proposal would have established an educational system that was largely independent of political oversight.[15]

The proposal sought a similar balance between symbolic deference and administrative independence in its approach to religious authorities. The rectors went beyond Rolland in calling for the exclusion of teaching orders and religious congregations from French schools, claiming that education could be made "truly national only by restricting the teaching profession to *maîtres* recognized by the nation, who had been authorized by a power that emanated from and is responsible to the nation."[16] They took care, however, to clarify that their aim was not to sever all ties between the Church and schools, but to improve upon the system that already existed, which they described as having been "established through the cooperation of spiritual and temporal authorities."[17] While the rectors argued that the state should oversee the recruitment, training, and certification of instructors, and that religious orders ought to be removed from their traditional positions, they nonetheless expected that instructors would be clerics and that religious instruction would remain the cornerstone of French education.

This proposal was at once ambitious and familiar: ambitious in its call for a genuinely national approach to educational reform and in its willingness to reverse the decisions of Louis XV and Louis XVI regarding the place of religious orders in French education; familiar in that their suggestions were essentially a reproduction of proposals issued during the 1760s, and so lacking the novelty that those proposals had possessed at the time of their own appearance. But this was only a first foray into the rejuvenated debate over education, and it was marked by the moment of its production and submission: the *mémoire* indicated that its authors thought there was a possibility of significant change, but were relatively modest in their sense of what that change might be.[18] In April 1789, neither a revolutionary politics nor a revolutionary pedagogy had yet emerged.

As that changed in summer 1789 and in the tumultuous years that would follow, administrators, faculty, and students found themselves trying to simultaneously understand and influence political developments that promised, or threatened, to transform education in France. The result was not – or at least was not initially – a flood of new or radical proposals to reinvent the schools, but a sense of deep and anxious uncertainty. When J. B. Dumouchel, the rector of the University of Paris (and a deputy in the Assembly), brought a delegation before his fellow deputies on 29 July, they offered little more than patriotic platitudes, struggling to imagine where the university might fit into the "majestic edifice" that the deputies were designing and of which educational reform promised to be but a part.[19] Over time, however, the new political possibilities and anxieties led those affiliated with French schools and universities – in Paris, Poitiers, and elsewhere – to offer a range of proposals about what sort of education might be appropriate to the new French order. They offered suggestions about the role that institutions inherited from the Ancien Régime might assume within that system (if any), about the place and purpose of education in the new political society, and about how to manage the transition from an inherited to an anticipated state of affairs.

This was true of the schools' internal regulations and pedagogical practices as well as their political ambitions and social functions. For example, in late 1789, students at the University of Paris petitioned the rector (Dumouchel) to have the curriculum updated, to replace dictated lectures with printed texts that would be commented upon and discussed in class, and for instruction to be offered in French rather than Latin. These were not particularly novel points in 1789, but the petition demonstrated the students' facility with revolutionary rhetoric and their sense that the new political environment would lead to new dynamics in the classroom and improved relations among members of the university community. Echoing national concerns, the students presented their requests as part of an attempt to reform the relationship between the members of a collective body and those who administered and governed that body and, more explicitly still, as part of an effort to make education answer the demands of representative government. They did so in explaining the petition's existence and again in arguing for instruction in the vernacular; regarding the latter, they asked: "having been habituated to using French in the study of reasoning, moral questions, and nature ... with what advantage will we not appear in those august assemblies which henceforth will arouse the ambition of all citizens, and to which each of us would be unworthy to be called if he had not had, beginning today, the noble ambition to prepare himself?"[20] Seeking to prepare themselves for a social and political order that was anticipated but undefined, these students took advantage of the institutional and discursive space opened up by the events of 1789. That their requests were so practical and so reasonable is striking; so too is the inaction of the faculty and administration, who discussed but did not act upon the petition. They were, presumably, awaiting word from the Assembly regarding the recently promised reforms.

The wait was long and frustrating. It was unclear who had and who should have immediate authority over the schools. The creation of political departments in autumn 1789 – and with that the establishment of departmental officials and authorities – seemed like it might prompt local initiatives to reform education, and in some places it did so.[21] But the relationship among political authorities, and between those authorities and the schools (not to mention the religious communities running many of those schools), remained unclear, leading to caution and confusion about the local administration of education.[22] Moreover, the continued prospect, and then promise, of a national system of public instruction meant that local efforts remained self-consciously provisional. Unsurprisingly, then, the results varied widely from town to town and region to region, ranging from administrative and institutional paralysis to relatively autonomous and ambitious attempts to reimagine how schools were run.[23] These approaches were presented as signs of deference to the Assembly's authority (in the case of paralysis), or as active and ongoing – but not presumptuous or pre-emptive – attempts to accommodate the new political order.

The need to balance anticipatory action and deferential patience was evident in a series of letters from the Faculty of Arts at the University of Paris to the deputies in the Assembly. In December 1790, members of the Faculty wrote to assure the deputies that they were working to overhaul the university's curricular emphases, internal practices, and recruitment procedures for staff and faculty. The rector, principals, professors, and *agrégés* stressed their "respectful submission to the law," their "zeal for the propagation and strengthening of the principles of the Constitution," and the steps they had taken or were taking to participate in and preserve the Revolution. They described new regulations making the *Declaration of the Rights of Man and Citizen* and the (promised) constitution the foci of the curriculum, requiring public lectures on Sundays to reinforce these lessons, and ordering the faculty to integrate the rights and responsibilities of citizenship more perfectly into the study of morals. They assured the deputies that instructors would be patriotic, qualified, and devoted to their role in "forming good citizens." Students would be required to wear the revolutionary cockade (and would not be permitted to enter classrooms without it), would have their reading materials regulated so as to prevent them from gaining access to anything that could "weaken or in any way alter" their attachment to the new government and its laws, and would be expected to participate in the university's "patriotic festival" on 4 May 1791. Lest the deputies mistake this for an exhaustive list, the faculty promised that further guarantees and illustrations of the university's devotion would be forthcoming.[24]

Among the memorandum's various ambitions, two are particularly striking. First is the emphasis on designing curricular and institutional norms that would attach students to the new regime and new laws intellectually, emotionally, and socially. The faculty emphasized their efforts to make the university's internal regulations reflect the new regime and to push their lessons beyond the schools' walls and into the public sphere. The second is the effort to balance a defense of the institutions and personnel already in place (and so a product of the Ancien Régime) with an acknowledgement of the inadequacy or impropriety of the Ancien Régime curriculum and practices.

A similar balance between historical apology and political anticipation was clear in a memorandum that the Faculty sent a few months later in which they again promised reform, defended themselves against criticisms regarding pre-revolutionary practices, and sought to justify receipt of continued support (and salaries) from the National Assembly. They claimed that under the Ancien Régime they had "worked at all times to perfect their teaching methods," at least insofar as circumstances would permit, and assured the deputies that they were "awaiting with pleasure the approaching moment when a national system of education [would] be organized," noting that while such a reform was beyond the faculty members' powers, it was not at all contrary to their wishes.[25] More specifically, they argued that while the materials traditionally taught in the Faculty of Arts, including the literature and languages of the Ancients, might seem obscure to some critics, these studies were important to the establishment and protection of an enlightened morality, to the inculcation of a "healthy love for one's country," and to the public education of a free people.²⁶ With these points in mind, they expressed hope and confidence that the deputies would use the nationalized lands to pay professors' salaries, to fund educational institutions, and to establish "*une propriété inattaquable*" to guarantee that the *collèges* and universities could fulfill their social and pedagogical mission in the years to come.²⁷

While the Faculty of Arts in Paris sought to anticipate and accommodate the deputies' shifting desires and expectations, others were less apologetic and less inclined to genuflect before the prospect of revolutionary change. As late as April 1791, long after the deputies' intention to overhaul the system of education had become clear, the administrators of the Collège Royal in Toulouse argued that they ought to be allowed to continue to function according to the administrative forms established by the February Edict of 1763 (discussed in Chapter 2). Their argument was supported by the departmental administrators of the Haute-Garonne, and it reflects not only the variety of political and pedagogical dispositions among the faculty and administrators of universities after 1789, but also growing frustration with the prolonged delay of possible reforms.²⁸

But such claims that the *collèges* should not have to change to accommodate the Revolution – or should be allowed to manage the change on their own terms – were greatly outnumbered by arguments that they were incapable of change and should be replaced with entirely new institutions (even if those new institutions were generally imagined as inhabiting the same buildings and drawing upon at least some of the same resources). Already in 1789, the Oratorian instructor Joseph Villier argued in his *Nouveau plan d'éducation et d'instruction publique* that it was necessary to "cut out [the education system's] problems from the root and to suppress every single one of the *collèges*; as violent as this remedy may seem, it is surely necessary."²⁹ A year later, Monsieur Degranthe, a professor at Collège Louis-le-Grand (and presumably a dissenter from the "official" letters sent by the Faculty of Arts), dismissed the laurels commonly bestowed upon the University of Paris, claiming that "if this university has eclipsed all others, it is due to the number and grandiosity of its privileges, rather than the wisdom or utility of the education it offers."³⁰ Degranthe described the reputations of the Ancien Régime institutions as having been "blackened in public opinion" and incurably associated with the "abuses, vices, and absurdities of the old system of education." In his lengthy pamphlet, *Abus de l'Ancienne Éducation* (discussed more fully below), Degranthe proposed that the new schools be called "*maisons d'éducation nationales*" and "*maisons polysophique nationales*," arguing that inherited terms like "*collège*" should be "banished" from the pedagogical lexicon.[31]

A similar argument that new institutions needed new names to escape the tarnished reputation of their Ancien Régime predecessors was presented by Alexandre Courtois in his January 1792 letter to the Assembly. Courtois, a departmental administrator in the Moselle, argued that the words "*collège*" and "*université*" should be replaced by "*lycée*" and "*gymnase*," giving rhetorical force to the break from the "pompous and extravagant ambitions" of the old educational order and a fresh start for institutions that, supported by public opinion, would lead the people to virtue.[32] Arguments like this echoed the increasingly prominent suggestion that history and the Revolution were at odds, as when the Directory of the Department of Paris derided the *collèges* in November 1791 as "gothic institutions" and "adversaries of the Constitution."[33]

Despite the heated political rhetoric, the question of what to preserve, what to reform, and what to "banish" was practical as well as political, and correspondents recognized that political and practical concerns were inextricably linked. As a group of Benedictines from the Loir-et-Cher put it:

> Economic wisdom surely requires that one maintain that which exists but does not impede development, that one not demolish the house when repairs will do. And yet this same wisdom that warns us against thinking that what presently fails could never become good also cautions us against thinking that because something has long existed, it must exist always.
> Possession must never be considered a right when it runs contrary to the purpose for which an institution was established.
> So, what is the purpose of education?[34]

As this note suggests, the reform of education could not be divorced from practical concerns any more than practical concerns could be quarantined from ideas about the nature, purpose, and future of political society. Administrators, instructors, students, and deputies quickly learned that, in the revolutionary pursuit of public instruction, material and ideational solutions were always provisional, each awaiting the problems posed by the other.

"Freed from the spirit of routine"

It was a common refrain in letters sent by administrators and instructors that the Revolution had liberated or energized them to rethink how education was organized and carried out in France. As in the letter from the Parisian Faculty of Arts noted above, these correspondents often mixed criticisms of Ancien Régime institutions or curricula with invocations of pre-revolutionary experience as a source of legitimacy. For example, a M. Arnauld, "*instituteur*," noted that his experience would allow him to help the deputies avoid the allure of chimerical plans or specious proposals. Experience, he claimed, had "become [his] patrimony." At the same time, the Revolution had served to "free [him] from the spirit of routine," and the coupling of pre-revolutionary experience with a reanimated imagination offered him a chance to "contribute to the improvement of a profession [he had] long embraced."[35]

Others offered a darker assessment of their pre-revolutionary experience. *Doctrinaires agrégés non-prêtres* in the Var and in Aix explained that they had long hoped for reform, but that "during a time of despotism and routine, when the public good counted for nothing and when innovations were treated as an offense, all such projects were doomed to fail."[36] Monsieur Paris, an Oratorian and academician who sent his *Projet d'éducation nationale* to the Assembly in 1790, claimed that the social conditions and inequalities of the Ancien Régime had made it impossible to offer any sort of meaningful education, but the Revolution had swept away such impediments and made it possible to reimagine at once society and the schools.[37] The novelty of the revolutionary moment was also stressed in the *Tableau d'un Collège en activité* sent to the Assembly by J.-F. Major, a professor in Bar-le-Duc: "Do not speak to me of Spartans; France is no Lacedaemonia. I ask you: has a people ever found itself in a position like that in which the French find themselves now?"[38]

Despite the apparent novelty of the moment, the correspondents' concerns were familiar: who should have access to schools (and at what levels); what should they be taught; who should instruct them and how should those instructors be recruited and certified; how would the system be funded? Their proposals were, for the most part, reasonable, focused on practical issues, and concerned to remain within the limits of what was possible given material, social, and institutional resources. This tendency is evident in the frequent discussion of financial limitations and the register of anticipated revenues and expenses with which many pamphlets concluded (sometimes before and sometimes after the *projets de loi* that R. R. Palmer identified as the customary embellishment of authors who "imagine[d] themselves as legislators").[39] Again, and as the Benedictines of the Loir-et-Cher noted, addressing such practical issues gave rise to questions about education's purpose and about its role in the regeneration of French society. As a result, and for all their practicality, these correspondents could not help but articulate views of the Revolution and anticipations of what French society might look like when the Revolution came to an end.

This interpenetration of practical and political concerns often led curricular reforms to be imagined and justified in political or social terms. Messieurs Girard and Roi, *maîtres-ès-arts* at the University of Bourges, for example, conceded that significant reforms needed to be undertaken at all levels of French education, and called for a number of measures to be taken so that the schools could better serve France's political, economic, and administrative needs. They promised that serving the state's practical interests would also lead schools to provide students with a better education. Their proposals included reducing the age at which students entered the schools (to 5), giving *pères de famille* priority as instructors, inverting the curriculum at the *collèges* so that logic preceded rhetoric, and encouraging the study of English and Italian in addition to French and Latin. They also called for greater emphasis on the study of mathematics, which they considered "indispensable." Finally, they called for the schools to provide a sort of social and political "apprenticeship," one that would include instruction in the new laws of the kingdom and the *Declaration of the Rights of Man and Citizen* and would be reinforced through the example of instructors who were "content with the Revolution and free of prejudices, who recognized no social divisions and would apply themselves to the task of forming young citizens."[40] With new curricular emphases, new personnel, and a new sense of purpose, Girard and Roi hoped that the schools could be made to resemble and to serve the new political order.

A similar desire that social, political, and pedagogical regimes mirror one another was evident in the proposal from M. Degranthe, a professor at Collège Louis-le-Grand noted briefly above. For Degranthe, the design of a new educational system was intimately related to the design of a new political order, a point he had stressed already in his *Projet d'un Plan d'Éducation Nationale, suivant la nouvelle division du Royaume* (1789), a work upon which he built in his *Abus de l'Ancienne Éducation* of 1790.[41] Degranthe's primary concerns in this later work were to defend the primacy of public over private education, to convince the aristocracy and social elites to send their children to public institutions rather than entrusting them to private tutors, and to outline a model for a public and national system of education.

According to Degranthe, there were three virtues that made public education more desirable than the private alternatives. First, public institutions could draw from a national pool of candidates, and so attract the best instructors. Second, they were better suited to forming pupils' characters. Third, they were more conducive to a spirit of *émulation*, which he described as "the source of all success."[42] The second and third of these were particularly important to his proposal and suggest broader themes in how Degranthe thought about education's role in the Revolution.

Degranthe argued that private education was ill-suited to preparing people for the demands of citizenship because it gave instructors and students incentives to avoid disagreement and debate and to venerate authority over accomplishment. He described private education as encouraging students to passively receive and regurgitate ideas presented by the instructor in exchange for the instructor's applause.[43] By contrast, public schools were likely to foster constructive competition and social dynamism because they compelled students of different social stations and temperaments to engage one another and to "make their character responsive to the character of others." If a student was naturally arrogant, he would be humbled by the others, if violent, he would be tamed, if miserly, generous, and in the end he would come to know the value of virtue: "In a word, it is by living in a well-run house with others that one learns to hate vice ... and to love and practice virtue."[44] Public schools were also more likely to foster a competitive spirit of emulation because, as he asked, "is there a motive for emulation more powerful for a young man who has talents than to have to compete against many others for a prize, and, [if successful], to have that crowd of others applaud his successes and his triumphs?"[45] Degranthe also turned to competition to improve the education offered in the schools. He argued that the government ought to establish a nationally uniform curriculum, but should directly oversee only half of the schools, entrusting the other half to independent instructors (an idea he first proposed in his 1789 pamphlet). The division would encourage a sense of competitive emulation among institutions and instructors, with the nation emerging as the primary beneficiary.[46]

Degranthe proposed a three-tier system of national education, beginning with *maisons d'éducation nationales* distributed throughout each department, and with particular attention to the need for schools in rural areas. Above these would be a *maison polysophique* in the chief city of each department and, above that, four extraordinary *maisons polysophiques* in Paris that would serve as a "center for the gathering of the best students from the eighty-three departments" of France.[47]

The first level of instruction, the *maisons d'éducation nationales*, would be subdivided into three classes, for students aged 5-9, 9-12, and 12-15. In the first class, students would learn how to read and write, how to draw and, as an "agreeable science," how to dance. In the second, students would continue their study of reading, writing and drawing (the last to the point of tracing maps), to which there would be added lessons in national and modern history as well as geometry. For their "agreeable sciences," students in the second class would learn to fence and would participate in military exercises. In the third (and final) class, students would study religion, morality, geometry, history and geography, as well as French and two additional languages. Degranthe designed these classes so that those who left school at age 9 had received the elementary skills and knowledge necessary for participation in society – the ability to read, write, and do basic calculations, as well as knowledge of the new constitution (through thrice-weekly political catechism exercises) – and so that those who remained through all three classes would be prepared for entry into a profession or, for those few who would continue in their studies, for entry into the *maisons polysophiques*.[48]

While he imagined that relatively few students would continue into the secondary schools, Degranthe thought it important that talent rather than wealth make the selection. To that end, he proposed that the state offer scholarships and the promise of a free education to reward those who showed particular merit or aptitude in the *maisons d'éducation nationales*. He called for the creation of 100 scholarships in each *maison polysophique*, to be awarded after a public competition open to all would-be students, rich and poor alike. The *maisons polysophiques* would educate only these *boursiers*, saving the schools from the burden and distraction of students who were uninterested in and ill-served by the demands of secondary education (a problem he thought common in the *collèges*).[49] Students at the *maisons polysophiques* would begin by studying logic (in French), rhetoric, physics and metaphysics, after which they would select from among four courses of specialized study: medicine and surgery; military studies; law; or architecture and design.[50]

A similar structure would apply to the four *maisons polysophiques* in Paris, the final "tier" in Degranthe's educational system. Each of those four establishments would be devoted to one of the four courses of specialized study and would bring together the 166 best students from around the country (each department would send two students to each of the four Parisian *maisons*). While their curricula matched the other *maisons polysophiques*, these four schools served a different function in Degranthe's system, one that illustrated at once the proposal's Ancien Régime roots and revolutionary character.

Echoing arguments presented in support of the *agrégation* in the 1760s, Degranthe claimed that the students at these Parisian *maisons polysophiques* would help to spread the benefits of the new educational system throughout France. He expected that after completing their studies, many of each cohort's 664 students would return to their respective departments and become instructors, thereby improving regional schools and repaying the nation for its investment in their education.[51] Just as the government of Louis XV and the parlements had hoped that the *agrégés* would serve as a sort of pedagogical vanguard, Degranthe claimed that the graduates of the Parisian *maisons polysophiques* would fill teaching vacancies across France, would set the standard of excellence for the new educational system, and would put the prestige of their education to use securing pedagogical and public benefits for the nation.

Despite the clear echoes of the *agrégation*, the politics underlying Degranthe's proposal more closely resembled Mirabeau's arguments for a *Lycée national* (discussed in Chapter 3). Mirabeau defended the cultivation of a "*jeunesse choisie*" in an elite Parisian institution not only for its role in educating the populace at large (that is, not only on the diffusionary terms of the *agrégation*), but also because it would embody a new, competitive, and meritocratic order. Like Mirabeau, Degranthe argued that the *maisons polysophiques* would put existing elites on notice that social status was now subject to competition and would be awarded not according to lineage, but in recognition of talents, skills, and accomplishments. For all of its infrastructural familiarity, Degranthe's proposal was a product of the Revolution.

Like many such attempts to reshape the social order, the establishment of a more meritorious elite and a more just and legitimate form of social hierarchy was recognized as a long-term project to which Degranthe (and Mirabeau) thought educational reform might contribute. Its ability to do so depended, however, upon the successful solution of more immediate problems; as J. F. Major noted in his *Tableau d'un Collège en activité*, how to establish and how to maintain a system of education were distinct questions, though they converged on the issue of how to recruit, train, and certify instructors.[52] Inadequately addressed after the expulsion of the Jesuits in the early 1760s, this was a familiar concern, and it provoked consistent and sustained attention in the proposals sent to the Assembly. Here again we see a general consensus that fundamental changes were on the horizon, but competing ideas about what changes were likely, what the respective roles of prescriptive design and dynamic competition ought to be, and about how the deputies and the schools might manage the interaction of political, social, institutional, and pedagogical forces.

The problem was at once persistent and pressing. The role of potential instructors was amplified by the view that schools offered an "apprenticeship" for social and political life and by the relative consensus that instructors exerted a great deal of influence as models their students might emulate. Describing the attributes of a desirable instructor was tantamount to describing the good citizen, again returning a practical problem to its roots in first principles. The Benedictines in the Loir-et-Cher described the selection criteria for instructors as "sufficient knowledge, good morals, and personal independence," and they encouraged authorities to esteem "wisdom above science, science above personality, personality above charm."[53] Monsieur Desbouis of Lyon, formerly a professor at the Collège de Sorèze (an *école militaire* in the Tarn), made a similar claim in the *Plan d'Éducation Nationale* of August 1790, writing that "in order to be a good instructor, one must have more than knowledge; one must also have a talent for teaching and an assiduous nature, good conduct and a particular genius for making students value what they are being taught."[54] The problem of recruiting and certifying good instructors thus had at least three elements: instructors were expected to be learned men, skilled teachers, and good role models.

A familiar desire to rationalize, standardize, and centralize the recruitment of instructors underlay J. F. Major's proposal for overhauling and "rejuvenating" the existing institutions. As he put it, his ambition was to "make education less arbitrary, so that instructors are no longer adrift, uncertain what they are supposed to be teaching, and so that students will no longer find themselves the victims of failed methods of instruction ... Instruction will be transformed."[55] His plan was, in essence, to reimagine and refashion the existing institutions, including the University of Paris, which he proposed renaming the École Nationale and transforming into a vast teachers' college for all of France. He claimed that the result would be a uniform system of instruction across France that would refocus instruction to make it more useful to society and to the state. To that end he called upon the deputies to establish a system in which all students would receive the same education until age 14 (focused on reading and writing in French, basic computation, and some literature as well as history, geography, cartography, and the principles of mathematics), and to establish four secondary schools in each district, offering instruction in agriculture and commerce, military and literary arts, the arts and useful sciences, and civic administration, respectively. Perhaps most important, however, was the role of the École Nationale (the reimagined University of Paris), which would design a uniform pedagogy, a "scientific method" for teaching the course of studies decreed by the deputies. Districts across France would send instructors to be trained (or re-trained) in Paris, and those instructors would re-emerge as "apostles of the Constitution" and of the new pedagogical order. Major thought that this plan would reinvigorate the university and address the clear disconnect between the unfulfilled promise of the *agrégation* and the demands of a national system of education.

Where Major sought to centralize and rationalize a system for training and then supplying instructors across France, others turned to the sorts of competitive dynamics that had characterized proposals like Mirabeau's and Degranthe's. Monsieur Miolan, for instance, *maître-ès-arts* in Aix, focused his November 1790 pamphlet *Sur les petites écoles* on establishing an educational infrastructure that would permit the state to control education while still benefiting from the dynamism and ambition that result from competition between instructors and between schools.[56] In short, Miolan sought to balance economic and professional liberalism with the desire for pedagogical uniformity.

Like Mirabeau, Miolan saw competition as likely to improve education because it would make instructors' livelihood dependent on their ability to offer an education that was valued by pupils and their parents. Again, like Mirabeau, Miolan proposed that the government rescind its promise of free education, arguing that making instructors depend on student fees would encourage them to improve their methods of instruction (so as to retain their students), and would encourage parents to pay greater attention to their children's education, thereby guaranteeing that students were diligent in their studies.[57] Unlike Mirabeau and other proponents of *enseignement libre*, however, Miolan did not think that the political authorities ought to leave that competition unregulated. Instead, he called for relatively robust legislative involvement, not only in the design of a new system of education, but also in its administration and maintenance.

Miolan's plan would have the state stipulate the youngest age at which one could become an instructor, test would-be instructors to ensure that they were sufficiently knowledgeable in the subjects they intended to teach, regulate the number of instructors permitted to work in any given location (so as to guarantee that there were enough teachers for the children of the village, town or city, and that there were enough students to keep teachers gainfully employed), and require that writers, mathematicians, or grammarians who offered specialized courses also offer general courses in reading and writing, thereby ensuring that students in all areas could acquire these basic and necessary skills. Because the goals of primary education – "to form men, and to make them useful to society and to themselves"[58] – were so important to the well-being of the state, it was imperative that the state encourage and ensure the perfection of the *petites écoles*. For this reason, while Miolan advocated a system predicated on *enseignement libre*, he stopped far short of a laissez-faire approach to education.

On issues of public morality and religion, Miolan contrasted his proposed system of (regulated) *enseignement libre* with the existing system, in which most instructors were clergymen or members of religious orders. Combining religious and instructional responsibilities was disadvantageous, he argued, because it meant that religious communities had to support priests who could not concentrate on their religious duties and because it divided clerics' attention between the ministry and the classroom. Because of these competing responsibilities it was not until a priest's "last years," after retiring from teaching, that he could devote all of his attention and energy to his religious calling. To remedy this, Miolan argued that clerics ought not to be engaged in education except in case of a severe shortage of qualified instructors.[59] Far from an affront to religious authorities, however, Miolan promised that this change would serve the interests of the Church, the schools, and even the priests themselves.

Others acknowledged more directly the disruptive professional, personal, and institutional consequences that were likely to follow from reform. As the academician and Oratorian Monsieur Paris noted in his *Projet d'éducation nationale* (1790), standardizing a new approach to education would also mean dismantling many elements of the inherited "system" and disrupting the lives of those who worked and studied in those institutions. Paris argued that the existing system of education was plagued by two fundamental flaws: first, far too many people lacked access to education; second, far too many people received an "indulgent" education focused on the belles-lettres and similar "*choses de luxe*."[60] Fixing this meant not only enrolling more students, but also changing curricula, eliminating many of the *collèges*, and redesigning the institutions and curricula of secondary and tertiary education. While he proposed the customary three-tier system of education, he proposed just one secondary school per department (offering sixty competitively selected students free instruction in natural history, history, geography, the physical sciences, philosophy, literature, mathematics, and languages), and then tertiary institutions tailored to the needs and resources of the various regions and departments (relatively widely available schools of medicine, engineering, and commerce, law schools in cities with major courts, military engineering academies near the frontiers, *écoles de marine* near port cities, etc.). He anticipated that among the consequences of this reorganization would be the obsolescence of many instructors then working in schools. Those who showed themselves capable of adjusting to the new expectations and curricula were welcome to continue in the reformed *collèges* after demonstrating their patriotism and talents to the municipal authorities. But he assumed that many would be given modest pensions and then either retire or pursue new and more useful professions.[61]

Where Degranthe, Miolan, Paris, and others framed the problem of how to recruit, train, and oversee instructors in terms of institutional efficacy and social utility, others saw the problem as a microcosm of France's transformation from a society of orders into a nation of citizens. While the logistics of placing instructors into classrooms were complicated by the anti-corporatist laws and the reorganization of the Church (noted in Chapter 3), it had become clear even before those laws were passed or enforced that the expectations regarding instructors' identities, skills, and methods would differ considerably from those of just a few years earlier. Moving from one set of expectations to another would pose political and cultural, as well as institutional and administrative, difficulties and, for those so positioned and so inclined, opportunities. This interplay of upheaval and opportunity was clear in nearly identical letters submitted just two days apart by groups of *doctrinaires agrégés non-prêtres* in Aix and in the Var (noted briefly at the start of this chapter).[62]

These *agrégés* acknowledged that there were real advantages to a system in which instructors were organized into corporate bodies collectively responsible for the training, certification, and discipline of their members; indeed, this had been part of the allure of handing *collèges* over to religious orders under the Ancien Régime. At the same time, these orders had reflected the Ancien Régime in much the same way that the new system of education was supposed to reflect and reinforce the new political and social order. For that reason, and despite the *agrégés'* recognition that many among the Regulars were good, patriotic, and virtuous citizens, the profession had been characterized by social hierarchy and injustice; as they put it: "we had our own aristocracy, our own *lettres de cachet*, our own despotisms, and even two distinct orders: the priests and the simple clerics." In terms reminiscent of Sieyès in *Qu'est-ce que le Tiers-Etat?*, they complained that while most of the work was carried out by clerics, "all of our estate's honors went to the priests; they enjoyed a monopoly over privileges and adopted pretensions of superiority, controlling provincial assemblies and dictating laws to their confreres ... The clerics constituted a majority among members of the congregation, but the priests occupied all of the chairs at the *collèges* except for a few in theology and in logic." They did not blame the priests personally, but rather the "absurdities and injustices" of Ancien Régime life. To remedy this, the *agrégés* proposed that the deputies dissolve the teaching orders but retain those instructors willing to continue in the new system, and that they make the *agrégation* the only determinant of status for instructors, establishing a civil and secular point of reference for all qualified instructors.[63]

As these *agrégés* realized, however, the problem of personnel extended well beyond the question of whether instructors would be organized as one or many corporate bodies. Where was this new system supposed to find qualified instructors whose values and priorities reflected a social and political order that was only just then coming into existence? They asked: "is it enough for an instructor to have pronounced once the word 'liberty?' What meaning will this word have for him? Can he be expected to have been devoted to the Patrie when no such thing really existed? What would 'civism' mean to him?"[64] The *agrégés* realized that the problem of recruiting, training, certifying, and overseeing instructors was as political as it was institutional or administrative, and addressing it meant wrestling once more with Rousseau's dilemma of the legislator: how could would-be instructors be expected to already have attributes that people were supposed to acquire by virtue of institutions, practices, and norms only then being established? For this reason, and unlike the vast majority of those who wrote to the Assembly (but perhaps echoing Helvétius in his more pessimistic moments), they argued that the reform of education had to follow from, rather than lead to, the transformation of political and civil society.

When these *agrégés* submitted their letters in spring 1790, they could not have known how deeply and how traumatically the problem of uncertain allegiances, dubious oaths, and civic distrust would upset the Revolution, not to mention the debate over educational reform. Within a year, the problem was endemic, unavoidable, and increasingly disruptive.

Impatience, uncertainty, and improvisation in educational reform

Trying to maintain and administer existing institutions while also anticipating, or at least not running afoul of, reforms pursued by national authorities was a source of considerable frustration for political and pedagogical administrators even before the Revolution. Indeed, this had been the case for much of the period after 1763, including the years after the establishment of the *agrégation* in 1766 (discussed in Chapter 2), when proposals to nationalize the recruitment, training, certification, and oversight of instructors complicated local efforts to actually staff and maintain schools.[65] But the disruptions and uncertainties of the Revolution were of a new sort, entangled from the first with deeply contentious political, social, cultural, and economic disputes and aggravated by uncertainties about who had the authority and capacity to implement change. The result in many places was a degenerative paralysis. In October 1790 in Valognes, for instance, political administrators and officials at the local *collège* wrote to the Assembly expressing their concern that necessary decisions were being postponed and pedagogical benefits forestalled because department officials were unwilling to approve even routine requests until the deputies announced the details of a national system. The petition in question was for approval to appoint a second chair in philosophy, at no increase to the school's budget, and it had been approved by the city, district, and *collège* officials, but still it was stalled.[66] The administrators in Valognes hoped that once they secured the reassurance of national authorities, they could soon get back to the work of reforming and improving education in the *collège*.

The mayor and citizens in Orléans were even more anxious and confused than their counterparts in Valognes, writing in February 1791 that the district authorities had shuttered the *collège* in anticipation of a national reform (despite the Assembly's provisional maintenance of the schools until a course of reform was settled upon). They noted that parents were frustrated by having to care for children they had expected to be at school and angry that their children's studies had been interrupted, and they expressed consternation at the prolonged uncertainty caused by the Assembly's failure to settle on a plan for reform. They concluded by expressing confidence that the deputies would soon remedy the situation, but their tone was more resigned than reassured; seeing their immediate problems as a result of uncertainty regarding the long-term plan, they waited, though not quite patiently.[67] Departmental authorities in the Côtes du Nord took precisely the opposite approach, responding to the resignation of professors at the Collège de St Brieuc by (provisionally) approving salaries for a new principal and new professors, noting that action was required to maintain the *collège* even provisionally.[68]

The problems faced by authorities in Orléans and in the Côtes du Nord were not at all rare. During the first half of 1791, insecurity stemming from the long-delayed promise of reform and the provisional status of the *corps enseignants*, uncertainty about how institutions were and would be funded, and hostilities resulting from the Civil Constitution of the Clergy and the clerical oath paralyzed both the existing institutions and the prospects for reform. The convergence of crises and uncertainties meant that even in those places where instructors or professors swore the clerical oath, the status of the schools and their place in the Revolution was unsettled and uncertain.[69] While experimentation and attempts to accommodate changing political and material circumstances continued, spring 1791 marked an important moment as the point at which the path from the institutional present to the promised future started to disappear.

Unlike the nationalization of Church lands or the ambiguous status of religious orders, the clerical oath forced clerics, political authorities, and educational administrators to wrestle with a choice that seemed to offer relatively little room for maneuver. As Timothy Tackett writes, "[b]y forcing the separation of the sheep and the goats among the French clergy, by imposing an absolute, unambiguous stance for or against the new constitution, the oath would come to reinforce and solidify the Manichaean universe of revolutionary politics."[70] Because the decision to swear or to not swear the oath was such a publicly visible one, clerics' decisions rippled through their communities, reinforcing or undermining the faith these communities had in the Assembly or in the clerics, and contributing to a dynamic in which "oath-taking and refusal formed a complex map of the politico-religious sensibilities of France, a map that was to be reflected in patterns of more violent dissent in the future."[71] In both the short- and long-term, the conflicts born of the Civil Constitution and the clerical oath would transform the history of the Revolution and of modern France. They also forced many instructors, professors, school administrators, and political authorities to wrestle with the fallout of a crisis that upended the debates over education and the maintenance, reform, or reinvention of the schools.

The conflicts and controversies surrounding the Civil Constitution (and then the clerical oath) exposed and aggravated the uncertain contours of academic governance, oversight, and administration and, in so doing, turned the problem of dealing with unsettled schools into a source of local conflicts and crises. This was most glaringly revealed at the University of Poitiers, where the Collège St Marthe was thrown into violent disarray in January and February 1791. The fallout from the Civil Constitution – and from the principal's refusal, along with five professors, to swear the clerical oath – initially appeared manageable, perhaps even to be handled in an amicable and peaceful manner. In a meeting of the university's tribunal on 22 January, the principal of the *collège*, M. Bernard, announced his intention to resign his post rather than swear the clerical oath, as did two professors of philosophy, the professor of rhetoric, and the professors of the IIIeme and IVeme. These relatively "patriotic refractories" announced that their resignation was offered in conformity with the law and was being presented to the tribunal so that the work of replacing them might proceed "without excessive interruption of the studies" being pursued at the *collège*, an institution for which they expressed continued affection and respect.[72] The tribunal then nominated provisional replacements for the non-juring professors, sent notification to the political authorities of the district and department, and made arrangements to install the new principal and instructors. Among attempts to navigate the upheaval caused by the Civil Constitution, this was as auspicious a start as could be hoped for in a *collège* with non-juring instructors.

The next day, however, the university's efforts ran into trouble when the district and department authorities were briefed on the steps being taken at the *collège*. The political authorities refused to recognize the university tribunal's jurisdiction over the vacant positions, claiming for themselves the right to install replacements. The university's delegation protested, citing Ancien Régime precedents as well as the Assembly's provisional maintenance of the teaching orders and existing institutions. As they saw it, the provisional maintenance had preserved the university tribunal's prerogatives regarding the appointment of provisional instructors and the recruitment and retention of more permanent replacements (though still under the "provisional" banner that accompanied all such efforts during this period). They protested that the local political authorities were misrepresenting the political situation at the *collège* by treating the non-juring professors as representative of the institution writ large, pre-empting the reform efforts of the National Assembly, improperly depriving the university of its rights, and proposing procedures for installing instructors that provided no guarantee that those instructors were qualified or suitable for their new responsibilities.[73] The points of conflict were at once procedural, political, and professional.

The district and department authorities were unmoved by the tribunal's arguments, and the competing authorities clashed again the next day when each tried to install its would-be instructors. As the rector and the lay faculty of the university describe the events of 24 January in letters to the Assembly, the university's provisional instructors were being presented to the students and other members of the *collège* when Michel-Pascal Creuzé, a municipal official (and later *conventionnel*), arrived with soldiers and asserted the political authorities' jurisdiction over the selection and instillation of new instructors.[74] Creuzé's forces were soon joined by national guardsmen and additional representatives of the department, district, and municipality, one of whom declared that they would no longer recognize the members of the tribunal as representatives of the university. Students apparently jeered the political authorities as they installed their preferred instructors, but the members of the university tribunal withdrew, thinking it better to pursue their appeal with the National Assembly than to risk escalating the altercation further.[75] Again their appeals were ineffective though, and the conflicts at this *collège* would persist until it was replaced by the newly established *école centrale* in 1795.[76]

While this case is notable for its violence, Poitiers was by no means alone in its experience of winter and spring 1791. The disruptive events of these months, and the relatively rapid deterioration of the *collèges* that resulted, are clear in an April 1791 letter from the departmental administrators of the Loir-et-Cher, who wrote to the Assembly frustrated by the dismantling of the existing *collèges* before the establishment of a new educational system. The Benedictine *collège* in Pont-Levoy – which had been home to one of the Benedictines whose letter was noted above – is described in this letter as important to the town and the community, esteemed by local families, and situated in sound and pleasant buildings. And on the verge of collapse. The Benedictines had left the *collège* after the April 15 law requiring the removal of non-juring priests from public functions, leading parents to withdraw their children and leaving the administrators "without any effective remedies at [their] disposal." Without qualified instructors to replace the Benedictines, and worried that anybody they installed would lack the confidence of the parents and the community, the administrators turned to the deputies to provide funds for the provisional maintenance of the school, for personnel to replace the newly absent instructors, and for a plan to integrate the existing schools into an educational regime "better adapted to the new constitution."[77] Departmental authorities did not fare much better when they stepped in, though they did manage to fashion a compromise enlisting three former Benedictines who had sworn the oath and who maintained the *collège* into the Terror, after which they were replaced when the school was more thoroughly republicanized.[78]

Likewise in Auch, where officials removed non-juring instructors in January 1791 and installed replacements, leading to the prompt departure of most students and a fight over jurisdiction among municipal, district, and department officials. In February, the municipal authorities claimed that they alone had the right to oversee the *collèges* and reaffirmed their installation of the replacement teachers.[79] That June, however, department authorities wrote to the Assembly complaining that they were forced to rely once again upon non-jurors because they could not find suitable replacements willing to swear the requisite oath; in cases where even this was not possible, they were forced to (reluctantly) close the schools.[80]

A similar dynamic was evident in Limoges, where officials complained that the need to replace at once almost the entire faculty of the city's *collège* undermined public confidence and led parents to withdraw their children, leaving half of the classes without any students and the others with enrollments as low as one, three, or seven students. The *collège* in Limoges had been controlled by the Jesuits, and was a prominent and prestigious institution in the seventeenth century. Despite a period of difficulties after the Jesuits' expulsion, the *collège* had managed to re-establish itself as important to the city and the surrounding towns, and had weathered the first years of the Revolution relatively well. With the dispute over the clerical oath, however, the situation "deteriorated rapidly and dramatically."[81] Given the expenses involved in maintaining the school, including salaries and accommodations for professors who were now largely without students and without purpose, the administrators proposed closing the *collège* until the Assembly completed its work on a national system of education, though they were hesitant to do so. Unlike the district administrators in Orléans, they did not want to make the de facto closure of the *collège* official without seeking clarification and clearance from Paris.[82] In the end, they managed to maintain the *collège*, though its troubles continued, and it seems that by 1794 the instructors were receiving salaries despite having no students to teach.[83]

If the clerical oath made it harder to imagine a future for Ancien Régime institutions, it also offered some would-be instructors a chance to reaffirm their commitment to the new politics and to clearly distinguish themselves from their non-juring (or reluctantly juring) colleagues. This approach was evident in a modified version of the letter sent by the *doctrinaires agrégés non-prêtres*, first received in spring 1790 (and noted above) but resubmitted in April 1791 by *agrégés* in Paris. Where the earlier version of the letter had highlighted the role of the *agrégation* in establishing uniform, meritocratic, secular, and national requirements for instructors, the 1791 letter added a concluding section stressing the authors' patriotism and loyalty, lauding the Civil Constitution of the Clergy for "reestablishing religion's primitive purity, making it more respectable and impressive, even to its enemies, and helping it to conform more perfectly to the spirit of the Gospels and the principles of our divine author."[84] Identifying themselves as among those who were "convinced that the new provisions would bring about the regeneration and purification of religion," the *agrégés* hoped to reassure the deputies that they could be entrusted with the regeneration of the nation as well.[85]

While the oath divided France deeply, perhaps even into "Two Frances" – (one clerical and anti-revolutionary, the other revolutionary and anti-clerical) – many of those who first wrestled with it sought to escape the unforgiving binary of acceptance or rejection.[86] This was true for those Tackett calls "patriot refractories" and for others we might call "reluctant revolutionaries," those who swore the oath but did so with some form of equivocation, caveat, or modification.[87] Cases of this sort put local and institutional administrators in an uncertain position as they tried to divine the relationship between the letter and spirit of the oath and to clarify the practical requirements of the new laws. In Châlons, for example, department authorities and administrators at the *collège* tried to determine whether the modified oaths sworn by ten instructors had been altered significantly enough to merit rejection and the subsequent removal of the instructors. Unsure how to proceed, and already struggling to fill the positions vacated by refractories, they asked the instructors to remain in their positions while transcriptions of the oaths as sworn were sent to the National Assembly for a determination of their legitimacy.[88]

Cases like these were further complicated by the difficulty of identifying just who was and who was not an agent of the state under the provisional educational regime. While the Assembly had indicated that the schools would be overseen and administered by political authorities, the institutions themselves continued in many places to reflect arrangements inherited from the Ancien Régime, and most of the personnel had come to their positions without substantive oversight by the state. Cleric-instructors could not work as state functionaries without swearing the oath, but until they swore the oath (and in some cases after), it was unclear whether or not some of them were in fact state functionaries.[89]

Were requirements designed for employees of a promised, but not yet realized, state system applicable to provisionally maintained members of Ancien Régime communities and institutions? Local officials had no easy answer to this, and their correspondence with Paris offered little help.

As problematic as communication with Parisian authorities was for local authorities and school administrators in the provinces, the problems they faced were not the result of distance alone. The same troubles plagued Jean-François Champagne when he became principal of Collège Louis-le-Grand in May 1791. Champagne took over the position after his predecessor refused to swear the oath (as did two other professors, with yet another having recently retired amid the tensions surrounding the oath); six days after becoming principal, Champagne wrote to departmental authorities in Paris describing a *collège* "in disarray" (as R. R. Palmer described it).[90] The principal, four assistant principals, several masters, chaplains, and the three aforementioned professors had recently left, though several of the non-jurors continued to live in buildings associated with the *collège*, making the dispute an interpersonal as well as administrative and political one. Champagne found his power to enforce changes in personnel hampered by Ancien Régime precedents and traditions (e.g., a building owned by the *collège* and inhabited by three former professors who had refused the oath was one over which "the principal ... has never had any power of inspection," leaving him powerless to remove the non-jurors from their rooms). His options were further limited by the prospect of antagonizing devout students (those "infected by the malady of fanaticism"), and his path forward was obscured by the lack of instruction from departmental and national authorities. He both opened and closed his letter imploring the department officials to "indicate ... the course [he] should follow," reinforcing the sense that while Champagne was committed to managing the various crises as they arose, those crises had overwhelmed the institution's ability to project a future for itself in the Revolution.[91]

The result of these many uncertainties, anxieties, and animosities was an aggravated sense of frustration with the Assembly for its inability to settle on a course of reform. The degeneration of many of the existing institutions seemed to reflect a conscious policy, a foretelling of the schools' destruction and the repudiation of the pedagogical institutions and traditions inherited from the Ancien Régime. As professors from the *collèges* in Nîmes noted regarding the *corps enseignants*: "While you have not yet stipulated a definitive form of public education, a number of your decrees have revealed the fate of [these bodies]: we have read their destruction in advance."⁹² The same seemed to be true for the institutions and organization of education, a problem that raised issues for the present as well as the future. The "provisional" status bestowed on these schools undermined confidence not just in their future, but in their value. As students in Sézanne put it, "while we await the long-anticipated results of your wise deliberations, a skeptical aversion to the old institutions has taken hold of our hearts and has paralyzed our youthful vigor." Writing in June 1791, they stressed the importance of establishing a new educational regime before the start of the new academic year so that they might benefit from a course of studies modeled on and appropriate to the new social and political order rather than waste another year in a course of studies that was at once useless and injurious.⁹³

"Brilliant, unacceptable, impractical, unconstitutional"

While the students' plea for a new system of education to take effect in autumn 1791 went unanswered, it was just three months after they wrote that the deputies in Paris finished work on the new constitution and Talleyrand presented what he hoped would be a conclusion to the debates over education. That proposal, discussed in Chapter 4, was left for the incoming deputies of the Legislative Assembly and, ultimately, passed over by the Committee of Public Instruction and by Condorcet (whose own plan for a system of public instruction, also discussed in Chapter 4, was drowned out by the coming of war in April 1792). While Talleyrand's presentation to the Assembly was in that sense inconsequential, it nonetheless reinforced the dynamics that had shaped the debate over education to that point, most crucially by establishing a clear set of measures to be evaluated and discussed by correspondents across France. Its publication and distribution gave focus to the debate over education and led to substantive responses and counter-proposals from correspondents across France (including the pamphlet submitted by Pierre Wouves discussed at the end of Chapter 5).

This was especially true for correspondents associated with the schools, as Talleyrand's proposal gave informed correspondents an image of the future to compare with the circumstances they had known in the past and the conditions in which they found themselves. It gave them a clear frame of reference within which to bring their experience to bear on the debate over reform. Among the more remarkable of these responses was a lengthy (seventy-four-page) printed pamphlet sent to the deputies in late 1791 by fourteen *maîtres de pension* in Paris who offered both laudatory and dismissive commentary on Talleyrand's proposal and demonstrated clearly the entanglement of practical, political, institutional, and constitutional concerns in the debates over education.[94] Their pamphlet was at once extraordinary and suggestive of the larger corpus of letters, proposals, requests, and complaints that flowed to the National Assembly from instructors, administrators, and students across France, and it offers a valuable opportunity to reflect on that corpus and correspondence more generally.

Writing shortly after the presentation of Talleyrand's proposal, the *maîtres* began their letter by invoking the constitution's two articles regarding education, recognizing Talleyrand's good intentions and essential patriotism, and then dismissing his proposed system as "inadmissible because it is impractical, impractical because it is unconstitutional, and unconstitutional because it is in contradiction with itself, resulting in miscalculations and injustices that would horrify the patriotic heart of its author if he even suspected their presence in his work."[95] The mix of admiration for Talleyrand and parts of his plan and despair at its inadequacies or impracticalities continues throughout, with the teachers' patriotism and civic sensibilities competing with their experience and sense of classroom realities as they assessed the plan that was supposed to "complete" the new constitution. They praised Talleyrand's proposal as "brilliant" and lauded its mobilization of "a thousand resources for helping the sciences and the arts to flourish in France." They endorsed his shift from classes to courses, allowing for instructors to offer more specialized instruction and students to benefit from a more coherent sequence of studies, and they singled out his "Institut national" as an "encyclopedic body, a fecund soil that would bear excellent fruit and enable the French to surpass all other peoples on Earth in their inventions," their agricultural production, and their wealth.[96] There was, it would seem, much to like in Talleyrand's proposal. Except, of course, that they thought it suffered from a fatal flaw at its most important point and failed to satisfy even the most basic requirements of the constitutional promise.

Like many participants in the debates over education, these teachers thought it important that the various institutions and levels of education be integrated into a coherent and uniform national system, claimed that the long-term "stability or ruin" of the constitution depended upon the fate of that system, and viewed primary education as the cornerstone of the reform project.[97] It was on this last point that they took issue with Talleyrand's proposed system, claiming that his misperceptions and miscalculations regarding primary schools fatally undermined the proposal and rendered it "unacceptable" under the new constitution. Unsurprisingly, then, the vast majority of their lengthy and detailed response to Talleyrand's proposal focused on primary schools and their role in regenerating French society.

The teachers' commentary on elementary education and the role of schools in the new political and social order oscillated between the philosophical and the practical, reinforcing the sense that these were mutually informative modes of thought. This seemed particularly true regarding primary schools, as those schools had to satisfy the constitutional promise of instruction in the "branches of education indispensable to all men" without presuming that students would continue on to secondary or tertiary levels of schooling. It was in the primary schools that students would learn the first principles of the constitution, would be introduced to the rights and responsibilities of citizenship, and would acquire the skills necessary to engage with and contribute to public debate through the written and spoken word. There too they would come to better know their religion (presumed to be Catholicism), would learn basic mathematics, would receive instruction in geography and history (including the principal events of the Revolution), and would acquire sufficiently useful skills to prepare them for entry into the professions.[98] On most of these points they agreed with Talleyrand, as they did that it was through the primary schools that the government would or would not fulfill its constitutional obligations regarding public instruction.

Where the teachers broke from Talleyrand was on the perpetually vexing issues of resources and personnel. They argued that Talleyrand provided for too few primary schools and too few instructors, was too lax in his requirements for their recruitment and vetting, too parsimonious in designating salaries and in distributing resources, and, ultimately, too detached from the realities of the classroom to describe a system of public instruction suitable to, and sufficient for, the new politics. The result, they claimed, was not just a proposal insufficient to the demands of national education, but a rupture between the principles and the practices of educational reform, one that threatened both the spirit and letter of the constitution.[99]

Their criticism focused on the need to provide not just educational access, but also a coherent plan for civic socialization. The teachers agreed with Talleyrand that festivals, public competitions, and the distribution of prizes would encourage emulation and help to promote civic sentiments, but they saw these public celebrations as complements to the interpersonal and emulative dynamics of the classroom.[100] Because students needed personal as well as collective instruction, and because their lessons would be shaped not just by texts and lectures but also by affective and emulative bonds with instructors, an insufficient number of teachers threatened to undermine both the curricular and the civic dynamics of public instruction.[101] To satisfy the promise enshrined in the constitution there would need to be many more instructors, they would have to be provided with adequate resources and a sufficient number of assistants, the size of schools would have to be capped (and so the total number of schools increased), expectations regarding instructors' qualifications and characters would have to change, and new systems for administering and overseeing the schools would have to be developed.

Some of their most impassioned commentary focused on the recruitment and retention of instructors. Emphasizing the influence that instructors would have as models to be imitated and emulated ("children are born imitators"), they highlighted the need for teachers to be "well educated, but especially in the art of communication ... without which erudition can accomplish little." Instructors should have to demonstrate purity of character and morals, irreproachable conduct, patience, kindness, tolerance, and sociability. Above all else, they should have to show that they are "truly citizens; that is, true patriots, sincere friends of the constitution, of the laws and the new order to which it has given rise."[102] Only then could they be entrusted with the care and instruction of future citizens.

Maintaining such a system would require a substantial investment of financial and administrative resources. It would require increasing instructors' salaries to a point that would make teaching a desirable profession or, at the very least, enough so that the salary was not a deterrent to otherwise desirable candidates. This meant rejecting Talleyrand's proposal for a graduated pay scale in which primary school teachers received lower salaries than their counterparts in secondary or tertiary institutions. They asked: "do primary school teachers have fewer physical needs than others? Or is it that their work is less respectable, valuable, or useful to society?"[103] Salaries would also have to be increased to attract instructors with families, as the hiring of celibate instructors threatened to undermine the sorts of social bonds that would prepare students for civil society.[104] The same social, political, and moral requirements would apply to the preceptors and monitors who would be hired to assist the teachers.[105]

The *maîtres de pension* recognized that what they were proposing represented a massive and largely new pedagogical infrastructure and a significant expense for the national treasury. To allay deputies' concerns, they provided estimates of the anticipated expenses for primary schools and for more advanced institutions as well. They estimated that the primary schools of Paris would cost slightly less than 1.3 million *livres* per year, and the system as a whole (at all levels) would require an annual investment of just over 31 million *livres* to maintain. They estimated, however, that the properties, *bourses*, rents, and related incomes from the Ancien Régime universities, *collèges*, academies, and other institutions would provide roughly two-thirds of that sum, requiring an additional annual investment of 10 million *livres*, which they thought a reasonable price to pay to fulfill a promise enshrined in the new constitution.[106]

The pamphlet submitted by these Parisian *maîtres de pension* is relatively unusual in its degree of specificity, its integration of philosophical, constitutional, and practical concerns, its sympathetic but distinctly critical assessment of the deputies' work, and its blunt presentation of what would be required to move beyond the slogans of educational reform. On each of these points, however, the pamphlet offers a distilled version of the broader corpus of letters, proposals, pleas, and suggestions flowing from schools across France to the deputies in Paris. Their premises, presumptions, and proposals are familiar, including the idea that the success of the schools and that of the constitution were intimately linked, their identification of primary education as the site of that relationship's most critical test, the perceived need for schools to both reflect and reinforce the new political and social environment, and in their sense that the principles of political reform and the practical problems of reforming schools were inseparable from one another. A new system of education could not satisfy the promise of the constitution if it could not be translated into practice, its translation into practice had to be informed by the realities of administration and instruction, and those in turn had to somehow embody and reflect the new social, political, and constitutional order.

It was perhaps fitting, then, that the Committee of Public Instruction under Arbogast and Condorcet began its work by requesting that officials across France send the Assembly information on the history and current state of affairs in the schools within each department.[107] Fitting, but fruitless, as Condorcet's proposal – like so many of the Legislative Assembly's designs for social, political, and economic regeneration – was forestalled by the coming of the war, the aggravation of political tensions that followed, and the collapse of the constitutional monarchy in the late summer of 1792. After the *journée* of 10 August, the fall of the monarchy, and the election of the National Convention, deputies, citizens, schoolmasters, and students would return to the work of reimagining education and reinventing the relationship between society and the schools. They did so proclaiming a clean break from the monarchical "Ancien Régime." Whether they would do the same for the ancien régime of education remained unclear.

Notes

1. Charles R. Bailey, *The Old Regime Collèges, 1789-1795: Local Initiatives in Recasting French Secondary Education* (New York, NY: Peter Lang, 1994).
2. Timothy Tackett proposes this way of reading such texts in his examination of clerical justifications regarding their decision to swear or not swear the clerical oath. Tackett, *Religion, Revolution, and Regional Culture*, 73.
3. The exceptions to this are Bailey, *The Old Regime Collèges, 1789-1795* and, more recently, Figeac-Monthus, *Les Enfants de l'Émile*, 39-43, 66-72. Bailey tends to retain the distinction between practical management of the schools and imagining or articulating systemic approaches to national reform, and Figeac-Monthus collapses these institutional voices into a broader discourse whereby authors legitimize their arguments by reference to their practical experience. Each is valuable, though neither captures the intersection of "located-ness" and political imagination discussed here.
4. On the relationship between discursive and social position, see Roger Chartier, "Letter: Why the Linguistic Approach can be an obstacle to the further development of historical knowledge. A reply to Gareth Stedman Jones," *History Workshop Journal*, 46 (1998), 271-272.
5. Sarah Knott, "Narrating the Age of Revolution," *The William and Mary Quarterly*, 73:1 (2016), 5, 23.
6. Palmer, *The Improvement of Humanity*, 91.
7. AN, AD/VIII//21, no. 8, *Mémoire sur l'éducation nationale par M. l'abbé Audrein ... présenté à l'Assemblée Nationale le 11 Décembre 1790* (Paris, 1791).
8. AN, F/17//1310, dossier 6, no. 53, Address to the National Assembly from the Doctrinaires agrégés non-prêtres de cinq collèges d'Aix, 6 May 1790, 3; AN, D/IV//66, dossier 1997, no. 8, Letter to the National Assembly from the Doctrinaires agrégés non-prêtres, professeurs de six collèges, à Draguignan, 8 May 1790, 3.
9. AN, D/IV//25, dossier 573, no. 1, *Extrait du Registre des Délibérations du Département des Côtes du Nord*, 9 March 1791; AN, AD/VIII//21, no. 14, M. Arnauld, *Éducation. Plan proposé aux Représentants de la Nation* (n.d. [1790], n.p.), 1-4.
10. Koselleck, *Futures Past*, 59.

11 "Mémoire de l'Université de Poitiers pour les Etats-Généraux de 1789," in Edmond Dreyfus-Brisac (ed.), *Revue internationale de l'enseignement*, T. 14 (Paris: Masson, 1887): 209–240.
12 Palmer suggests that the authors of this proposal were probably among those consulted by Rolland d'Erceville as he prepared his speech and then text. Palmer, *The Improvement of Humanity*, 72.
13 "Mémoire de l'Université de Poitiers pour les Etats-Généraux de 1789," 228.
14 Ibid., 214, 234–235.
15 This is particularly evident in the proposal's argument about how to make the universities' oversight of their districts most effective. Ibid., 236.
16 Ibid., 213, 221–228.
17 Ibid., 209.
18 A similar sense that universities were willing to embrace the emerging idea of social and institutional reform is evident in the *cahiers de doléances* submitted by the University in Orléans; see Rideau, "Un corps séparé," 95–97.
19 AP 8: 303–304. This presentation is also described in R. R. Palmer, *The School of the French Revolution: A Documentary History of The College of Louis-le-Grand and its Director, Jean-François Champagne, 1762–1814* (Princeton, NJ: Princeton University Press, 1975), 86–87.
20 Quoted in Palmer, *The School of the French Revolution*, 88–91.
21 Bailey, *The Old Regime Collèges, 1789–1795*, 46.
22 For example, AN, D/IV//5, dossier 42, 1–10, Questions regarding public instruction submitted by officials in the Bouches-du-Rhone, 1790–1791. These inquiries describe anxieties in Aix-en-Provence about the relationship among political authorities on matters of educational oversight. Similarly, departmental authorities in the Bas-Rhin and municipal authorities in Strasbourg worried that problems regarding oversight of schools would lead to broader confusion about local administrative arrangements and hierarchies: AN, D/IV//6, dossier 95, nos 3–9, Questions submitted by departmental officials in the Bas-Rhin, 1790–1791. In August 1790, Target, writing on behalf of the constitutional committee, left the relationship between political authorities and religious orders administering schools to the discretion of the departmental authorities in Yonne: AN, D/IV//7, dossier 111, no. 14, Questions submitted by departmental authorities in Yonne, August 1790.
23 Bailey, *The Old Regime Collèges, 1789–1795*, 46–52.
24 *Arrêté pris par MM. les Recteur, Principaux, Professeurs & Agrégés de la Faculté des Arts de l'Université de Paris, assemblés au Collège de Louis-le-Grand, le 18 Décembre 1790* (Paris, n.d.), 1–3.
25 *Mémoire de la Faculté des Arts de l'Université de Paris, au sujet des traitemens qu'elle espère de l'Assemblée Nationale, pour ceux de ses Membres qui sont employés à l'Education publique* (Paris, n.d.), 1.
26 Ibid., 2–3.
27 Ibid., 12.

28 Archives Municipales de Toulouse, 1R7, 1-4, Mémoires from the Bureau d'Administration du Collège Royal in Toulouse to the National Assembly, April 1791.

29 Joseph Villier, *Nouveau plan d'éducation et d'instruction publique, dédié à l'Assemblée nationale, dans lequel on substitue aux Universités, Séminaires et Collèges, des établissemens plus raisonnables, plus utiles, plus dignes d'une grande Nation* ... (Angers: Imprimerie de Mame, 1789), 12.

30 Degranthe, *Abus de l'Ancienne Éducation, dévoiles et reformés par les progrès de la Raison, par M. Degranthe, au Collège de Louis-le-Grand* (Paris, 1790), 35.

31 Ibid., 1.

32 AN, F/17//1309, dossier 2, no. 14, Letter from Alexandre Courtois, administrator in the Département de la Moselle, to the National Assembly, 20 January 1792.

33 Quoted in Palmer, *The School of the French Revolution*, 114-115. On the relationship between concepts of historical lineage and the revolutionary present, see especially Bronislaw Baczko, *Lumières de l'utopie* (Paris: Payot, 1978).

34 AN, D/IV//34, dossier 838, no. 3, Letter from M. Robert, M. Dibon, and M. Gallais, ancien Benedictines, n.d. [late 1790-early 1791], 15.

35 AN, AD/VIII//21, no. 14, *Éducation. Plan proposé aux Représentants de la Nation, par M. Arnauld, instituteur* (n.n., n.d. [1790]), 3-4.

36 AN, F/17//1310, dossier 6, no. 53, Address to the National Assembly from the Doctrinaires agrégés non-prêtres de cinq collèges d'Aix, 6 May 1790, 2-3; AN, D/IV//66, dossier 1997, no. 8, Letter to the National Assembly from the Doctrinaires agrégés non-prêtres, professeurs de six collèges, à Draguignan, 8 May 1790, 3.

37 AN, AD/VIII//21, no. 13, *Projet d'éducation nationale par M. Paris, de l'Oratoire, de plusieurs Académies & Sociétés Littéraires* (Paris, 1790), 3-4. Similar claims were made by academicians in Orléans (AN, D/IV//38, dossier 1004, no. 2, Letter from seven academicians from the Académié de peinture in Orléans, n.d. [1791]), and by M. Serane, an instructor in Paris (AN, F/17//1310, dossier 7, no. 99, Letter to the National Assembly from M. Serane, de Paris, 7 July 1791), and by many others.

38 AN, AD/VIII//21, no. 9, *Tableau d'un Collège en activité, par J. F. Major, Professeur au Collège de Bar-le-Duc, suivant son projet sur l'instruction publique adressé le 15 octobre au Comité de Constitution* (Bar-le-Duc, 1790), 15.

39 Palmer, *The Improvement of Humanity*, 91. For a few among many such examples, see AN, AD/VIII//21, no. 13, *Projet d'éducation nationale par M. Paris*, 17-24; AN, AD/VIII//21, no. 9, *Tableau d'un Collège en activité par J.F. Major*, 1790, 19; AN, AD/VIII//21, no. 25, *Observations sur le rapport que M. Talleyrand Périgord... suivies d'un Plan d'Instruction primaire national, présentés à l'Assemblée Nationale, par les Maîtres de Pension de Paris* (Paris,

1791); AN, D/IV//25, dossier 573, no. 1, *Extrait du Registre des Délibérations du Directoire du Département des Côtes du Nord*, 9 March 1791; AN, D/IV//49, dossier 1401, no 6, *Moyen de faire distribuer gratuitement l'instruction aux enfans de cette capitale sans charger la commune, proposé à l'Assemblée Nationale par les maîtres de Pension de Paris*, 18 June 1791. This was especially true after traditional sources of revenue were nationalized and then, later, lost or sold. For example, AN, D/IV//48, dossier 1377, no. 6, Petition from a collège in Alençon requesting financial support, 12 August 1791.

40 AN, F/17//1310, dossier 7, no. 89, *Nouveau Plan d'Éducation Nationale*, submitted by MM. Girard and Roi, Maîtres-ès-Arts de l'Université de Bourges, & Maîtres de Pension à Nevers, 15 September 1790.
41 M. Degranthe, *Projet d'un Plan d'Éducation Nationale, suivant la nouvelle division du Royaume, en soixante-quinze ou quatre-vint-cinq Départemens* (Paris, 1789).
42 Degranthe, *Abus de l'Ancienne Éducation*, 9–10.
43 Ibid., 12.
44 Ibid., 10.
45 Ibid., 11.
46 Ibid., 46, 51–52.
47 Ibid., 19–20.
48 Ibid., 36–37.
49 Ibid., 39–40. Those students who wanted to continue their education but were not awarded a bourse (and whose parents could afford to pay for them to do so), could continue their education as "externs" at the *grands maisons d'éducation nationales*, where courses would be offered that were analogous to those offered in the *maisons polysophiques*.
50 Ibid., 38, 41–43.
51 Ibid., 43–44.
52 AN, AD/VIII//21, no. 9, *Tableau d'un Collège en activité, par J.F. Major*, 9–14.
53 AN, D/IV//34, dossier 838, no. 3, Letter from M. Robert, M. Dibon, and M. Gallais, ancien Benedictines, 8–9.
54 AN, F/17//1310, dossier 7, no. 81, *Plan d'Education Nationale présenté par M. Desbouis*, August 1790.
55 AN, AD/VIII//21, no. 9, *Tableau d'un Collège en activité, par J. F. Major*, 9–11.
56 AN, F/17//1310, dossier 7, no. 95, *Projet sur les petites écoles*, submitted by M. Miolan, November 1790.
57 Ibid., 2.
58 Ibid., 1.
59 Ibid., 2–4.
60 AN, AD/VIII//21, no. 13, *Projet d'éducation nationale, par M. Paris*, 7.
61 Ibid., 8–17, 25–27.

62 AN, F/17//1310, dossier 6, no. 53, Address to the National Assembly from the Doctrinaires agrégés non-prêtres de cinq collèges d'Aix, 6 May 1790; AN, D/IV//66, dossier 1997, no. 8, Letter to the National Assembly from the Doctrinaires agrégés non-prêtres, professeurs de six collèges, à Draguignan, 8 May 1790.

63 AN, F/17//1310, dossier 6, no. 53, Address to the National Assembly from the Doctrinaires agrégés non-prêtres de cinq collèges d'Aix, 6 May 1790, 3–6; AN, D/IV//66, dossier 1997, no. 8, Letter to the National Assembly from the Doctrinaires agrégés non-prêtres, professeurs de six collèges, à Draguignan, 8 May 1790, 3–7.

64 AN, F/17//1310, dossier 6, no. 53, Address to the National Assembly from the Doctrinaires agrégés non-prêtres de cinq collèges d'Aix, 6 May 1790, 3–6; AN, D/IV//66, dossier 1997, no. 8, Letter to the National Assembly from the Doctrinaires agrégés non-prêtres, professeurs de six collèges, à Draguignan, 8 May 1790, 3–7.

65 Philippe Marchand, "Recrutement et formation des regents des collèges du Nord au 18e siècle: réalité et projets," in Baker and Harrigan (eds), *The Making of Frenchmen*, 483–492.

66 AN, D/IV//41, dossier 1112, no. 4, Letter from the administration of the Collège de Valognes, requesting a second chair in Philosophy, October 1790.

67 AN, D/IV//38, dossier 1004, no. 3, Letter from citizens in Orléans protesting the proposed suspension of their collège, 3 February 1791, 2–3. The general climate of uncertainty regarding education in Orléans was evident in another letter written to the Assembly, at roughly the same time, by the local *Académie de peinture* defending its utility and petitioning the deputies to confirm their support with additional resources. AN, D/IV//38, dossier 1004, no. 2, Letter from seven academicians from the Academié de peinture in Orléans, n.d. [1791]).

68 AN, D/IV//25, dossier 573, no. 1–2, Letters from the Directory of the Département des Côtes du Nord to the National Assembly, 12 March 1791.

69 Bailey, *The Old Regime Collèges, 1789–1795*, 10. Bailey cites the cases of *écoles militaires* in Tournon and in Effiat where Oratorian instructors overwhelmingly swore the oath but then wrote to the Assembly bemoaning the uncertainty of the situation in which they found themselves.

70 Tackett, *Religion, Revolution and Regional Culture*, 6. While Tackett may be right in the aggregate, that the willingness of many teachers to embrace the legislation "greatly enhance[d] the continuity of education during the early years of the Revolution" (47–48), the disruptive uncertainty to which it gave rise complicated efforts to imagine how the provisionally-maintained schools might be incorporated into a more permanent system. On this, see Bailey, *The Old Regime Collèges, 1789–1795*, 72.

71 David Andress, *French Society in Revolution, 1789–1799* (Manchester:

Manchester University Press, 1999), 90. On the publicity of the oath-swearing ceremonies and priests' explanations of their decisions, see Tackett, *Religion, Revolution and Regional Culture*, 59–74.

72 AN, D/IV//67, dossier 2026, no. 3, *Extrait des Registres des Délibérations du Tribunal de l'Université de Poitiers*, 22 January 1791, 1–3. R. R. Palmer briefly notes the unrest in Poitiers, but emphasizes the increasingly enthusiastic republicanism of the period after the declaration of war in April 1792 rather than the attempts to navigate the crises of winter 1791. Palmer, *The Improvement of Humanity*, 108–109.

73 AN, D/IV//67, dossier 2026, no. 2, Letter to the National Assembly from faculty members of the University of Poitiers, January 1791, 1; AN, D/IV//67, dossier 2026, no. 4, Letter from the rectors and professors of the University of Poitiers to the National Assembly, n.d., 3.

74 AN, D/IV//67, dossier 2026, no. 3, *Extrait des Registres des Délibérations du Tribunal de l'Université de Poitiers*, 22 January 1791, 5; AN, D/IV//67, dossier 2026, no. 4, Letter from the rectors and professors of the University of Poitiers to the National Assembly, n.d., 3.

75 AN, D/IV//67, dossier 2026, no. 4, Letter from the rectors and professors of the University of Poitiers to the National Assembly, n.d., 4. While Bailey describes this episode as illustrating that "local officials could indeed act promptly, effectively, and cooperatively in administering the oath and in replacing the non-jurors, even without being sure of the procedures to be followed," the scene described by the university officials suggests a less benign view of the process. Bailey, *The Old Regime Collèges, 1789–1795*, 73.

76 Palmer, *The Improvement of Humanity*, 108–109.

77 AN, D/IV//36, dossier 937, no. 3, Letter to the National Assembly from departmental authorities in the Loir-et-Cher, 30 April 1791, 2–3.

78 Palmer, *The Improvement of Humanity*, 111–112.

79 The case to this point, but not including the June 1791 letter to the Assembly, is described in Bailey, *The Old Regime Collèges, 1789–1795*, 75.

80 AN, D/IV//31, dossier 740, no. 4, Letter from departmental authorities in Gers, 4 June 1791. On the broader phenomenon of retaining non-juring priests for lack of replacements, see Andress, *French Society in Revolution*, 91.

81 Bailey, *The Old Regime Collèges, 1789–1795*, 156–160.

82 AN, D/IV//68, dossier 2055, nos 2–3, Two letters from departmental administrators in the Haute-Vienne, 27 March 1791. A similar inquiry came in August 1791 from department authorities in the Orne and the administrators of a *collège* in Alençon, who said that the *collège* would soon have to close due to financial difficulties caused by the disappearance of Ancien Régime sources of revenue and the inaction of the Assembly on plans to replace them. AN, D/IV//48, dossier 1377, nos 6, 8, 12 August 1791.

83 Bailey, *The Old Regime Collèges, 1789–1795*, 165–168.

84 AN, D/IV//49, dossier 1401, nos 1-2, Letter from doctrinaires non-prêtres to the National Assembly, received 28 April 1791. On the generally enthusiastic response of doctrinaires or agrégés non-prêtres to the Revolution, see Bailey, *The Old Regime Colleges, 1789-1795*, 68.
85 Tackett, *Religion, Revolution and Regional Culture*, 298.
86 On the oath's role in the "division" of France, see Tackett, *Religion, Revolution and Regional Culture*; Claude Langlois, "La Rupture entre l'Eglise catholique et la Révolution," in François Furet and Mona Ozouf (eds), *The French Revolution and the Creation of Modern Political Culture, vol. 3: The Transformation of Political Culture, 1789-1848* (New York, NY: Pergamon Press, 1989): 375-390. John McManners suggests that the oath aggravated an existing division rather than creating a new one. See John McManners, *The French Revolution and the Church* (New York, NY: Harper & Row, 1969), 49-50.
87 Tackett, *Religion, Revolution and Regional Culture*, 31, 64.
88 AN, D/IV//41, dossier 1147, nos 1-2, Description of the administration and performance of the civic oath by professors at the Collège in Châlons, May 1791.
89 AN, D/IV//31, dossier 740, no. 4, Letter from departmental authorities in Gers, 4 June 1791, 2. This phenomenon is noted in McManners, *The French Revolution and the Church*, 48.
90 Palmer, *The School of the French Revolution*, 108.
91 Ibid., 108-110.
92 AN, D/IV//31, dossier 740, no. 8, Letter from doctrinaires professeurs du Collège de Nîmes about public instruction and the constitution, 29 August 1791, 3-4.
93 AN, D/IV//41, dossier 1145, no. 4, Letter from students enrolled in the Collège de Sezanne, 14 June 1791, 1-2.
94 AN, AD/VIII//21, no. 25, *Observations sur le rapport que M. Talleyrand-Périgord... présentés à l'Assemblée Nationale, par les Maîtres de Pension de Paris* (Paris, 1791).
95 Ibid., 1-2.
96 Ibid., 3-4.
97 Ibid., 4-5, on national uniformity, see 44-47.
98 Ibid., 6-8, 31-32.
99 Ibid., 8-9.
100 Ibid., 46-49.
101 Ibid., 16.
102 Ibid., 35-37.
103 Ibid., 22-23.
104 Ibid., 34-35. The teachers criticized celibacy as a form of "egoism" and as grounds for exclusion from any position that would require putting the interests and well-being of others or of society before oneself.

105 Ibid., 47–49.
106 Ibid., 69–72.
107 Louis Grimaud, *Histoire de la liberté d'enseignement en France depuis la chute de l'Ancien Régime jusqu'à nos jours* (Paris: Arthur Rousseau, 1898), 23.

7

Republican instruction: an elusive ideal

The first years of the French Republic dazzle with the festivals, celebrations, ceremonies, proclamations, and spectacles that seemed to define republican pedagogy. Politics, and political pedagogy, seemed to be everywhere, as legislators "aimed to draw upon all the means of education and of propaganda to disseminate the 'universal' principles of morality and ideology."[1] These were also the years in which violence was most inescapably present as a complement and counterpart to public instruction and republican zeal.[2] Political regeneration and civic obligation were the order of the day, and the republicanization of France and the French people seemed to transcend boundaries of private and public, personal and political.

At times, the *conventionnels*' debates over education themselves took on the air of spectacle, and they can seem to demand explanation (as opposed to explication) in a way that the arguments put forward by Talleyrand and Condorcet do not. To note just one example (albeit a famous and extraordinary one): on 13 July 1793 Robespierre presented a proposal, attributed to the Jacobin martyr Michel Lepeletier, that all children between the ages of 5 and 12 be taken from their families and raised in boarding schools where they would be subject to an immersive program of moral and political indoctrination.[3] That even a few members of the Convention thought the children of France should be forcibly displaced and raised in such an environment is, at the least, an engaging and bewildering tale to tell.

But as J.-F. Major, a professor from Bar-le-Duc, had reminded the deputies of the Assembly in 1790 (in a pamphlet noted in Chapter 6):

the French were not Spartans, and France was no Lacedaemonia.⁴ This remained true under the Republic, and proposals like Lepeletier's never occupied a central place in the debates over education.⁵ Instead, and despite invocations of Lepeletier's neo-Spartan ghost, the practical pursuit of public instruction continued among *conventionnels*, local authorities, schoolmasters, and citizens across France.

Public instruction continued to represent an attempt to synthesize the acquisition of skills and habits necessary for political participation with the cultivation of civic sentiments, emotions, and attachments that would make politics both possible and sustainable. As a would-be teacher from Dijon noted in a letter of 6 Thermidor, year II, the aim was to "excite emulation, develop [students'] talents, and inspire republican virtues and good morals" while ensuring that those virtuous students could "speak, reason, and write" well enough to participate actively in political affairs.⁶ This local ambition was mirrored in Gilbert Romme's more programmatic statement, presented in 1793 on behalf of the Committee of Public Instruction and noted in Chapter 3: public instruction needed to be a "source of both enlightenment and of virtue" so that society and the new polity might thrive.⁷

Of course, the problem of nurturing virtuous political participation had changed since Mirabeau, Sieyès, and others first discussed how to give public instruction institutional form. This was true in both material and political terms, and each would shape what public instruction meant under the National Convention. And yet, while the concerns of 1792, 1793, and beyond were new, they were not unfamiliar; deputies and political commentators in 1789 had also worried about how to distinguish legitimate from illegitimate forms of political participation (and legitimate from illegitimate incidences of political violence), about the loyalties of a population that was being asked to embrace a new political order, and about the threats of political intrigue and conspiracy (real and imagined). By 1792–93, these concerns were magnified by the experience of the preceding years and by anxieties about the sustainability of new political institutions in the face of wars both foreign and, after spring 1793, domestic. Nonetheless, as a Citoyen Mulard noted in his letter of 22 Nivôse, year II (11 January 1794), the coming of the Republic mirrored the spring and summer of 1789 in the suddenly renewed possibilities for reform and reinvention, and so offered an opportunity for the *conventionnels* to focus again on establishing a national system of public instruction.⁸

The republican debates over education proceeded on three (familiar) fronts, focusing on what we might call civic, primary, and systemic elements of reform. The first of these is evident in the increased emphasis on extra-institutional or civically performative modes of instruction. The targets of these efforts were the immediately political populace and the civic community as such. The second front – primary education – is clear in the renewed focus on the education received by very young children (in the home, with tutors or parents, and then in schools), the drafting and dissemination of elementary texts, and the cultivation of rudimentary skills and basic knowledge.[9] The third – the systemic – saw continued attempts to design and establish a multi-tiered and national system of public instruction, to translate the inherited institutions, ideas, and (sometimes) personnel into instruments of republican pedagogy.

Each of these foci has antecedents in Ancien Régime debates and in proposals from the first years of the Revolution. Each is also characterized by the perceived need for (and apparent experience of) a radical departure from the recent past, the need to realize and reinforce the break from the Ancien Régime(s). But declaring themselves free of the monarchy did not spare the *conventionnels* from the material, political, and institutional difficulties that had plagued earlier attempts at reform, and the tension between inherited circumstances and a new ideological landscape continued to shape plans for social and political regeneration in important and revealing ways.

A changing tenor in an ongoing debate

The reform of education raised directly the problem of revolutionary process, of how already existing social, political, economic, and cultural institutions could manage the crises of the present while also giving rise to a fundamentally different order of things. While this had been true since 1789, the problem seemed more and more vexing in the early months and years of the Republic. As a result, and in light of mounting crises in 1792–93, the reform of education attracted both attention and scorn. Some saw in education a path to a more peaceful and stable future. Joseph Chénier, for instance, claimed in November 1793 that the "surest means by which to restore calm to the Republic is to organize education."[10] Others, like Marat, mocked efforts at educational reform as akin to "planting trees so that they may bear fruit for the future nourishment of soldiers who are already dying of starvation."[11] Marat's point resonated both inside the Convention and beyond, and the crises of revolution and of war transformed how *conventionnels* and others thought about the role of the schools in remaking French society.[12]

One result was an intensified focus on education's role in the formation and preservation of political community, including greater emphasis on the education of adults (those shaping the political present) and young children (those who would inhabit the political future but had little, if any, meaningful experience of the Ancien Régime or the constitutional monarchy). It also led to uncertainty and ambivalence regarding the reform of institutions like the *collèges* and universities, institutions that would shepherd children from their present into the nation's future. This, in turn, led to important changes in the debates over public instruction, including a more explicit and more emphatic focus on socialization and on education's role in stabilizing the social order. A particularly clear indication of this emerged in the debates over female education, where arguments separating the education of girls from the reform of schools (and so from the education of boys) were increasingly explicit. Under the Convention, the Committee of Public Instruction returned to an almost entirely "naturalist" notion of sexual difference, arguing that men were destined for public life and political affairs and women for home and hearth, and that plans for education should reflect this "necessity." The formal education of girls – even at the elementary level – largely disappeared from the Committee's debates, and when girls or women were mentioned, it was generally to extol a woman's contributions to the Republic as *"la mère gardienne des bonnes mœurs."*[13] Where Talleyrand thought that girls should be educated so that they might "recognize and appreciate those [benefits] they were given by" the constitution, the *conventionnels* hoped that women might focus on what they could give to the Republic (that is, children).

The turn from institutional to interpersonal concerns was symptomatic of a broader shift in the *conventionnels'* emphases as they focused increasingly on the cultivation of civic sentiments and communal bonds for men and women, old and young. Where proposals had focused in the first years of the Revolution on integrating this civic work into the curricula, routines, and rituals of existing institutions, *conventionnels* and their correspondents were increasingly wary of relying on the schools to socialize citizens. If public instruction had aimed initially to offer an "apprenticeship" in participatory politics and representative government, its purpose under the Convention seemed to change, serving now as an incubator of republican devotion.

Perhaps the most famous statement of this came in Rabaut Saint-Étienne's 21 December 1792 speech to the Convention. In an oft-quoted passage, Rabaut distinguished between "public instruction," which aimed to "enlighten and exercise the mind," and "national education," which would "form the spirit." He described the former as carried out primarily in the classroom, giving rise to knowledge, and reserved for those with aptitude and opportunity, whereas the latter relied upon festivals, public games, and communal celebrations, and its lessons were necessary for all. The two were "sisters" but, he claimed, unequal, and national education was the more important sibling.

The speech offered a critique and counterpoint to Condorcet's proposal (discussed in Chapter 4 above), and it is often cited as evidence of the Convention's preference for indoctrination over education.[14] It is worth noting, however, that Rabaut's argument was as much about the temporality of revolutionary change as it was about pedagogy and politics. He prefaced his comments by acknowledging the critical importance of instruction and emphasizing the need for a "solid theory of instruction" based on three underlying principles: man is capable of perpetual improvement; this improvement depends upon the acquisition and dissemination of knowledge; the enlightenment of men contributes to the improvement of government and of society. The problem lay not in instruction per se, but in the immediacy of the Republic's problems and the time it would take for instruction to pay dividends. Echoing Marat, Rabaut argued that "the fruits of this instruction are for our descendants to enjoy, but we need institutions for the present. We must in an instant elevate our morals to match our laws, [we must] affect a revolution in citizens' hearts and minds just as we have in the conditions of government."[15] Rabaut's speech hinged on something like Mona Ozouf's distinction between "miraculous" and "laborious" models of regeneration, and it reflected the *conventionnels'* anxiety about the process of revolution rather than a widely or firmly held set of pedagogical commitments.[16]

For Rabaut, Chénier, and others, the political turmoil around them reflected not only the existence and influence of conspirators or counter-revolutionaries, but also the problem of politics breaking out in a society that had not been prepared by the right sort of education. This contributed to the apparent need to educate not only children, but adults, and to offer them similar sorts of lessons. As Nicholas Hentz wrote, "if the present generation had been raised within the Republic, public instruction could be limited to the young; that, however, is not the case … It is not enough that the [present generation] be disabused of their previous beliefs, they must also be instructed."[17] Echoing this, a Citoyen Flavigny worried that parents in the countryside understood the new political principles no better than their children, and officials in the Loire asked for the Convention's permission to enroll adults in primary schools alongside school-aged children.[18]

Freeing French society from its "aristocratic spirit" and Ancien Régime attachments was a symbolically (and sometimes physically) violent act, and that violence came increasingly to shape the conceptual parameters within which education was debated.[19] Social and political regeneration was not as simple as substituting one set of allegiances or attachments for another though; the *conventionnels* had to not only depict the monarchy, aristocracy, and Ancien Régime society in a negative light and the Republic in a positive one, but also to define the forms of political practice, engagement, and behavior that were acceptable within the new Republic.[20] It was not enough to make the people "republicans"; they had to be made republicans of a particular sort, and their republicanism had to be manifest in the patterns of their daily lives.[21] The polyvalence of this endeavor, and the changing political tenor with which it was pursued, is evident in the renewed focus on the role of language in French political life. Attempts to make the French speak French, and to make the French language foster a republican community, were taken up in revealing ways by some of the Republic's most important figures, including the Abbé Grégoire, Condorcet, and the Abbé Sieyès.

Since at least mid-century, the idea of a uniform French language that was reinforced and reproduced through standardized instruction in schools had appealed to those who wanted to translate the abstract "nation" into a meaningful political, social, and cultural community. They imagined linguistic unity as an instrument of political unity, linguistic disunity as a source and symptom of political, cultural, or social division. These efforts encountered two competing and quite different adversaries: the languages of Antiquity (especially Latin) and the many regional dialects (patois) spoken in eighteenth-century France. Unlike Latin, which might be replaced through curricular reform, the patois operated and reproduced themselves outside the formal curricula and confines of the schools, and so replacing them with a uniform national vernacular was thought to require and to promise a transformation of French society. It was Grégoire who would most visibly shepherd this ambition into the Revolution.[22]

In the August 1790 questionnaire with which Grégoire announced his project and solicited information from correspondents and readers across France, he presented it as a complement to the debates over education and educational reform, the "education of the rural population" and the "universalization of the French language" each being an essential and effective means by which to "support the constitution."[23] Indeed, in its tone and process, the launch of Grégoire's inquiry echoed many of the political ambitions of the Revolution's first years: it was solicitous of public contributions, inclusive in its vision of French society, and relatively non-coercive in its approach. By the time Grégoire presented his findings to the Convention in June 1794, however, much had changed. The work had come to be defined in terms of securing loyalty and eradicating political "error," its tone more violent and less trusting than four years earlier.[24] He argued that "the people must know the laws in order to sanction and obey them," and that the persistence of dialects was causing people near the borders to establish "dangerous relations" with France's enemies. Conspirators, he claimed, were able to draw upon linguistic divisions among the people to build support for their "counter-revolutionary machinations." Even those patois-speaking populations who did not succumb to counter-revolutionary overtures were alienated from the revolutionary community and denied the enlightenment and moral improvement that the Republic offered, instead remaining subject to the "most absurd prejudices, which bring with them the most grievous consequences."[25] The change in tone was not unique to Grégoire; it is evident also in Bertrand Barère's January 1794 *Rapport et projet de décrets sur les idioms étrangers et l'enseignement de la langue française*, where foreign languages and patois were associated with counter-revolution or foreign plots, linguistic diversity was thought to serve the interests of "despots," and linguistic unity was presented as a prerequisite not only for the efficacy of the laws, but also the mutual surveillance among citizens that would protect the Republic.[26] Teaching people the national language and "annihilating" regional dialects had become part of a process by which recalcitrant populations could be, if not forced (as in Rousseau's famous phrase), at least prepared to be free.

There were some efforts to push back against this coercive and uncompromising approach to language, most notably the work undertaken by Condorcet, Sieyès, and Julien Duhamel to reinforce language's role in making "civilized conflict" and open political discussion possible. Between late 1792 and mid-1793, Condorcet, Sieyès, and Duhamel worked on their *Journal d'instruction sociale*, the first issue of which appeared on 1 June 1793. The journal aimed to integrate education in natural law, civic law, and political economy and, in so doing, to make possible a "peaceful and consensual republican order."[27] This required attention to language, to the coherence or incoherence of terms used in political discussions, and to the adverse consequences that follow from confusions or misunderstandings born of imprecise language.[28] Far from coercing univocality or closing off disagreement, the journal sought to clarify points of discussion, to make room for "salutary doubts" and constructive debates, and to engender a more refined and public application of reason to politics.[29] The historical moment belonged, however, to projects like Grégoire's and fears such as Barère's, as became clear when the *Journal d'instruction sociale* folded after just five weeks and six issues, and when Condorcet went into funereal hiding very shortly thereafter.

The attention to language that drove Grégoire's work and the *Journal d'instruction sociale*, and the underlying concern with political community and communication that animated these projects, both reflected and fed off a broader anxiety about the nature and character of a republican public. This anxiety gave rise to some of the Revolution's most famous pedagogical efforts, including the dramatic festivals of the year II, the politicization of ephemera, the proliferation of political songs, the spread of political catechisms, increased attention to the theater and public spaces as sites of political instruction, attempts to change how people dressed and spoke to one another, and even how time and space were organized and experienced. The new approach to a public pedagogy was manifest in proposals like that presented by Lakanal on behalf of the Committee of Public Instruction in June 1793, of which roughly 40 percent is devoted to the more than thirty festivals being proposed.[30] While some of the attributes of this pedagogy are familiar, we are clearly looking at a difference in kind as well as degree when we compare 1790 with the first years of the Republic. But the difference is not total, nor did it come all at once.

The festival was, as Rabaut and others remarked, a form of instruction that performed the "unity" of the people, could address broad swaths of the population simultaneously, and could be coordinated at both the local and national level. After August 1792, festivals and civic celebrations were increasingly enlisted in efforts to spread "civic virtue throughout society [so as] to ensure that passions destructive of republican harmony were extirpated from the adult population."[31] But unity was not all they performed. They also offered both instruction in and models of participatory citizenship. They offered an opportunity to single out noteworthy individuals or those who merited special recognition, and they permitted the public a chance to participate in the performance of republican politics as spectators, members of the procession, or speakers.[32] They were occasions on which people engaged one another and their communities outside of the supposedly paradigmatic split between the personal and the public.[33] Their efficacy was thought to rely not only on the power of political symbols and sensations, but also the social dynamics of emulation and performance.[34] Children, for example, were often enlisted to give speeches, perform dramas, or sing songs that they had prepared in the classroom, as at the Fête de la Jeunesse in Vif on 20 ventôse, year III (10 March 1795).[35] Similarly, at the Fête de la Réunion held on 10 August 1793 in the Haute-Marne, prizes were awarded to those children who had best recited the *Declaration of the Rights of Man and Citizen*, a competition over which a tribunal of local deputies presided.[36]

For adults too, the festivals offered an opportunity for the community and/or the state to single out those who merited special recognition without necessarily setting them apart from the broader social unit. Even the stern and generally catechismic proposal submitted by Charles Le Roy in fructidor, year III (which called for "all games and diversions to be prohibited" during the festival), included plans to award prizes to those who wrote the best hymns and simple songs on civic-related themes.[37] Such prizes, whether for children or adults, served to mediate the tension between individual merit, civic equality, and social integration, and to do so without reanimating the "realm of distinctions" that marked Ancien Régime festivals.[38] They were in this sense inheritors of the "economy of emulation" that Jeremy Caradonna has highlighted in the Ancien Régime *prix de vertu*, a connection reinforced in episodes like the awarding of the *prix d'émulation* to a Citoyenne Hurard in Rouen in 1793.[39]

The festivals thus sought to encourage not just obedience, but civic performance, public participation, and preparation for engaged citizenship (though they offered little sense of what "engaged citizenship" might look like in later practice). Even as political anxiety and illiberal impulses came to dominate revolutionary politics, public instruction – including festivals and civic celebrations – preserved at least some sense that the recognition of meritorious individuals and the establishment of communal bonds could be synthesized, that personal achievement and civic solidarity could be reconciled, and that the social force of emulative esteem could bring together educational institutions, local populations, and the national community.[40] For this project to succeed, however, the work of extraordinary and festive occasions would have to be complemented by quotidian and "curricular" forces: regeneration was going to require routine as well as revelation.

Texts, teachers, and trusts: familiar problems in unfamiliar circumstances

If the festivals, catechisms, and ephemera of the Republic presented citizenship and the Revolution in frequently spectacular terms (and in contrast with spectacularly sinister foes), the actual work of revolution nonetheless required practically minded efforts to establish new institutions for the production and reproduction of republican society. As they had in 1789, many of the participants in the republican debates over education saw matters of political principle in decidedly practical terms, imagining political transformations and institutional adjustments as part and parcel of the revolutionary process. The rekindled discussions of public instruction seemed to offer a renewed opportunity to engage with the institutions of revolutionary society, and letters about education continued to find their way to Paris from officials, administrators, and citizens across France.

The most frequent refrain in these letters was impatience regarding the delayed establishment of public instruction. This impatience was clear even before the fall of the constitutional monarchy on 10 August 1792, as the Legislative Assembly faced rising levels of discontent about their inaction on education. In Marseille, for instance, the Jacobin-affiliated *Manuel du laboureur et de l'artisan* highlighted education as symptomatic of the Legislative Assembly's more general failure, writing: "The Legislative Assembly has not only neglected to attend to the most urgent measures needed to assure public welfare, it has also disdained to take the time to organize a system of national education. Corrupt men! They have considered only their own self-interest!"[41]

The impatience continued into the Republic as correspondents pressured the *conventionnels* to make progress and scolded them for the time lost by their predecessors. Already in autumn 1792, the professors and principals of the Parisian *collèges* argued that over the preceding years "our morals, our ideas, our laws: all have changed. Only education remains the same," and in January 1793 a Citoyen Gazagnaire wrote, "you have long promised us the organization of primary schools. And from time to time I have even read in the papers that the Committee of Public Instruction has put together a report. But still nothing ..."[42] The *Société académique* in Tours asked in August 1793 that the *conventionnels* turn their attention to education and, tired of oratory, requested that the legislators "speak no more of Greeks and of Romans, but rather of the French in the eighteenth century."[43]

More constructively, correspondents submitted plans for institutional reform or proposals for new pedagogical practices. They submitted texts they had drafted, as when Citoyen Dubessey sent along a *"catéchisme politique,"* or Citoyen Thiébault presented his *Petit Catéchisme républicain à l'usage des enfants.*[44] Others sought to improve classroom instruction, as when Citoyen Terrilon offered a method that he claimed could teach children to read in just four months, or when Citoyen Coulon submitted his method for teaching children to write (along with a request for a job implementing that method).[45] More broadly, correspondents raised two issues that had long been central to the debates over education: the need to recruit, train, and oversee instructors, and the need to draft or disseminate appropriate texts.

The problem of texts illustrated the interplay of centralized and decentralized efforts at reform. Since summer 1789, correspondents had requested that national authorities establish a uniform corpus of instructional materials, especially those communicating and explaining the new political and social institutions.[46] They had also been sending exemplars and abstracts for consideration, hoping to influence, participate in, or benefit from the legislators' work. But no standard set of texts had materialized, and the fall of the constitutional monarchy and the proclamation of the Republic seemed to require that the project begin anew. Unsurprisingly, then, the first year of the Republic saw renewed attention to the problem of texts. Correspondents inquired about when they could expect texts from the state, complained that they were still using works from the Ancien Régime, proposed stocking public and schools' libraries with books and manuscripts confiscated from *émigrés*, suggested establishing a company of learned men to draft suitable texts, and submitted their own works for consideration.[47] As these correspondents emphasized, it was education – and especially texts – that would transmit the Republic's principles and character to future generations after the "courage and enthusiasm" of its first moments waned.[48]

This sentiment found an echo in Grégoire's January 1794 announcement that the Convention would hold a competition to select elementary texts for the new pedagogical regime.[49] Arguing that the process of educating citizens started while the newborn child was still in his or her parents' arms, Grégoire emphasized the need for simple and appealing works that would lay the moral, intellectual, and emotional groundwork for the education children would later receive in schools.[50] The *concours* aimed to produce texts suitable for parents or nurses of very young children and for use in the primary schools, creating a textual bridge from familial to formal instruction and bringing greater uniformity to the first lessons of children's lives.[51] These texts were to offer instruction in reading, writing, and speaking the national language, elementary mathematics and practical geometry, the measurement of time, distance, and weights, the principles of geography, the principles of republican morality and the principal texts of the Revolution (the *Declaration of the Rights of Man and Citizen*, the Constitution, and the *Annales du Civisme* proposed by Grégoire in September 1793 and already being produced by the Convention).[52]

The integration of technical and moral instruction, the attempt to establish good habits in infancy that would be maintained and reinforced in the schools, and the sense that the schools were preparatory for participation in civil society indicate the continued relevance of public instruction as a political pedagogy. The Republic needed new texts, but it had largely inherited its sense of what those texts should aim to do. And yet, despite the familiarity of the genre and the continued arrival of submissions in spring and summer 1794, the Committee of Public Instruction found itself that autumn without suitable texts for either primary instruction or more specialized subjects. On 22 October 1794, the Committee called the *concours* to an unsuccessful conclusion, claiming that none of the submissions had been satisfactory and appointing specific authors to draft the necessary texts.[53] While later competitions would result in more satisfactory outcomes and in the distribution of prizes and pensions, this first attempt stalled, leaving the work of the newly appointed authors to be subsumed into the short-lived *École Normale*, which was imagined as a revolutionary factory devoted to the "production" of primary instructors.[54] That, too, was proving a vexing problem for the *conventionnels*.

Finding, vetting, installing, and retaining teachers had been a problem since 1762, and for more than thirty years efforts to reform or reinvent the schools had run aground on the issue of who could be entrusted with such influence, how those people would be recruited and overseen, and what limitations could be placed upon their affiliations and their professional activities. No issue had done more to define the "education question" during these decades, as the emulative dynamics of the classroom and the social, political, cultural, and economic influence attributed to educational regimes had combined to make instructors the *sine qua non* of educational reform.

The "instructor question" illustrates again how much the *conventionnels*' options remained limited by the legacy of the Ancien Régime and the constitutional monarchy. Since 1789, the problem of personnel had been shaped by the sometimes complementary and sometimes contestatory nexus of national legislation and local expediency, by political ideologies and material circumstances, and by the relationship between religious and political institutions. These issues proved particularly vexing when it came to disentangling the schools from the supposedly dismantled religious orders.

Religious orders had been suppressed in February 1790, but those devoted to instruction had been maintained. Controversies surrounding the Civil Constitution of the Clergy and the clerical oath had aggravated tensions between secular authorities and clerical instructors and, as we saw in Chapters 3 and 6, many schools were left after spring 1791 with only provisionally maintained or dubiously credentialed instructors. Others were left without instructors at all.[55] Elsewhere, however, members of the "secular" teaching orders had remained in their positions and sworn the clerical oath (in its original or slightly modified forms). Their continued presence was offered as a sign of their loyalty to the nation, but still they worked knowing that their status was tenuous at best, as professors in Toulouse complained in late 1792 or early 1793.[56]

The problem was exacerbated by one of the Legislative Assembly's last actions concerning education. On 18 August 1792, the deputies voted to disband all of the provisionally maintained ecclesiastical orders, including those devoted to education. They did so even as they recognized the utility of these orders, noting in the preamble that "a free state cannot suffer the existence of any corporation, not even those that serve the nation through their teaching."[57] While the Assembly offered individual members of these orders a chance to remain in their provisional positions, and ordered the departmental officials to nominate provisional replacements for those who did not do so, the suppression of these congregations alienated and ostracized many instructors and made settling the "instructor question" even more difficult.

Local officials and administrators continued to struggle under the Republic, as they had under the constitutional monarchy, to translate piecemeal legislative guidance into practices for an inherited but only provisionally maintained system. The result was often confused exasperation. In the Haute-Garonne in October 1792, administrators worried that the salaries paid to provisionally maintained former members of religious congregations violated regulations regarding the payment of provisionally maintained professors, and their counterparts in Rouen wondered in May 1793 how to adjudicate competing claims for payment from professors, instructors, and others occupying provisional positions in the patchwork of educational institutions.[58] In response to these sorts of financial pressures and uncertainties, other correspondents sought to revitalize the call for a competitive system of *enseignement libre*, familiar from the proposals of Mirabeau and others in the first years of the Revolution. Citoyen

Pocheron, for example, proposed in November 1793 that the guaranteed salary for instructors should be reduced considerably, forcing them to rely at least in part on student fees and, with that, to take greater care in their work and more interest in their students' success.[59]

Others focused more intently on the identity of would-be instructors and on the boundaries of those the Convention would consider acceptable. The competing purposes at which correspondents worked is evident in letters received by the Convention just two months apart, the first complaining in November 1793 that ex-nobles were ineligible to serve as instructors, arguing that those who renounced their noble status and embraced the Republic should be allowed to contribute to the public regeneration of morals, and the second emphasizing in January 1794 that the Convention needed to devote far more attention to purging unsatisfactory or unsuitable instructors (including ex-nobles) who might weaken or undermine their students' attachment to the Patrie.[60]

The *conventionnels* themselves struggled to clarify the nature and scale of the problem, as we see in a November 1792 letter from Gilbert Romme to Jean-Marie Rolland, then Minister of the Interior. Romme complained that the "spirit of ornamentation and aristocracy" continued to reign at several schools despite the law of 18 August. He demanded that greater vigilance be maintained in executing the law, and reminded Rolland that the Convention could be called upon to provide whatever additional legislative measures might be necessary to complete the elimination of error and aristocratic sentiment. Finally, he threatened that suppression might be necessary if adequate progress was not made, but only of especially recalcitrant schools.[61] Romme's letter is remarkable for two reasons: first, because it so clearly entangled the fate of the school with the "spirit" of its instructors and, second, because of the explicitly contingent view of how reform measures would be pursued. The fate of the schools would be decided, he thought, on something like a case-by-case basis, with local conditions and legislative measures evolving in response to one another. Progress was elusive, however, and both the problem and the pursuit of local solutions were ongoing a year later when the Convention voted on 3 October 1793 to allow local authorities to remove instructors deemed unwilling or incapable of properly meeting their professional obligations.[62]

If texts and teachers represented projects on which any new system of public instruction would depend, they in turn depended on the Convention's ability to solve an equally familiar though even more fundamental problem: finances. The tension among institutional expectations, national ambitions, and immediately pressing concerns had shaped the debate over financing a new system of education since at least November 1789, when the lands attached to the *collèges* and similar institutions had been nationalized but not sold. This had led many to expect that even if they were not maintained as properties of the individual institutions, those lands would be used to fund a national system of education. This presumption underlay the proposals put forward by Talleyrand in 1791 and by Condorcet in 1792, and it served as a starting point – stated or unstated – for the discussion of finances in many of the letters and proposals submitted to the Assembly. On 8 March 1793, those lands were put up for sale.[63]

This sale represented a turning point in the debates over how education would be funded, and it seems like a moment that should offer us insight into the trajectory of republican thinking about the schools. From here it seems like a short and logical leap to the September 1793 vote suppressing the *collèges* and universities (discussed below), an impression supported by Joseph Fouché's claim that "this law [of 8 March 1793] would overcome the timidity of previous legislation, which had been 'afraid to overthrow the foundations of past errors with one blow.'"[64] But the apparent trajectory from earlier "half-measures" to Fouché's final blow is misleading. Alongside his call for legislative temerity, Fouché also called for the Convention to "show ... its love for the sciences by devoting special funds to their support," and the law of 8 March itself included an exemption for those buildings and lands actually being used for instruction or lodging. The picture is muddled further still by the Convention's decree, the very next day, that preference in filling vacant bourses at the *collèges* should be shown to the children of those who had "taken up arms in defense of the patrie," indicating that at least some *conventionnels* continued to support the *collèges* and supposed that they would be preserved in the coming months and years.[65]

The hope that the sale of these lands would not destroy the *collèges* was reinforced in August 1793 by the Minister of the Interior, Dominique Joseph Garat, who expressed his desire that the law of 8 March not disrupt the schools any more than necessary. He asked that the Convention compel the departments to provide him with the information he needed to pay the salaries of professors and instructors so as to avoid interrupting instruction.[66] A month later, and in the face of numerous letters complaining that professors were not being paid, that the *collèges* were not receiving the money due them, and that the schools would have to close if funds were not forthcoming, the Convention heard a proposal to fund "the salaries owed to the professors of the *collèges* and other establishments of public instruction in France" and to provide for the *bourses* owed to students in those establishments.[67] The proposal also stipulated that the "professors [would] choose from among themselves a representative to explain to all of their students the Declaration of Rights and the constitutional act," echoing promises the Faculty of Arts at the University of Paris had been making since 1790.[68] The proposal was approved the following day, 4 September.

Eleven days later, the Convention voted to suppress the *collèges* and universities inherited from the Ancien Régime.

An ambivalent break

The hopes of Garat and Fouché notwithstanding, by summer 1793 the schools were in a deplorable state. As Joseph Lakanal noted that July in a meeting of the Committee of Public Instruction: "the Convention is barraged with complaints and requests related to public instruction. The schools, the *collèges*, the universities are almost all closed, if not by law, then in fact, except for those few that have maintained a sad appearance of continued activity." Taking stock of the Revolution's work on education, he conceded that "after four years [of Revolution], children have been largely left to themselves. While I do not think the old methods of instruction were great ... I worry about the effects [this long suspension of instruction] will have on the generations to come."[69]

Attacks on the universities, academies, and *collèges* shared in the hyperbole that characterized the political vocabulary of the Terror and struck at institutions and individuals alike.[70] That the universities and *collèges* were outdated corporations, that their members suffered from an *esprit de corps* antithetical to republican society, and that their internal organization was "aristocratic" were well-established lines of attack. Claude-Laurent Masuyer, in his criticism of Condorcet's proposal for a Société nationale (which Masuyer claimed would simply reproduce the institutions of the Ancien Régime under another name), described the academies as "truly aristocratic-academic *parlements*," and academicians as "a society of men who have no occupation other than to be, or at least to make people believe them to be savants, who, looking down from chairs, dispense reputations and rewards, and who idly cast the shadow of their laurels, whether deserved or not, across the entirety of the Republic."[71] Similarly, shortly after the suspended vote to suppress the *collèges* in September 1793 (discussed below), Citoyen Rolin warned the Convention that at Collège de l'Égalité (formerly Louis-le-Grand), "almost all of the professors are or were aristocrats," and the principal – Jean-François Champagne – was a "corruptor" of young boys. Rolin wrote that at the *collège*, "not only do [students] do nothing in their classes, but they are almost all corrupted by the Regent of the house ... he is seen about Paris at all hours of day and night, and even sneaks into [the students'] chambers to corrupt them, sleeping with them when he catches them unaware." He also denounced M. Cillaux of the Collège de Lisieux for "the most revolting lack of civic-mindedness; he almost never attends the public assemblies ... [and] offers a very peculiar sort of education to the boys lodged with him."[72]

Even when they escaped condemnation as instruments of political or sexual corruption, it became very difficult to articulate a place in republican society for educational institutions inherited from the Ancien Régime. The schools and those who worked in them faced increasingly strident attacks, including claims that savants and scholars were, by their nature, antithetical to or incompatible with the ideals of the Republic. For example, in his *Sur l'Instruction publique* of 1793, Nicholas Hentz effectively wrote the academicians and savants out of the Republic's social and political landscape: "it is not the savants who have won here. Look at the sans-culottes, or at the patriots: are they savants? Now look at the academicians, these men of grand phrases, these *érudits*; and now I ask you, are they republicans?"[73] Similarly, J.-M. Coupé declared in the Committee of Public Instruction's session of 2 July 1793 that under the Ancien Régime, "all of France's savants and artists were corrupted and made into royalists, and [Jacques-Louis] David alone remained worthy of Rome, of Athens, and of the French Republic."[74] Even Grégoire claimed in August 1793, as he proposed that the academies be suppressed, that such institutions had been "infected" by the aristocratic and feudal spirit of the Ancien Régime, describing them as institutions that would "forever bear the imprint of despotism, whose organization is an attack upon equality, [and] who fight against meaningful reform."[75]

But these condemnations reflected the fluctuations of political rhetoric as well as longstanding or committed anti-corporatism. There were exceptions even to such clear condemnations, as when Grégoire claimed – in the same speech – that the scientific academies had performed "services of singular importance to the nation" and so deserved an exemption from the impending suppression.[76] While the proposed exemption was rejected by his colleagues, Grégoire was not alone in thinking that once the most caustic voices subsided, institutions much like the more "useful" of the Ancien Régime academies would be (re-)established. On 24 August, barely a fortnight after the Convention voted to suppress the academies, the Minister of the Interior, Jules-François Paré, tried to secure funds with which to continue paying the former secretary of the Royal Academy of Architecture, Michel-Jean Sedaine, arguing that "after a short while, a new system of schools will be organized ... [and Sedaine] will likely return to his position."[77]

The *collèges* encountered a similarly ambivalent form of condemnation. On 15 September 1793, in the motion proposing their suppression, Jean Bon Saint-André described the *collèges* as a "shrine to the barbarity of the Middle Ages, a hideout of the prejudices built up over centuries."[78] Such critiques were not rare, and Saint-André's motion drew upon a legacy of even more incendiary proposals, as when an unidentified speaker proposed to the Paris Commune that they should "light fire to the archives of the *collèges*, after having noted everything they found there that relates to feudalism."[79] But their actual fate was not so dramatic or so definitive.

The *conventionnels* approved the motion to suppress the universities and the *collèges* on 15 September, but they returned to the subject the next day, suspending the measure and postponing definitive action. They took up the issue again a month later, and they voted for suppression again on 20 October, though in a modified form (this time the *petites écoles* were to be suppressed as well).[80] But the decrees were unclear about the nature, timeline, and purpose of suppression. The initial motion to suppress was conditional upon the *conventionnels* settling on a program for national reform and establishing new institutions (again, organized in a three-tier pyramid of necessary and then useful subjects), and the accompanying proposal indicates that the anticipated outcome was a reshuffling of institutional resources rather than an act of republican vandalism or anti-corporatist dismantling. The confusion regarding suppression, reinvention, and replacement was evident in the shifting conjugations of the decrees' central clauses, which sometimes indicated that suppression would follow after the establishment of the new schools ("*les collèges ... seront supprimés*") and at other times presented suppression as anticipating and preparing for the establishment of the new schools ("*les collèges ... sont supprimés*").[81] During these weeks, seals were placed upon the doors of the *collèges* and universities, were removed, and were then placed there again, offering a material expression of the *conventionnels'* ambivalence.

This ambivalence left local officials, schools administrators, and would-be reformers (including political clubs and societies) in limbo, increasingly unable to reconcile the institutions they oversaw with the political and material realities around them. In many places this contributed to paralysis and the continued process of institutional dissolution, though elsewhere administrators took it upon themselves to act, establishing provisional courses of instruction and asking approval rather than permission from the authorities in Paris.[82] In Toulouse, for example, local authorities worked in late 1793 and early 1794 to consolidate the existing institutions and resources and to anticipate what the National Convention might do.[83] They cited the preamble to the *Declaration of the Rights of Man and Citizen* regarding ignorance's role in public misfortune and noted the contribution of public instruction to the public good. They outlined a wide range of courses to be offered, including instruction in the *Declaration of the Rights of Man and Citizen*, the Constitution, and the principles and responsibilities of republican citizenship, but also mathematics, logic, physics, French grammar and orthography, chemistry, belles-lettres, the "philosophical history of peoples," geography, natural history, and the military sciences. In the buildings that had housed the *Académie des Sciences* they would hold courses in botany, medicine, physiology, the veterinary sciences, and related subjects. Other classes would be held in museums, libraries, the former *Académie de peinture et arts*, gardens, and other public spaces.[84] This was far from being a "system" of public instruction, but it did not purport to be, aiming instead to preserve the public role of the schools while waiting – again – for a definitive course of action from Paris.

Efforts such as these required wrestling with continued uncertainty about the status of provisionally maintained instructors and working to secure increasingly elusive funds and resources, but also trying to anticipate where the Convention might turn next in its debates and demands.[85] Some correspondents regretted the failure of Condorcet's proposal (or perhaps the clarity of a single proposal, whatever it might have been), and many lamented the need to reconcile apparently irreconcilable directives coming from Paris.[86] The situation was summarized nicely by professors in Toulouse who wrote to the Convention during the Republic's first months to inquire about their salaries and their students' scholarships: "our position is rendered grim by the continued uncertainty regarding whether or not our *collège* will be destroyed."[87] A year later, and even after the votes of September and October 1793, the situation remained much the same.

The plans to suppress and replace the *collèges*, universities, and *petites écoles* were never realized, though the Department of Paris did prevent the *collèges* under its jurisdiction from opening in October 1793.[88] They nonetheless represent an important moment in the revolutionary debates over education. The *conventionnels* had voted almost unanimously for a break from the institutional past, for rejection and replacement rather than reform and reorganization. They broke the imagined link between the past and future of education, and while instructors, administrators, and local officials worked to maintain the schools until they could be replaced, the debates in the Convention were no longer tethered to the institutions inherited from the Ancien Régime.

But no break is clean, and the *conventionnels*, like political and pedagogical administrators across France, continued to wrestle with the material, social, political, and legislative conditions inherited from the Legislative Assembly. That "inheritance" continued to shape the pursuit of public instruction even as the *conventionnels* turned to the design of new institutions appropriate to what they declared would be an entirely new polity.

Persistent questions and questionable conclusions: Bouquier and beyond

On 18 June 1793, in an attempt to expedite the establishment of new schools, the Convention had created a Commission of Public Instruction that was to focus on the institutional demands of reform, especially those related to primary instruction. Despite its relatively clear mandate, this body – known as the Commission of Six – found its work hampered by many of the tensions that shaped the broader debates over education, leading to competing institutional voices and legislative indecision.

In an effort to break the stalemate, the Commission's membership was enlarged (to nine) and its efforts were rejuvenated after the uncertain denouement of September 1793. Its members were prominent figures in the Convention and were familiar with the debates over education; they had initially included Robespierre (who left when he joined the Committee of Public Safety nine days after the Commission of Six was formed), Grégoire, Bourdon, and Lakanal, and, among the supplementary members added in September, Gilbert Romme, Arbogast, and Guyton Morveau (who had dropped the aristocratic "de" as revolutionary politics required).[89] Still, the group remained divided over whether the state was responsible for instruction beyond the elementary level, a dispute that became clear in the debates preceding the Convention's approval of a modified and abridged version of a proposal presented by Gabriel Bouquier in December 1793.[90]

Bouquier's plan echoed his colleagues' broader concerns about political association, social organization, and political publicity; it also reflected their anti-corporatism and their emphasis on political spectacle and performance. He promised that his plan would "banish forever any idea of academic corporatism, scientific societies, and pedagogical hierarchies." He claimed that it was based upon the principles of the Constitution, namely "liberty, equality, and brevity." In keeping with the idea that politics were a form of pedagogy (particularly when the education one sought to offer was so distinctly political), he claimed that

> the most wonderful schools, the most useful and simple, where the young receive an education that is truly republican are, no doubt, the public sessions of the departments, the districts, the municipalities, the tribunals, and, above all, the popular societies. It is from these pure sources that the young gain knowledge of their rights, of their responsibilities, of the laws, and of the morals of a republic.[91]

Similarly, he emphasized the pedagogical importance of festivals, theaters, and civic games, and he called for the buildings confiscated from the Church to be turned over to local authorities so that they could be put to use for these sorts of activities.[92] At least on these points, Bouquier's proposal reflected the Convention's preoccupation with performances of civic devotion acted out under the watchful eye of a suspicious and centralized state.

But his proposal also echoed those of Talleyrand, Mirabeau, and others from the first years of the Revolution. It included a system of *enseignement libre*, arguing that all citizens ought to be permitted to open a school once they had registered their desire to do so with the local authorities, specified what sort of school it is they intended to open, and produced a *certificat de civisme*. It sought to further delegate political responsibility to local authorities by stipulating that while the Convention would oversee the production and distribution of elementary textbooks, including the *Declaration of the Rights of Man and Citizen*, the Constitution, and a *Tableau des actions héroïques ou vertueuses*, the practical work of overseeing education would be entrusted to local officials, whether by municipality or section, and to "fathers, mothers, tutors and curators ... [that is] to the citizens."[93] Finally, like his predecessors in the National Assembly, Bouquier aimed to balance the obligations of the state, the interests of society, and the needs of the citizenry with a curriculum that included and accommodated various courses and levels of study, each receiving support from the state to the degree that it was considered necessary, useful, or merely desirable. This would include a system of universal, free, but not compulsory primary instruction, as well as a bifurcated system of secondary instruction, one part of which would be state funded and devoted to the "useful" sciences, the other offering courses in more "elective" or "agreeable" sciences and administered by the state but funded through student fees (to be supplemented by need-based scholarships for meritorious students). Echoing arguments put forward by Mirabeau and Talleyrand, he claimed that a system of elementary education would fulfill the state's obligations, but noted that French society and the French state had an interest in developing higher levels of education as well.[94] He also called for the state to support popular societies, public games, and local festivals in their efforts to cultivate a sense of civic unity and political community.

Bouquier's proposal aimed to reconcile the broader ambitions of public instruction with the narrower imperatives of its political moment. The synthesis was unstable though, and his plan came under attack from a number of his colleagues in the Convention. Michel-Edme Petit described the division among the *conventionnels* during the December 1793 debates:

> We all want a system of free national education; but some want primary schools and no more; others want secondary schools but ignore primary schools; some want schools in each commune, others schools in each canton ... others don't want any sort of formal schools at all, imagining that because they've learned what they know by miracle, others should learn in much the same manner.[95]

The lack of clear priorities and uncertainty about what might be practicable led to competition for scarce resources, which Petit identified as the real problem at hand. In the end, the Convention passed a version of the Bouquier Law that was far less ambitious than the Bouquier proposal had been, preserving only those articles that dealt with primary education, and even those in modified forms.

The most important change was the introduction of compulsory attendance at the elementary level, amending the law so that parents who chose to keep their children out of the state-funded primary schools incurred a prohibitively steep fine.[96] On other points, the final law incorporated suggestions or priorities presented by other *conventionnels* during the debates of November and early December 1793. These included provisions for instructors to be vetted and certified as "eligible" by local authorities (as proposed by Gilbert Romme), and more explicit efforts to attract instructors with practical (as opposed to pedagogical) experience and expertise, as suggested by Petit.[97] The law also stipulated that instructors would be salaried by the nation, but their salaries would depend upon the number of students enrolled in their classes, balancing the nation's responsibility to provide free instruction with the incentives that were supposed to come from competition.[98] The result, as Petit had argued it must be, was a course of reform that would proceed piecemeal and with a considerable degree of local autonomy.[99]

In practice, this meant that a great deal of the promised education would never materialize, an outcome confirmed by a government survey in October 1794.[100] Trying to gauge to what degree the Bouquier Law had been put into effect, the Committee of Public Instruction found that fewer than 10 percent of the reporting districts had a full retinue of schools, and the vast majority (227 of 350 districts) "gave [either] no report or reported no schools or few."[101] It also meant, because of the law's silence regarding whether or not clerics could be appointed as instructors (a remarkable silence in a moment of avowed dechristianization), that much of the education that was offered would be carried out by instructors about whom authorities had suspicions or concerns. The resulting and competing problems of absent or inappropriate instructors would dominate the "education question" in 1794, returning the debates over education to the conditions of its origins in the 1760s.[102]

More striking than the desultory results of the Bouquier Law's implementation, however, is the ideological uncertainty evident in the Convention's debates and decrees. Anti-corporatist rhetoric and egalitarian imperatives competed with a resilient sense that advanced courses of study served at once public, private, and political interests. Demands for laissez-faire approaches to education were coupled uneasily with the need to scrutinize and oversee instructors, and the language of national sovereignty, political centralization, and cultural uniformity culminated awkwardly in the delegation of administrative and organizational decisions to local authorities. The civic festivals and public performances that were supposed to be the lynchpin of republican education were among the parts of Bouquier's proposal dropped from the Convention's decree. If this was, as Palmer speculates, a compromise fashioned or at least sanctioned by the Committee of Public Safety, its primary virtue seems to have been denying and ignoring points of conflict rather than enshrining a particularly "Jacobin" approach to education.[103]

Read in light of the competing proposals and unproductive compromises that characterized its approval and implementation, the Bouquier

Law offers little clarity as to where the "education question" stood in 1794. In this respect, it is symptomatic of the period then drawing to a close. The *conventionnels* never managed to articulate a distinctly republican model of public instruction, much less a coherent or plausible system of republican education. Their proposals were marked by imprecise relationships among national and local institutions and authorities, uncertainty about the state's role in primary and secondary education, and uneven steps towards a system to provide instructors for the nation.

These points reflect anxieties not just about the schools and about the aims of education, but about the political order to which education was supposed to contribute.[104] Addressing them would require a vision of France's political, cultural, and social future, a clear sense of how the people, the nation, and the state should engage one another, and a plausible idea of where the Revolution was headed. The *conventionnels* did not settle these points; they no more solved the problem of public instruction than they did the problem of politics.

Notes

1 Serge Bianchi, *La Révolution culturelle de l'an II: élites et peuple (1789-1799)* (Paris: Aubier, 1982), 153.
2 Terror's role as guarantor and instructional model is discussed in Ronald Schechter, "The terror of their enemies: reflections on a trope in eighteenth-century historiography," *Historical Reflections/Réflexions Historiques*, 36:1 (2010): 53-75.
3 *AP* 68: 661. The plan is reprinted in James Guillaume, *Procès-verbaux du Comité d'Instruction publique de la Convention nationale*, T. 2, 34-61. The plan was not an accurate or a complete presentation of Lepeletier's views on education, as Palmer notes. Palmer, *The Improvement of Humanity*, 138.
4 AN, AD/VIII//21, no. 9, *Tableau d'un Collège en activité, par J. F. Major*, 15.
5 Livesey, *Making Democracy in the French Revolution*, 173.
6 AN, F/17//1010D, no. 3923, J. Toussaint, *Plan d'Instruction*, 6 thermidor, an II.
7 Romme, *Rapport sur l'instruction publique, considérée dans son ensemble*, 9-11.
8 AN, F/17//1009, 1810, Letter from C. Mulard to the National Convention, 22 Nivôse, an II (11 January 1794), 1-2.
9 Michel Manson, *Les Livres pour l'enfance et la jeunesse sous la Révolution* (Paris: INRP, 1989).
10 *AP* 78: 373.

11 Marat's quip comes from a December 1792 debate following upon the presentation of a plan for primary schools presented by Lanthenas. See Compayré, *Histoire critique des doctrines de l'éducation en France*, T. 2, 348; Barnard, *Education and the French Revolution*, 105; Kaplan, "Virtuous competition among citizens," 245.
12 Robert J. Vignery, *The French Revolution and the Schools: Educational Policies of the Mountain, 1792-1794* (Madison, WI: State Historical Society of Wisconsin, 1965), 34.
13 Pauline Léveillé, "L'Image des femmes dans les proces-verbaux du Comité d'Instruction Publique," in Marie-France Brive (ed.), *Les Femmes et la Révolution française: actes du colloque international, 12-13-14 avril 1989, Université de Toulouse-le Mirail* (Toulouse: Presses universitaires du Mirail, 1989), vol. 1, *Modes d'action et d'expression nouveaux droits – nouveaux devoirs*, 461-471; Carlo Pancera, "La Tendre Mère," in Brive (ed.), *Les Femmes et la Révolution française*, 473-479. Also Joan Landes, *Visualizing the Nation: Gender, Representation, and Revolution in Eighteenth-Century France* (Ithaca, NY: Cornell University Press, 2001); and Jennifer Ngaire Heuer, *The Family and the Nation: Gender and Citizenship in Revolutionary France, 1789-1830* (Ithaca, NY: Cornell University Press, 2005), esp. 17-126.
14 For example, Bell, *The Cult of the Nation in France*, 1-3.
15 *AP* 55: 345-347.
16 Mona Ozouf, "Regeneration," in François Furet and Mona Ozouf (eds), *A Critical Dictionary of the French Revolution*, trans. by Arthur Goldhammer (Cambridge, MA: Harvard University Press, 1989): 781-791.
17 Nicholas Hentz, *Sur L'Instruction publique* (Paris, 1793), 3.
18 AN, F/17//1010A, 3031, Letter from C. Flavigny, 21 floréal an II (11 May 1794); F/17//1010A, 2492, Letter from officials in the Département de la Loire regarding education, 11 germinal an II (31 March 1794).
19 Ozouf, *Festivals and the French Revolution*, 104-105.
20 Hunt, *Politics, Culture, and Class in the French Revolution*, 68-69.
21 A view of nationalism roughly akin to this is suggested in Philip S. Gorski, "Nation-ization Struggles: A Bourdieusian Theory of Nationalism," in Philip S. Gorski (ed.), *Bourdieu and Historical Analysis* (Durham, NC: Duke University Press, 2013): 242-265.
22 Sepinwall, *The Abbé Grégoire and the French Revolution*, 90-136.
23 As quoted in Michel de Certeau, Dominique Julia, Jacques Revel, *Une politique de la langue: La Révolution française et les patois: l'enquête de Grégoire* (Paris: Gallimard, 2002), 27. For Grégoire's questions, see 13-16, and for some of the responses, 185-273. For other responses, see Augustin Gazier, *Lettres à Grégoire sur les patois de France, documents inédits sur la langue, les mœurs et l'état des esprits dans les diverses régions de la France au début de la Révolution, suivie du rapport de Grégoire à la Convention* (Paris: Durand et Pedone-Lauriel, 1880). For the report itself, Henri Grégoire, *Rapport sur*

la nécessité et les moyens d'anéantir les patois et d'universaliser l'usage de la langue française (Paris: Imprimerie nationale, n.d.).
24 On revolutionary concern with language, see Sophia A. Rosenfeld, *A Revolution in Language: The Problem of Signs in Late Eighteenth-century France* (Stanford, CA: Stanford University Press, 2001), esp. 123-180; Bell, *The Cult of the Nation in France*, 182-197.
25 De Certeau, Julia, Revel, *Une politique de la langue*, 335-337.
26 Bertrand Barère, *Rapport et projet de décrets sur les idiomes étrangers et l'enseignement de la langue française* (pluviôse, an II), in Baczko, *Une education pour la démocratie*, 427-437.
27 Jean-Antoine-Nicolas de Caritat, marquis de Condorcet, Emmanuel-Joseph Sieyès, Jules [Julien]-Michel Duhamel, *Journal d'instruction sociale* (Paris, 1793), 2; Rosenfeld, *A Revolution in Language*, 160.
28 Condorcet, Sieyès, Duhamel, *Journal d'instruction sociale*, 2-3.
29 Ibid., 4, 11; Velicu, *Civic Catechisms and Reason in the French Revolution*, 103.
30 Joseph Lakanal, *Projet d'éducation du peuple française: le 26 juin 1793, présenté à la Convention nationale, au nom du Comité d'Instruction publique par Lakanal* (Paris, 1793).
31 Kaplan, "Virtuous competition among citizens," 241. For a discussion of competing views about whether *émulation* was compatible with the sort of civil society (and civil harmony) at which the Revolution should aim, see Martin S. Staum, *Minerva's Message: Stabilizing the French Revolution* (Quebec City: McGill-Queen's University Press, 1996), 132-134, as well as Shovlin, *Political Economy of Virtue*, 59-62.
32 Kaplan, "Virtuous competition among citizens," 245-246.
33 Livesey, *Making Democracy in the French Revolution*, 198-201.
34 Ihl, *Le Mérite et la République*.
35 AN, F/17//1010D, 9478, Description of the Fête de la Jeuneesse (20 Ventôse, an III), submitted to the National Assembly, March 1795.
36 *AP* 72: 276-277.
37 AN, F/17//1010D, 5, no. 10724, Proposal for a system of public instruction, submitted to the National Convention by Charles Le Roy, September 1795.
38 Ozouf, *Festivals and the French Revolution*, 3.
39 Jeremy L. Caradonna, "The monarchy of virtue: the prix de vertu and the economy of emulation in France, 1777-1791," *Eighteenth-Century Studies*, 41:4 (2008): 443-458. Hurard's prize is in the archives of the Institut national de recherche pédagogique, in Mont Saint-Aignan, no. 2003-1561.
40 Compare Rosanvallon, *The Demands of Liberty*, 22.
41 Quoted in Kennedy, *The Jacobin Clubs in the French Revolution*, 107.
42 AN, F/17//1002, 119, Letter from the principals and professors of the collèges of Paris, 1792; AN, F/17//1004, 367, Letter from C. Gazagnaire, January 1793.

43 AN, F/17//1005, 733, Letter from the Société académique de Tours, 6 August 1793. Similarly impatient missives include F/17//1001, 1, Letter from a committee of "citoyens libres" in the city of Auray, 21 September 1792; F/17//1001, 36, Letter from the Tribunal de Commerce in Issoudun to the National Convention, October 1792; F/17//1001, 38, Letter from the permanent sections of Besançon to the National Convention requesting the prompt organization of public instruction, 10 October 1792; F/17//1002, 101, Letter from C. LeMur to the National Convention, 4 November 1792; F/17//1004, 305, Letter from the citizens of the city of Agen, December 1792; F/17//1004, 323, Letter from C. Legendre, Director of the École Chrétienne, to the National Convention, 23 December 1792; F/17//1004, 353, Members of the General Council of the Département de Calvados to the National Convention, 11 January 1793; F/17//1004, 381, Citizens of St. Yrieix to the National Convention, January 1793; F/17//1009, 1763, Letter from C. Blargas to the National Convention, 14 Nivôse an II (3 January 1794).

44 AN, F/17//1002, 118, Letter from C. Dubessey submitting a political catechism, 21 October 1792; F/17//1010C, 3226, Republican catechism submitted by C. Thiebault, floreal an II (12 May 1794).

45 AN, F/17//1002, 103, Letter from C. Terrilon of Plombières-en-Vosges, submitting a method to teach children to read in four months, 1 November 1792; F/17//1002, 125, Letter from C. Coulon to the National Convention submitting a description of a method to teach children to write, 11 November 1792.

46 Morange and Chassaing, *Le Mouvement de réforme de l'enseignement en France*, 108.

47 AN, F/17//1002, 102, Letter to the National Convention from C. Jean-François Christophe Hervieu, procureur of the commune of Coutances, 1 November 1792; F/17//1002, 119, Letter from the principals and professors of the collèges of Paris, 1792; F/17//1002, 148, Letter from C. Berger, professor in Lyon, regarding elementary texts, 1792; F/17//1002, 192, Letter from citizens in the district of Marcigny-sur-Loire regarding texts confiscated from the property of émigrés, 25 November 1792; F/17//1006, 1101, Letter from C. Pocheron regarding instructors' salaries, 28 brumaire an II (18 November 1793); F/17//1007, 1255, Letter from C. Demonceaux, instituteur, requesting new elementary texts, 16 frimaire an II (6 December 1793); F/17//1009, 1816, Letter to the National Convention from students at the Collège de Condrieu in the Rhône, 1793.

48 AN, F/17//1001, 38, Letter from the permanent sections of Besançon, 10 October 1792; F/17//1006, 1082, Letter from the Société républicaine de Vervins, 22 brumaire an II (12 November 1793); F/17//1007, 1220, Letter from the Commune de Paris to the National Convention, 5 December 1793; F/17//1009, 1810, Letter from C. Mulard to the National Convention, 22

nivôse an II (11 January 1794); F/17//1010A, 2422, Letter from C. Vigner to the National Convention, 8 germinal an II (28 March 1794).

49 Henri Grégoire, *Rapport sur l'ouverture d'un concours pour les livres élémentaires de la première éducation*, 3 pluviôse, an II (Paris, 1794).
50 Ibid., 3, 8.
51 Ibid., 8.
52 Ibid., 9. On the *Annales du Civisme* and the production of the *Recueil des actions héroiques et civiques des républicains français*, see Henri Grégoire, *Rapport sur les moyens de rassembler les matériaux nécessaires à former les annales du civisme & sur la forme de cet ouvrage: séance du 28 septembre 1793, l'an deuxième de la République* (Paris, 1793); Emmet Kennedy, *A Cultural History of the French Revolution* (New Haven, CT: Yale University Press, 1989), 355–356.
53 AN, F/17//10102, dossier 6, folder 4, 9 Committee of Public Instruction announces closure of the *concours des livres élémentaires*, 1 brumaire an III (22 October 1794).
54 Julia, *Les Trois Couleurs du tableau noir*, 156.
55 Hunt, *Politics, Culture, and Class in the French Revolution*, 69.
56 AN, F/17//1001, no. 93, 6, Mémoire from four maîtres and chaplains at the collèges des boursiers in Toulouse; this Mémoire can be dated to sometime between August 1792 and February 1793, as it mentions the law of 18 August 1792 and a follow-up letter which refers to this text is dated 25 February 1793 (AN, F/17//1001, no. 93, Letter from professors in Toulouse). For an example of the complications brought on by the uncertain status of these instructors, see AN, F/17//1004, no. 331, Letter from the professors at the Collège de Bergues, St Vinox, to the National Convention, 18 January 1793.
57 *AP* 48: 350.
58 AN, F/17//1001, 63, *Extrait des Registres des Arrêtes du Directoire du Département de Haute Garonne*, 13 October 1792; F//17//1001, 9 & 9bis, Letters from municipal authorities in Rouen to the National Convention, May 1793.
59 AN, F/17//1006, 1101, Letter from C. Pocheron to the National Convention, 28 brumaire an II (18 November 1793).
60 AN, F/17//1006, 1196, Letter from C. d'Auburtin condemning the exclusion of ex-nobles from serving as instructors, 13 November 1793; F/17//1009, 1756, Letter from the commune of Branscourt calling for a purge of unsatisfactory instructors, 19 nivôse an II (8 January 1794).
61 AN, F/17//1001, 92, Copy of the letter from Gilbert Romme to Rolland, Minister of the Interior, 14 November 1792.
62 *AP* 75: 494.
63 On this, see Palmer, "How five centuries of educational philanthropy disappeared," 186–189.

64 Kennedy, *A Cultural History of the French Revolution*, 159.
65 ADHG, 1 L 1004, 13, *Decret de la Convention nationale, du 9 mars 1793... Relatif aux bourses vacantes dans les Collèges* (Toulouse, 1793), 1.
66 AN, F/17//1005, 786, Mémoire from the Minister of the Interior to departmental officials regarding the law of 8 March 1793, dated 4 August 1793.
67 See, for example, the letter written by Jean-François Champagne, director of Collège Louis le Grand, to the Committee of Public Instruction on 29 May 1793, reproduced in Palmer, *The School of the French Revolution*, 132–134, as well as AN, F/17//1143, dossier 2, no. 15, Letter from the administrators of the district of Bordeaux to the Minister of the Interior, 13 Germinal an II (2 April 1794).
68 Guillaume, *Procès-verbaux du Comité d'Instruction publique de la Convention nationale*, T. 2, 357.
69 Guillaume, *Procès-verbaux du Comité d'Instruction publique de la Convention nationale*, T. 1, 568.
70 Tackett, *The Coming of the Terror in the French Revolution*, 276–279.
71 Claude-Laurent Masuyer, *Discours sur l'organisation du l'instruction publique et l'éducation nationale en France: examen et réfutation du système proposé successivement par les citoyens Condorcet et G. Rome* [sic], *au nom du Comité d'instruction publique de l'Assemblée législative et de la Convention nationale* (Paris: Imprimerie nationale, 1793), 61, 88.
72 AN, F/7//3688 (3), 99, Observations from C. Rolin, 19–20 September 1793; F/7//3688 (3), 108, Observations from C. Rolin, 21 September 1793.
73 Hentz, *Sur L'Instruction publique*, 1.
74 Guillaume, *Procès-verbaux du Comité d'Instruction publique de la Convention nationale*, T. 1, 533.
75 *AP* 70: 519.
76 For the exception that Grégoire proposed for the Académie des Sciences (but which was not accorded), see *AP* 70: 522–523. This was a line of argument that had been prepared in the preceding months by Lakanal and Lavoisier; see Hahn, *The Anatomy of a Scientific Institution*, 237–240.
77 AN, F/17//1005, 778, Petition from Jules-François Paré, Minister of the Interior, 24 August 1793.
78 *AP* 74: 234.
79 *Le Moniteur Universel*, 13 août 1793, no. 225.
80 Barnard, *Education and the French Revolution*, 124–126; Palmer, *The Improvement of Humanity*, 160–170.
81 *AP* 74: 135, n. 1.
82 For example, AN, F/17//1002, 134, Inquiry from departmental administrators in Lot to the National Convention, 16 November 1792; F/17//1001, no. 98 (bis), 2; F/17//1004, 342, "Plan d'études" proposed for the Collège de Nancy, 1793.

83 ADHG, 1 L 1016, proposal for a provisional reorganization of education in Toulouse, 1793.
84 ADHG, 1 L 992, Provisional organization of instruction in Toulouse, 22 Nivôse an II (11 January 1794), 1; the courses were presented as a public poster, 1 L 992, 10.
85 For the uncertain status of provisional instructors, see AN, F/17//1001, 63; F/17//1001, 9 & 9bis; on the problem of competing plans and demands, F/17//1004, 391; F/17//1010B, 2754, Letter from the Société des Amis de la Liberté et de l'Égalité in Autun, 17 germinal an II (6 April 1794).
86 On regret regarding the failure of the Condorcet plan, AN, F/17//1001, 98 (bis), 2. A similar view is presented in the *Projet d'Éducation* submitted by a Citoyen Odoard-Fantin in November 1792. Odoard-Fantin claims that Condorcet's plan would be ideal for "calmer" times, but unworkable in the tumultuous present. AN, F/17//1002, 126, Letter from C. Odoard-Fantin to the National Convention, November 1792. On the difficulty of anticipating the imperatives to come from the political authorities, AN, F/17//1001, 93, Mémoire presented by four maîtres and chaplains at the collèges des boursiers in Toulouse, n.d. [late 1792–early 1793], 6.
87 AN, F/17//1001, 93, Mémoire presented by four maîtres and chaplains at the collèges des boursiers in Toulouse, n.d. [late 1792–early 1793].
88 Palmer, *The Improvement of Humanity*, 170. The Convention continued to honor its commitments to the teaching personnel and students of these *collèges*, effectively paying the salaries and scholarships of instructors and students who were being prevented from teaching and studying.
89 Ibid., 137, 169.
90 G. Bouquier, "Rapport et projet de décret formant un plan général d'instruction publique, par G. Bouquier, membre de la Convention nationale et du Comité d'instruction publique," in Guillaume, *Procès-verbaux du Comité d'Instruction publique de la Convention nationale*, T. 3, 56–62; 191–196.
91 Ibid., 57.
92 Ibid., 60.
93 Ibid., 57–60. Vignery describes this as a system of "support without interference by the state." Vignery, *The French Revolution and the Schools*, 113. On this, see also Palmer, *The Improvement of Humanity*, 180.
94 Guillaume, *Procès-verbaux du Comité d'Instruction publique de la Convention nationale*, T. 3, 60–61. Cf. Palmer, *The Improvement of Humanity*, 179.
95 *AP* 81: 241.
96 For the debate over, and objections to, the Bouquier proposal, see Guillaume, *Procès-verbaux du Comité d'Instruction publique de la Convention nationale*, T. 3, 92–97, 150–157. On the amendments to Bouquier's articles for primary instruction, see Palmer, *The Improvement of Humanity*, 181.
97 *AP* 81: 706. This caused some confusion as instructors and municipal author-

ities tried to determine what sort of relationship they were supposed to have with one another under the new law. For example, AN, F/17//1010A, 2417, Letter from instructors at the Collège d'Orange to the National Convention, 4 germinal an II (22 March 1794).

98 *AP* 81: 706. This too led to confusion and criticism, as in the letter from the Jacobin club in Autun who criticized this arrangement for giving instructors an incentive to enroll as many students as possible, thereby spreading their attention too thin and depriving those students of the attention they needed and deserved. AN, F/17//1010B, 2754, Letter from the Société des Amis de la Liberté et de l'Égalité in Autun, to the National Convention, 17 germinal an II (6 April 1794).

99 The turn to piecemeal reform is suggested by the final comment before discussion of Bouquier's proposal concluded, as Pierre Philippeaux asked that all documents pertaining to the reform of primary schools be published and disseminated without delay so that the Convention could move on to the next steps towards reform. *AP* 81: 707.

100 In those cases where schools were established and then maintained, the successful reform often reflected the zeal of a local administrator of political club rather than the coherence of the proposal or sufficiency of resources. Local efforts by Jacobin clubs during this period are discussed in Kennedy, *The Jacobin Clubs in the French Revolution, 1793–1795*, 145–150.

101 Kennedy, *A Cultural History of the French Revolution*, 160–161; similar statistics are cited in Palmer, *The Improvement of Humanity*, 182–183.

102 Across France, schools struggled to find suitable instructors, often finding that the only way to staff schools was to hire former priests. These problems are evident in a slew of letters to the Convention regarding ad hoc arrangements and attempts to balance political and practical imperatives. Examples can be found at ADHG, 1 L 993, 43, 44, Assessment of candidates for positions as instructors, 1 germinal an II (21 March 1794); AN, F/17//1010A, 2620, Officials in Carcassonne concerned about the lack of a qualified female instructor, germinal an II; F/17//1010A, 2437, Letter from the Société populaire de Phalsbourg, germinal an II; 2469; Letter from administrators in Vézelise complaining of an insufficient number of candidates for positions as instructors, 30 ventôse an II (20 March 1794); F/17//1010A, 3045 Administrators in the district of Nevers to the National Convention, 23 floréal an II (12 May 1794); F/17//1010A, 3129, Letter from officials in Rouen to the Convention requesting permission to appoint an ex-priest as a professor in the botanical gardens, 9 prairial an II (28 May 1794); F/17//1010B, 2725, Officials in the canton of Contigné to the National Convention requesting information about the permissibility of appointing ex-priests, 27 germinal an II (16 April 1794); F/17//1010B, 2774, Administrators in the commune of Aigle, regarding limits on school personnel, 9 floréal an II (28 April 1794); F/17//1010B, 2785, Letter from officials

in the commune of Bu regarding the employment of married ex-priests, floréal an II. See also Kennedy, *A Cultural History of the French Revolution*, 160–161; Palmer, *The Improvement of Humanity*, 182–183.
103 Palmer, *The Improvement of Humanity*, 181.
104 Livesey, *Making Democracy in the French Revolution*, 170–172, 187–188; Palmer, *The Improvement of Humanity*, 243.

Conclusion
Politics: real, pursued, and promised

In October 1794, when the academic year would normally have been starting up again, the schools of the French Republic lacked instructors, students, and funds, not to mention a clearly defined role in French society and a sense of pedagogical or political purpose. Political authorities were unwilling or unable to settle on a coherent plan to reform or replace the existing institutions. The prospect that those authorities would seek to establish a uniform system of national education both hung over and motivated local attempts at reform or reinvention. Critics and commentators emphasized the role of education in shaping the national character and in defining the political order even as they disagreed fundamentally about what that character and order ought to be. The echoes of the mid-1760s were clear in the closing months of the Convention and the first years of the Directory, and on many points it seemed that the revolutionary debates had yielded little progress. As late as 1798–99, the Directory's Council on Public Instruction decided that the nation's textbooks "would have to be rewritten, but only after the philosophical principles of a republican education had been identified."[1] It is tempting, then, to accept François Guizot's nineteenth-century assessment and dismiss the debates of these years as "phantoms soaring over ruins."[2] This, however, misses much of what made these debates, and these years, so important.

A generation before 1789, the expulsion of the Jesuits had entangled the practical work of education in debates over the nature, character, and mutability of the social and political orders. It sparked a debate about who could shape the nation's collective future and how they might do so, establishing an institutional and conceptual nexus where competing futures could be imagined, articulated, and scrutinized. Thinking about the reform of education served a number of (sometimes overlapping) political and ideological functions during these years, as participants in the debates over education used descriptions of the schools – existing or anticipated – as microcosmic representations of French society and social relations, the state and political administration, and the role of the public in French politics. Because of this, the post-expulsion debates helped to solidify the idea, expressed earlier by Montesquieu and others, that a nation's political and educational regimes should reflect and reinforce one another, that education was critical to civil society's role in producing and reproducing a viable political order. At the same time, the debates of the 1760s and 1770s were an affair largely reserved for the initiated, the *parlementaires*, *philosophes*, ministers, members of *le monde*, and, to a lesser degree, professors and school administrators. It was an affair that "engaged ... the political and intellectual *elites* of the country."[3]

Even for those elites, the prospect of transforming French politics and society through the schools seemed to depend on the monarch – or, in some cases, the parlements – being willing and able to impose reform. This was one reason Helvétius was so pessimistic; his faith in the power of education was expansive, but his faith in the Ancien Régime state waned, as did his confidence in a populace that lacked the interest and awareness that might make progress possible. Rousseau's assessment was roughly the same, and the record of reform in the 1760s and 1770s offers little reason to reconsider. Indeed, it suggests that inaction on education was symptomatic of a broader paralysis in the French polity.

After 1789, however, the prospect of transformative changes in French politics, culture, and society was not an abstraction upon which to reflect, but an apparent inevitability with which people would have to reckon. The reform of education seemed suddenly like a necessary component of, and complement to, social and political change, a point emphasized by legislators in the Assembly and correspondents across the country. These participants in the revolutionary debates over education had inherited the Enlightenment view that systems of education and of governance should mirror one another, and they wed that view to the new sense of "possibilism" unleashed by the Revolution.[4]

The reorganization of education offered revolutionary legislators and commentators a specific set of cultural and institutional concerns on which to focus, established contextual parameters within which to imagine and articulate a social and political future, and seemed to provide a plausible way of thinking about how the revolutionary present might lead to any such future. The "education question" made explicit the problem of revolutionary process, of how inherited institutions could give rise to radically new successors and how people who had not been prepared in advance could be at once educated for and enlisted in political society. In this, the debates over education and politics were emblematic of the Revolution's encounter with revolutionary time, with new ways of thinking about how past, present, and future might relate to one another, and about how action in an uncertain present might give shape to an as-yet-undefined future.[5]

Almost all of the initial proposals for reform – even those that proposed replacing or reinventing the Ancien Régime schools – took the existing institutions and expectations as the starting point for thinking about a system of public instruction. When participants in these debates focused on the financial and material resources required for a national system of education, the personnel needed for the schools, the subjects to be taught and the texts used, or the professional and political lives for which students should be prepared, they started with an assessment of the *petites écoles*, *collèges*, and universities as they existed in 1789 (and they often offered a more favorable assessment of these institutions than later debates might suggest). What they could imagine and what they aimed to achieve were bound from the start by what they saw before them and what they had to hand, and the reform of education served as an important point of convergence for ideological or political ambitions and practical or material limitations.

At the same time, proposals for a reformed system of education allowed those who participated in these debates to express what they thought the Revolution could or should be. Describing the attributes of suitable instructors, the need for administrative reforms in the schools, and the sort of curriculum best suited to prepare students for their future as citizens offered a chance to flesh out a theory of citizenship, a sense of how French society, politics, and industry should work, a vision of political practice, and a microcosm of representative governance. It also offered people a chance to reflect upon the changes sweeping France, to think about what might be taking shape around them. This was especially clear prior to the presentation of the constitution in September 1791, as legislators and correspondents across France shared in the refrain that a new system of education must both prepare for and reflect a constitutional regime that was only then emerging. Education's role as a preparatory and proxy institution allows us to examine how people thought about and understood the new politics in how they approached the schools and their reform. When deputies, citizens, political societies, teachers, and students described what "public instruction" might mean, they gave voice to ideas about what political society might be.

The vision of public instruction that took shape in the first years after 1789 represented an ambitious attempt to prepare French society for the travails and uncertainties of contestatory politics. This vision anticipated political disputes and disagreements among an informed and engaged citizenry, hoping to preserve the national community amid such disputes by nurturing the ameliorative bonds of civic sentiment; in its integration of *éducation* and *instruction* it acknowledged that a civil political culture was not a naturally occurring phenomenon, and that neither virtue nor reason would suffice alone. This politico-pedagogical ideal was reflected in calls to reform the curriculum, but it was even more clearly evident in proposals to give students primary (if not final) responsibility in managing and adjudicating points of contention and in increased attention to the socializing function of education. Participants in these debates explored new ways of organizing and orchestrating power, recasting professors and instructors as learned role models rather than imperious experts or impersonal judges, reimagining administrative and disciplinary authority as the responsibility of student-citizens working in concert with school officials, and re-presenting social hierarchies as the result of meritocratic and emulative competition among students. They anticipated that these organizational reforms would be complemented by a program of civic instruction that would simultaneously illustrate and nurture affection for the new national regime. On each of these points the constitutive elements were familiar, but – the revolutionaries hoped – regenerated.

These proposals served as complement and corollary to the constitutional design of new political institutions, a way to think about civil society's role in a system of representative and participatory government. Especially after the rejection of the binding mandate in summer 1789, the question of how and where legitimate political discourse took place was thrown into sharp relief. Even as some deputies and commentators moved to distance the legislators' work from the public's commentary, to insulate the representatives from the represented, others tried to imagine how new social dynamics and political practices might establish a substantive role for the public in the new politics. Situating the reform of education within the problem of representation, they recognized that participatory politics required not just institutional avenues through which the public could learn about and communicate with the state (a free press, the publicity of legislative debates and decisions, the right to petition the government, regular elections, etc.), but also the widespread acquisition of specific skills and basic forms of knowledge (especially the abilities to read and write, but also numeracy, basic geography, rudimentary knowledge of the sciences, and some form of civics), the promotion of particular social and civic habits (staying abreast of the political issues of the day, attending public forums, voting, etc.), and the cultivation of specific civic sentiments that would be rooted in everyday life and reinforced by festive occasions. Aiming to address all of these points, public instruction took shape as a polyvalent approach to education, a political pedagogy that sought to integrate the acquisition of skills, the cultivation of virtue, and the socialization of citizens.

Shared foci were by no means the same as consensus though, and each of these points gave rise to substantive disagreements. After all, what knowledge and which skills should citizens have? Which forms of political participation are legitimate, necessary, and fruitful, and which exceed the boundaries that make "representative" governance workable? How much debate and disagreement can be tolerated before social ties fray or falter? Reforming education would require not just answering these questions, but translating those answers into institutional norms that could be established and maintained within the constraints set by human, political, and material circumstances.

And so ideological and material imperatives became intertwined in the debates over education. The content of new curricula and the character of (possibly new) instructors were expected to ensure or undermine the Revolution's achievements, diffuse or dilute revolutionary principles, and establish or erase the Revolution's legacy. These risks and rewards operated on different, and sometimes competing timelines, and the reform of education gave rise to a localized version of the Legislator's dilemma described by Rousseau. The theory of public instruction that emerged after 1789 held that an appropriate system of education could prepare the citizenry to participate in political debates and could establish the civic bonds necessary to preserve the national and political community when those debates turned contentious, but the pursuit of this pedagogical ideal was only possible because political disputes and disagreements were already shaking France. For the constitutional regime to survive, it seemed that the people had to have in the present attributes that public instruction could only give them in the future.

What was true of the people was true of the schools as well. Establishing a new system of public instruction seemed to depend on the transformation of institutions, practices, and personnel inherited from a repudiated but all-too-recent past. In that, it occupied a point of contact between what Mona Ozouf described as the revolutionaries' "miraculous" and "laborious" approaches to regeneration. Instruments of laborious regeneration, the schools (and those associated with the schools) would have to themselves benefit from a miraculous transformation.[6] To put the point somewhat differently: the regenerative transformation of French society relied upon the idea that people – both individually and collectively – were shaped by their experience and their education, but the practical work of educating the next generation of citizens would have to be entrusted to people whose own education and experiences bound them to the old regime. This was one of the reasons that recruiting, vetting, and overseeing instructors was so central to the "education question" even before the disputes over the Civil Constitution of the Clergy and the clerical oath shattered the provisional maintenance of the educational status quo ante: those best positioned to turn the schools into instruments of revolutionary regeneration were themselves products of a decidedly un-revolutionary education.

A remarkably wide range of commentators noted this problem (including many of the instructors themselves), and they did so with candor and with confidence that it could and would be solved. They proposed new incentive structures to entice the many instructors that would be needed, new systems of vetting and overseeing those instructors to guarantee their aptitude and moral character, and new pedagogical emphases to break the stultifying routine of the Ancien Régime. And yet, even as many correspondents agreed that these were the appropriate foci for reform, each point gave rise to its own disputes and disagreements, embedding the reform of education within broader disputes about the political, religious, economic, and administrative character of France. Similarly, disputes broke out regarding the administration and allocation of resources, the production and distribution of texts, the location and administration of schools, and the role of the state in settling these questions. These were issues on which proposals were scrutinized, and upon which they faltered. They were also the stuff of practical political work, as deputies and correspondents sought to realize a national system of public instruction despite the limitations imposed by material, financial, or human resources and the deep uncertainty that plagued attempts to anticipate France's national future.

The limitations and disruptions of these years undermined those efforts, and the pursuit of public instruction was in many ways a failure.

Nonetheless, the tension among political regeneration, the practical work of institutional reform, and the instability born of dramatically unsettled circumstances makes the debate over education a valuable window onto broader questions about the Revolution and its evolution over time. Of course, as with any such "window," the view is limited, and there is much that defined the Revolution that is not visible in the debates over education. That said, there are several points on which the history traced above is suggestive.

The debates over education suggest a public pursuit of representative government and participatory politics that extended well beyond the design and establishment of formal political institutions and far beyond the Assembly's walls. Politics posed social and cultural problems as well as legislative and legal ones, and the debates over education reflect a model of thinking about the constitution and constitutional politics that focused on how citizens would interact with one another, how and when they would encounter the state, how and where their political judgments would be communicated and conveyed, and how they would respond to the conflicts that accompany collective political engagement. Each of these would shape the new political order, and each was a point of concern in the reform of education.

Tracing the debates over education beyond the Assembly's (or Convention's) walls also suggests that the pursuit of a contestatory and participatory model of politics was more sustained, more practical, and more nuanced than we might suppose when tracing the Revolution's descent into the Terror or noting the *conventionnels*' inability to settle upon a course of reform. Amid shifting ideological currents, and despite a persistent lack of guidance from Paris, local officials, members of political clubs, instructors and administrators in the schools, and private citizens continued to work towards a system of public instruction that they hoped might help to realize and sustain a new political order. Such efforts were, of course, uneven, and attention to them does not dilute the illiberalism of the year II or the violence of the Terror. But it does remind us that the Revolution was not one thing, playing out on one historical track.

This, too, reminds us that the attempts to reform education took place within a polity in motion, and that the attempts to cultivate a new politics in the classroom took shape at the same time that citizens in Paris and across France were fashioning and improvising a new politics in political clubs, in the press, and in the streets.[7] While this is most strikingly evident in the disruptions that followed from the Civil Constitution of the Clergy and again after the fall of the Legislative Assembly, it was true from the start. The interplay of anticipation, instability, and improvisation that shaped the debates over education was evident in the relative quiet of summer 1789, as deputies, administrators, professors, students, and concerned citizens took stock of the revolutionary events that would remake society and would inevitably shape the reform of education. It is clear also in their trial-and-error approach to local problems, the continued attempts to fashion a viable set of reforms even as the national authorities disagreed and became distracted by national and international developments, and in the contributions offered anew after each dramatic turn in local or national affairs. Those who participated in the revolutionary debates over education encountered their efforts as elements of a historical process, their experiences as "evidence of history" unfolding. The work of politics led people to think of their lives as at once historically constructive and, at the same time, subject to the contingencies of an increasingly unstable world.[8] They would have recognized well Marx's famous observation that "men make their own history, but they do not make it just as they please."[9]

In this, the debates over education reflected one of the most important consequences of the French Revolution: the location of historical and ideological forces in familiar institutions and quotidian affairs. The French Revolution helped to transform modern politics not by creating political ideologies or abstractions, but by situating politics in the social, material, institutional, and interpersonal spaces of people's lives, in places like schools. The national community and its collective future would be forged in those spaces, for better or worse, and by virtue of decisions made by people operating with imperfect knowledge in uncertain circumstances. That this description seems apt more than 200 years later suggests the enormity of the revolutionary project, the importance of its legacy, and the promise – and peril – of modern politics.

Notes

1 Livesey, *Making Democracy in the French Revolution*, 183.
2 Quoted in Palmer, *The Improvement of Humanity*, 123.
3 Chartier, Compère, Julia, *L'Éducation en France du XVIe au XVIIIe siècle*, 208. Emphasis added. This sense is reinforced by recent findings about the social composition of Enlightenment networks of debate and discussion. See Maria Teodora Comsa, Melanie Conroy, Dan Edelstein, Chloe Summers Edmondson, and Claude Willan, "The French Enlightenment network," *Journal of Modern History* 88 (2016): 495–534.

4 Darnton, "What was revolutionary about the French Revolution?," 27.
5 Ozouf, "Regeneration," 789; Peter Fritzsche, *Stranded in the Present: Modern Time and the Melancholy of History* (Cambridge, MA: Harvard University Press, 2004), 18-20, 201-203.
6 Ozouf, "Regeneration," 781-791.
7 Micah Alpaugh, *Non-Violence and the French Revolution: Political Demonstrations in Paris, 1787-1795* (Cambridge: Cambridge University Press, 2015).
8 Fritzsche, *Stranded in the Present*, 13.
9 Karl Marx, *The Eighteenth Brumaire of Louis Bonaparte* (New York, NY: International Publishers, 2004), 15.

Bibliography

Primary sources

Manuscript sources were drawn from the following archival collections:
Archives nationales de France (AN)
    AD/VIII//21
    C/II//8 – C//II//16
    D/IV//4 – 70
    F/7//3688
    F/17//1001 – 1012
    F/17//1143
    F/17//1309 – 1310
    F/17//10102
    H/3//2528
    M/198
Archives Départemental de la Haute-Garonne (ADHG)
    1 (L) 992
    1 (L) 993
    1 (L) 1004
    1 (L) 1016
Archives Municipales de Toulouse
    1(R) 7
Bibliothèque de la Sorbonne, Archives de l'Université de Paris (AUP)
Institut national de recherche pédagogique (Mont Saint-Aignan)

Published primary sources

Bourdon de la Crosnière, Léonard, *Plan d'un Établissement d'Éducation Nationale, autorisée par Arrêt du Conseil du 5 Octobre 1788, sous le titre de Société Royale d'Émulation* (Orléans, 1788).

La Chalotais, Louis-René de Caradeuc de, *Compte rendu des Constitutions des Jésuites... les 1, 3, 4, et 5 décembre 1761, en exécution de l'arrêt de la cour du 17 août précédent* (1762).

La Chalotais, Louis-René de Caradeuc de, *Essai d'éducation nationale, ou Plan d'Études pour la jeunesse* (1763).

La Chalotais, Louis-René de Caradeuc de, *Second Compte rendu sur l'appel comme d'abus des Constitutions des Jésuites ... les 21, 22, et 24 mai 1762* (1762).

Condorcet, Jean-Antoine-Nicholas de Caritat, marquis de, *Condorcet: Political Writings*, Steven Lukes, Nadia Urbinati (eds) (New York, NY: Cambridge University Press, 2012).

Condorcet, Jean-Antoine-Nicholas de Caritat, marquis de, *Écrits sur l'instruction publique*, Charles Coutel and Catherine Kintzler (eds), vol. 1 (Paris: Edilig, 1989).

Condorcet, Jean-Antoine-Nicolas de Caritat, marquis de, Emmanuel-Joseph Sieyès, Jules [Julien]-Michel Duhamel, *Journal d'instruction sociale* (Paris: 1793).

Condorcet, Jean-Antoine-Nicholas de Caritat, marquis de, *Œuvres de Condorcet*, A. Condorcet O'Connor and M. F. Arago (eds), Tome VII (Paris: Firmin Didot frères, 1847–49).

Condorcet, Jean-Antoine-Nicolas de Caritat, Marquis de, *Selected Writings*, Keith Michael Baker (ed.) (Indianapolis, IN: Bobbs-Merrill Co., 1976).

Degranthe, *Abus de l'Ancienne Éducation, dévoiles et reformés par les progrès de la Raison, par M. Degranthe, au Collège de Louis-le-Grand* (Paris: 1790).

Dreyfus-Brisac, Edmond (ed.), *Revue internationale de l'enseignement*, T. 14 (Paris: Masson, 1887).

Duclos, Charles Pinot, *Considérations sur les mœurs de ce siècle* (Paris: 1784).

Dupont de Nemours, Pierre-Samuel, "Mémoire au Roi, sur les Municipalités, sur la hiérarchie qu'on pourrait établir entre elles, et sur les services que le gouvernement en pourrait tirer," in Anne-Robert Jacques Turgot, *Œuvres de Turgot*, T. II (Paris: Guillaumin, 1844), 502–550.

Épinay, Louise Florence Pétronille Tardieu d'Esclavelles, marquise de, *Les Conversations d'Emilie*, Rosena Davison (ed.) (Oxford: Voltaire Foundation, 1996).

Faculté des Arts, Université de Paris, *Arrêté pris par MM. les Recteur, Principaux, Professeurs & Aggrégés de la Faculté des Arts de l'Université de Paris, assemblés au Collège de Louis-le-Grand, le 18 Décembre 1790* (Paris: Imprimerie de Seguy-Thiboust, n.d.).

Faculté des Arts, Université de Paris, *Mémoire de la Faculté des Arts de l'Université de Paris, au sujet des traitemens qu'elle espère de l'Assemblée Nationale, pour ceux de ses Membres qui sont employés à l'Education publique* (Paris: Imprimerie de Seguy-Thiboust, n.d.).

Galiani, Ferdinando, and Louise d'Épinay, *Correspondance*, vol. III, mars 1772–mai 1773, Georges Dulac and Daniel Maggetii (eds) (Paris: Persée 1992).

Gazette nationale, ou Le Moniteur Universel (Paris: 1789–1810).

Gazier, Augustin, *Lettres à Grégoire sur les patois de France, documents inédits sur la langue, les mœurs et l'état des esprits dans les diverses régions de la France au début de la Révolution, suivie du rapport de Grégoire à la Convention* (Paris: Durand et Pedone-Lauriel, 1880).

Genlis, Stéphanie Félicité, comtesse de, *Adèle et Théodore, ou Lettres sur l'éducation; contenant tous les principes relatifs aux trois différens plans d'éducation des princes, des jeunes personnes, & des hommes* (Paris: Lambert, Baudouin, 1782).

Genlis, Stéphanie Félicité, comtesse de, *Les veillées du château, ou cours de morale à l'usage des enfans*, 2 vols. (Dublin: Chez Wogan et Jones, 1795).

Grégoire, Henri Jean-Baptiste, *Rapport sur l'ouverture d'un concours pour les livres élémentaires de la première éducation*, 3 pluviôse, an II (Paris: Imprimerie nationale, 1794).

Grégoire, Henri Jean-Baptiste, *Rapport sur les moyens de rassembler les matériaux nécessaires à former les annales du civisme & sur la forme de cet ouvrage: séance du 28 septembre 1793, l'an deuxième de la République* (Paris: Imprimerie nationale, 1793).

Guillaume, James (ed.), *Procès-verbaux du Comité d'Instruction publique de l'Assemblée législative* (Paris: Imprimerie nationale, 1889).

Guillaume, James (ed.), *Procès-verbaux du Comité d'Instruction publique de la Convention nationale* (Paris: Imprimerie nationale, 1891–1958).

Guyton de Morveau, Louis-Bernard, *Mémoire sur l'Education publique, avec le prospectus d'un collège, suivant les principes de cet ouvrage* (1764).

Haffner, Isaac, *De l'Éducation littéraire ou, Éssai sur l'organisation d'un Établissement pour les hautes sciences* (Strasbourg: La Librairie Académique, 1792).

Helvétius, Claude-Adrien, *De l'Homme, de ses facultés intellectuelles, et de son éducation* (Londres, 1773) [re-printed by Geneviève et Jacques Moutaux (eds), Librairie Arthème-Fayard, 1989].

Hentz, Nicholas, *Sur L'Instruction publique* (Paris: 1793).

Laclos, Pierre-Ambroise-François Choderlos de, "Des Femmes et de leur éducation," in Laclos, *Oeuvres complètes*, Laurent Versini (ed.) (Paris: Bibliothèque de la Pléiade, 1979).

Lakanal, Joseph, *Projet d'éducation du peuple française: le 26 juin 1793, présenté à la Convention nationale, au nom du Comité d'Instruction publique par Lakanal* (Paris: 1793).

Masuyer, Claude-Laurent, *Discours sur l'organisation du l'instruction publique et l'éducation nationale en France: examen et réfutation du système proposé successivement par les citoyens Condorcet et G. Rome* [sic], *au nom du Comité d'instruction publique de l'Assemblée législative et de la Convention nationale* (Paris: Imprimerie nationale, 1793).

Mavidal, J., E. Laurent, and E. Clavel (eds), *Archives parlementaires de 1787 à 1860: Recueil complet des débats législatifs et politiques des Chambres françaises. Première série, 1787 à 1799* (Paris: P. Dupont, 1875). [*AP*]

Mercure de France, par une société de gens de lettres, novembre 1777, no. 15 (Amsterdam, 1777).

Mirabeau, Honoré Gabriel Riqueti, comte de, *Travail sur l'éducation publique, trouvé dans les papiers de Mirabeau l'ainé* (Paris: Imprimerie nationale, 1791).

Montesquieu, Charles Baron de, *The Spirit of the Laws* (New York, NY: Cosimo Press, 2011).

Philipon de la Madelaine, Louis, *Vues Patriotiques sur l'éducation du peuple, tant des villes que des campagnes* (Lyon: Chez P. Bruyset-Ponthus, 1783).

Rabaut Saint-Étienne, Jean-Paul, *Projet d'éducation nationale* (Paris: Imprimerie nationale, n.d.).

Rolland d'Erceville, Barthélemy-Gabriel, "Compte Rendu aux Chambres assemblées, par M. Rolland, des différens Mémoires envoyés par les Universités sises dans le Ressort de la Cour, en exécution de l'Arrêt des Chambres assemblées, du 3 Septembre 1762, relativement au plan d'Étude à suivre dans les Collèges non dépendans des Universités, & à la correspondance à établir entre les Colleges & Universités. Du 13 Mai 1768," in Barthélemy-Gabriel Rolland d'Erceville, *Recueil de plusieurs des ouvrages de M. le président Rolland* (Paris: Chez P.G. Simon & N.H. Nyon, 1783).

Romme, Gilbert, *Rapport sur l'instruction publique, considérée dans son ensemble; suivi d'un Projet de décret sur les principales bases du plan général de l'instruction publique, présenté à la Convention nationale, au nom du Comité d'instruction publique* (Paris: Imprimerie nationale, 1793).

Rousseau, Jean-Jacques, "Considerations on the Government of Poland," in Rousseau, *The Plan for Perpetual Peace, On the Government of Poland, and other writings on History and Politics*, Christopher Kelly (ed.) (Hanover, NH: Dartmouth University Press, 2005).

Rousseau, Jean-Jacques, "Discourse on Political Economy" in *Basic Political Writings*, Donald A. Cress (ed.) (Indianapolis, IN: Hackett, 1987).

Rousseau, Jean-Jacques, *Émile, ou de l'Éducation* in *Œuvres de J.J. Rousseau*, T. XVIII (Amsterdam: Chez Marc-Michel Rey, 1773).

Rousseau, Jean-Jacques, *The Social Contract, Or Principles of Political Right*, trans. G. D. H. Cole (New York: Cosimo Press, 2008).

Talleyrand-Périgord, Charles-Maurice de, *Rapport sur l'instruction publique, fait au nom du Comité de Constitution à l'Assemblée nationale, les 10, 11 et 19 septembre 1791* (Paris: Imprimerie nationale, 1791).

Villier, Joseph, *Nouveau plan d'éducation et d'instruction publique, dédié à l'Assemblée nationale, dans lequel on substitue aux Universités, Séminaires et Collèges, des établissemens plus raisonnables, plus utiles, plus dignes d'une grande Nation* ... (Angers: Imprimerie de Mame, 1789).

Voltaire (François-Marie Arouet de), *Œuvres complètes de Voltaire*, Tome 41 (Paris: L. Hachette, 1876–1900).

Secondary sources

Albertone, Manuela, "Du Pont de Nemours et l'instruction publique pendant la Révolution: de la science économique à la formation du citoyen," *Revue Francaise d'Histoire des Idées Politique* – Les Physiocrates et la Révolution, 20 (2004): 353–371.

Albertone, Manuela, "Physiocracy" in Alan Charles Kors (ed.), *Encyclopedia of The Enlightenment* (New York, NY: Oxford University Press, 2003), vol. 3, 283–284.

Allain, Ernest, *La Question d'Enseignement en 1789 d'après les cahiers* (Paris: Librairie Renouard, 1886).

Alpaugh, Micah, *Non-Violence and the French Revolution: Political Demonstrations in Paris, 1787–1795* (Cambridge: Cambridge University Press, 2015).

Andress, David, *French Society in Revolution, 1789–1799* (Manchester: Manchester University Press, 1999).

Aston, Nigel, *Religion and Revolution in France, 1780–1804* (Washington DC: The Catholic University of America Press, 2000).

Baczko, Bronislaw, *Ending the Terror: The French Revolution after Robespierre*, trans. by Michel Petheram (New York, NY: Cambridge University Press, 1994).

Baczko, Bronislaw, *Lumières de l'utopie* (Paris: Payot, 1978).

Baczko, Bronislaw, *Une éducation pour la démocratie: textes et projets de l'époque révolutionnaire* (Genève: Librairie Droz S. A., 2000).

Baecque, Antoine de, *Corps de l'histoire: Métaphores et politique (1770–1800)* (Paris: Calmann-Lévy, 1993).

Bailey, Charles R., *French Secondary Education, 1763–1790: The Secularization of ex-Jesuit Collèges* (Philadelphia, PA: The American Philosophical Society, 1978).

Bailey, Charles R., *The Old Regime Collèges, 1789–1795: Local Initiatives in Recasting French Secondary Education* (New York, NY: Peter Lang, 1994).

Baker, Keith Michael, *Condorcet: From Natural Philosophy to Social Mathematics* (Chicago, IL: University of Chicago Press, 1974).

Baker, Keith Michael, "Enlightenment and the Institution of Society: Notes for a Conceptual History," in *Main Trends in Cultural History: Ten Essays*, Willem Melching and Wyger Velema (eds) (Atlanta, GA: Rodopi, 1994): 95–120.

Baker, Keith Michael, "French political thought at the accession of Louis XVI," *Journal of Modern History*, 50:2 (1978): 279–303.

Baker, Keith Michael, *Inventing the French Revolution: Essays on French Political Culture in the Eighteenth Century* (Cambridge: Cambridge University Press, 1990).

Barnard, H. C., *Education and the French Revolution* (Cambridge: Cambridge University Press, 1969).

Barnett, S. J., *The Enlightenment and Religion: The Myths of Modernity* (New York, NY: Manchester University Press, 2003).

Belhoste, Bruno, "Un espace public d'enseignement aux marges de l'université: les cours public à Paris à la fin du XVIIIe siècle et au début du XIXe siècle," in Thierry Amalou and Boris Noguès (eds), *Les Universités dans la ville: XVIe-XVIIIe siècle* (Rennes: Presses universitaires de Rennes, 2013): 217–234.

Bell, David A., *The Cult of the Nation in France: Inventing Nationalism, 1680–1800* (Cambridge, MA: Harvard University Press, 2001).

Bianchi, Serge, *La Révolution culturelle de l'an II: Élites et peuple (1789–1799)* (Paris: Aubier, 1982).

Bickart, Roger, *Les Parlements et la notion de la souveraineté nationale au XVIIIe siècle* (Paris: F. Alcan, 1932).

Blackman, Robert H., "What does a deputy to the National Assembly owe his constituents? Coming to an agreement on the meaning of electoral mandates in July 1789," *French Historical Studies*, 34:2 (2011): 205–241.

Bloch, Jean H., *Rousseauism and Education in Eighteenth-century France* (Oxford: Voltaire Foundation, 1995).

Bloch, Jean H., "Rousseau and Helvétius on innate and acquired traits: the final stages of the Rousseau-Helvétius controversy," *Journal of the History of Ideas*, 40:1 (1979): 21–41.

Bond, Elizabeth Andrews, "Circuits of practical knowledge: the network of letters to the editor in the French provincial press, 1770–1788," *French Historical Studies*, 39:3 (2016): 535–565.

Brockliss, L. W. B., *French Higher Education in the Seventeenth and Eighteenth Centuries: A Cultural History* (Oxford: Clarendon Press, 1987).

Brouard-Arends, Isabelle, "Les Géographes éducatives dans Adèle et Théodore de Madame de Genlis," in Nathalie Ferrand (ed.), *Locus in fabula: La Topique de l'espace dans les fictions françaises d'Ancien Régime* (Leuven: Peeters, 2004): 573–582.

Brubaker, William Rogers, *Citizenship and Nationhood in France and Germany* (Cambridge, MA: Harvard University Press, 1992).

Brubaker, William Rogers, "The French Revolution and the invention of citizenship," *French Politics and Society*, 7:3 (1989): 30–49.

Brunot, Ferdinand, *Histoire de la langue Française: Des Origines à nos jours*, T. VII: *La Propagation du français en France jusqu'à la fin de l'Ancien Régime* (Paris: Armand Colin, 1967).

Buisson, Ferdinand (ed.), *Nouvelle Dictionnaire de pédagogie et d'instruction publique* (Paris: Hachette, 1911).
Burson, Jeffrey D., "Reflections on the pluralization of Enlightenment and the notion of theological Enlightenment as process," *French History*, 26:4 (2012): 524–537.
Campbell, Peter R., "Introduction," in Peter R. Campbell (ed.), *The Origins of the French Revolution* (New York, NY: Palgrave Macmillan, 2006): 1–34.
Caradonna, Jeremy L., *The Enlightenment in Practice: Academic Prize Contests and Intellectual Culture in France, 1670–1794* (Ithaca, NY: Cornell University Press, 2012).
Caradonna, Jeremy L., "The monarchy of virtue: the prix de vertu and the economy of emulation in France, 1777–1791," *Eighteenth-Century Studies*, 41:4 (2008): 443–458.
Carter, Karen E., *Creating Catholics: Catechism and Primary Education in Early Modern France* (Notre Dame, IN: University of Notre Dame Press, 2011).
Carter, Karen E., "'Les garçons et les filles sont pêle-mêle dans l'école': gender and primary education in Early Modern France," *French Historical Studies*, 31:3 (2008): 417–443.
Certeau, Michel de, *The Practice of Everyday Life*, trans. Steven Rendall (Berkeley and Los Angeles, CA: University of California Press, 1984).
Certeau, Michel de, Dominique Julia, and Jacques Revel, *Une politique de la langue: La Révolution française et les patois: L'Enquête de Grégoire* (Paris: Gallimard, 2002).
Chambliss, J. J., "Condorcet," in J. J. Chambliss (ed.), *Philosophy of Education: An Encyclopedia* (New York, NY: Routledge, 1996): 105–107.
Chartier, Roger, "Letter: Why the Linguistic Approach can be an obstacle to the further development of historical knowledge. A reply to Gareth Stedman Jones," *History Workshop Journal*, 46 (1998): 271–272.
Chartier, Roger, *The Cultural Origins of the French Revolution*, trans. Lydia G. Cochrane (Durham, NC: Duke University Press, 1991).
Chartier, Roger, Marie-Madeleine Compère, and Dominique Julia, *L'Éducation en France du XVIe au XVIIIe siècle* (Paris: Société d'Édition d'énseignement Supérieur, 1976).
Chisick, Harvey, *The Limits of Reform in the Enlightenment: Attitudes towards the Education of the Lower Classes in Eighteenth-Century France* (Princeton, NJ: Princeton University Press, 1981).
Cock, Jacques de, *Mirabeau et la naissance du régime parlementaire* (Lyon: Fantasques éditions, 1999).
Compayré, Gabriel, *Histoire critique des doctrines de l'éducation en France depuis le seizième siècle* (Paris: Hachette, 1880).
Comsa, Maria Teodora, Melanie Conroy, Dan Edelstein, Chloe Summers Edmondson, and Claude Willan, "The French Enlightenment network," *Journal of Modern History*, 88 (2016): 495–534.

Cowans, Jon, *To Speak for the People: Public Opinion and the Problem of Legitimacy in the French Revolution* (New York, NY: Routledge, 2001).
Cumming, Ian, *Helvetius: His Life and Place in the History of Educational Thought* (London: Routledge, 1955).
Darnton, Robert, "What was revolutionary about the French Revolution?" in Peter Jones (ed.), *The French Revolution in Social and Political Perspective* (London: Arnold, 1996): 18–29.
DeJean, Joan, *Tender Geographies: Women and the Origins of the Novel in France* (New York, NY: Columbia University Press, 1991).
Dornier, Carole, "Morale de l'utilité et lumières françaises: Duclos, considérations sur les mœurs de ce siècle (1751)," *Studies on Voltaire and the Eighteenth Century* (SVEC), 362 (1998): 169–188.
Downs, Gregory P., *Declarations of Dependence: The Long Reconstruction of Popular Politics* (Chapel Hill, NC: University of North Carolina Press, 2011).
Doyle, William, *Aristocracy and its Enemies in the Age of Revolution* (New York, NY: Oxford University Press, 2009).
Echeverria, Durand, *The Maupeou Revolution: A Study in the History of Libertarianism: France, 1770–1774* (Baton Rouge, LA: Louisiana State University Press, 1985).
Edelstein, Dan, *The Enlightenment: A Genealogy* (Chicago, IL: University of Chicago Press, 2010).
Ferrone, Vincenzo, *The Enlightenment: History of an Idea*, trans. Elisabetta Tarantino (Princeton, NJ: Princeton University Press, 2015).
Figeac-Monthus, Marguerite, *Les Enfants de l'Émile? L'effervescence éducative de la France au tournant des XVIIIe et XIXe siècles* (New York, NY: Peter Lang, 2015).
Fitzsimmons, Michael, *The Remaking of France: The National Assembly and the Constitution of 1791* (New York, NY: Cambridge University Press, 1994).
Friedland, Paul, *Political Actors: Representative Bodies and Theatricality in the Age of the French Revolution* (Ithaca, NY: Cornell University Press, 2002).
Frijhoff, Willem, and Dominique Julia, *École et société dans la France d'Ancien Régime. Quatre Exemples: Auch, Avallon, Condom et Gisors* (Paris: Armand Colin, 1975).
Fritzsche, Peter, *Stranded in the Present: Modern Time and the Melancholy of History* (Cambridge, MA: Harvard University Press, 2004).
Froeschlé, Michel, *L'École au village: Les Petites Écoles de l'Ancien Régime à Jules Ferry* (Nice: Serre, 2007).
Furet, François, *Penser la Révolution française* (Paris: Éditions Gallimard, 1978).
Furet, François, *Revolutionary France, 1770–1880*, trans. Antonia Nevill (Oxford: Oxford University Press, 1992).
Furet, François, and Jacques Ozouf, *Reading and Writing: Literacy in France from Calvin to Jules Ferry* (Cambridge: Cambridge University Press, 1982).

Gauchet, Marcel, *La Révolution des pouvoirs: La Souveraineté, le peuple et la représentation, 1789–1799* (Paris: Gallimard, 1995).

Gay, Peter, *The Enlightenment: The Science of Freedom* (New York, NY: W. W. Norton & Co, 1969).

Gill, Natasha, *Educational Philosophy in the French Enlightenment: From Nature to Second Nature* (Farnham, England: Ashgate Publishing, 2010).

Goldgar, Anne, *Impolite Learning: Conduct and Community in the Republic of Letters, 1680–1750* (New Haven, CT: Yale University Press, 1995).

Goldstein, Jan, *The Post-Revolutionary Self: Politics and Psyche in France, 1750–1850* (Cambridge, MA: Harvard University Press, 2005).

Gontard, Maurice, *L'Enseignement primaire en France de la Révolution à la loi Guizot (1789–1833): Des Petites Écoles de la monarchie d'ancien régime aux écoles primaires de la monarchie bourgeoise* (Paris: Société d'Édition 'Les Belles Lettres', 1959).

Goodman, Dena, *Becoming a Woman in the Age of Letters* (Ithaca, NY: Cornell University Press, 2009).

Goodman, Dena, "Public sphere and private life: toward a synthesis of current historiographical approaches to the old regime," *History and Theory*, 31:1 (1992): 1–20.

Goodman, Dena, *The Republic of Letters: A Cultural History of the French Enlightenment* (Ithaca, NY: Cornell University Press, 1996).

Gorski, Philip S., "Nation-ization Struggles: A Bourdieusian Theory of Nationalism," in Philip S. Gorski (ed.), *Bourdieu and Historical Analysis* (Durham, NC: Duke University Press, 2013): 242–265.

Gottlieb, Anthony, *The Dream of Enlightenment: The Rise of Modern Philosophy* (New York, NY: W. W. Norton & Company, 2016).

Goubert, Pierre, and Michel Denis, *1789: Les Français ont la parole... Cahiers de doléances des états généraux* (Paris: Julliard, 1964).

Graff, Harvey J., *The Legacies of Literacy: Continuities and Contradictions in Western Culture and Society* (Bloomington, IN: University of Indiana Press, 1987).

Grandière, Marcel, *L'Idéal pédagogique en France au dix-huitième siècle* (Oxford: Voltaire Foundation, 1998).

Grateau, Philippe, "Les Français et l'instruction d'après les cahiers de doléances de 1789," in Alain Croix, André Lespagnol, and Georges Provost (eds), *Église, éducation, lumières: Histoires culturelles de la France, 1500–1830* (Rennes: Presses universitaires de Rennes, 1999): 139–145.

Grimaud, Louis, *Histoire de la liberté d'enseignement en France depuis la chute de l'Ancien Régime jusqu'à nos jours* (Paris: Arthur Rousseau, 1898).

Grossman, Mordecai, *The Philosophy of Helvétius, with Special Emphasis on the Educational Implications of Sensationalism* (New York, NY: Columbia University Press, 1926).

Gruder, Vivian R., *The Notables and the Nation: The Political Schooling* of the French, 1787–1788 (Cambridge, MA: Harvard University Press, 2007).

Habermas, Jürgen, The Structural Transformation of the Public Sphere: An Inquiry into a Category of Bourgeois Society, trans. Thomas Burger (Cambridge, MA: MIT Press, 1989).

Hahn, Roger, The Anatomy of a Scientific Institution: The Paris Academy of Sciences, 1666–1803 (Berkeley and Los Angeles, CA: University of California Press, 1971).

Halévi, Ran, "The monarchy and the elections of 1789," The Journal of Modern History, 60 (1988): S75–S97.

Heuer, Jennifer Ngaire, The Family and the Nation: Gender and Citizenship in Revolutionary France, 1789–1830 (Ithaca, NY: Cornell University Press, 2005).

Hirschman, Albert O., The Passions and the Interests: Political Arguments for Capitalism before Its Triumph (Princeton, NJ: Princeton University Press, 1977).

Hont, István, "Commercial Society and Political Theory in the Eighteenth Century: The Problem of Authority in David Hume and Adam Smith," in Willem Melching and Wyger Velema (eds), Main Trends in Cultural History: Ten Essays (Atlanta, GA: Rodopi, 1994): 54–94.

Hudson, David, "In defense of reform: French government propaganda during the Maupeou Crisis," French Historical Studies, 8:1 (1973): 51–76.

Huet, Marie-Hélène, Rehearsing the Revolution: The Staging of Marat's Death 1793–1797 (Berkeley and Los Angeles, CA: University of California Press, 1982).

Hufton, Olwen H., Women and the Limits of Citizenship in the French Revolution (Toronto: University of Toronto Press, 1992).

Hunt, Lynn, Politics, Culture, and Class in the French Revolution (Berkeley and Los Angeles, CA: University of California Press, 1984).

Hyslop, Beatrice Fry, A Guide to the General Cahiers of 1789: With the Texts of Unedited Cahiers (New York, NY: Octagon Books, 1936).

Ihl, Olivier, Le Mérite et la République: Essai sur la société des émules (Paris: Gallimard, 2007).

Israel, Jonathan, A Revolution of the Mind: Radical Enlightenment and the Intellectual Origins of Modern Democracy (Princeton, NJ: Princeton University Press, 2010).

Israel, Jonathan, Enlightenment Contested: Philosophy, Modernity, and the Emancipation of Man, 1670–1752 (New York, NY: Oxford University Press, 2006).

Iverson, John, "Introduction: emulation in France, 1750–1800," Eighteenth Century Studies, 36:2 (2003): 217–223.

Jainchill, Andrew, Reimagining Politics after the Terror: The Republican Origins of French Liberalism (Ithaca, NY: Cornell University Press, 2008).

Julia, Dominique, "Les Professeurs, l'église et l'état après l'expulsion des Jésuites, 1762–1789," in Donald N. Baker and Patrick J. Harrigan (eds), The Making of

Frenchmen: Current Directions in the History of Education in France, 1679–1979 (Waterloo, Ontario: Historical Reflections Press, 1980): 459–481.

Julia, Dominique, *Les Trois Couleurs du tableau noir: La Révolution* (Paris: Éditions Belin, 1981).

Kafka, Ben, *The Demon of Writing: Powers and Failures of Paperwork* (New York, NY: Zone Books, 2012).

Kaplan, Nira, "Virtuous competition among citizens: emulation in politics and pedagogy during the French Revolution," *Eighteenth-Century Studies*, 36:2 (2003): 241–248.

Kennedy, Emmet, *A Cultural History of the French Revolution* (New Haven, CT: Yale University Press, 1989).

Kennedy, Michael L., *The Jacobin Clubs in the French Revolution: The Middle Years* (Princeton, NJ: Princeton University Press, 1988).

Kintzler, Catherine, *Condorcet: L'Instruction publique et la naissance du citoyen* (Paris: Le Sycomore, 1984).

Knott, Sarah, "Narrating the Age of Revolution," *The William and Mary Quarterly*, 73:1 (2016): 3–36.

Kors, Alan Charles, *D'Holbach's Coterie: An Enlightenment in Paris* (Princeton, NJ: Princeton University Press, 1976).

Koselleck, Reinhart, "Crisis," trans. Michaela W. Richter, *Journal of the History of Ideas*, 67:2 (2006): 357–400.

Koselleck, Reinhart, *Futures Past: On the Semantics of Historical Time*, trans. Keith Tribe (New York, NY: Columbia University Press, 2004).

Ladd, Jr., Everett C., "Helvetius and D'Holbach: 'La Moralisation de la politique'," *Journal of the History of Ideas*, 23:2 (1962): 221–238.

Landes, Joan, *Visualizing the Nation: Gender, Representation, and Revolution in Eighteenth-Century France* (Ithaca, NY: Cornell University Press, 2001).

Landes, Joan, *Women and the Public Sphere in the Age of the French Revolution* (Ithaca, NY: Cornell University Press, 1988).

Langlois, Claude, "La Rupture entre l'Eglise catholique et la Révolution," in François Furet and Mona Ozouf (eds), *The French Revolution and the Creation of Modern Political Culture, vol. 3: The Transformation of Political Culture, 1789–1848* (New York, NY: Pergamon Press, 1989): 375–390.

Larsen, Anne R., and Colette H. Winn (eds), *Writings by Pre-revolutionary French Women* (New York, NY: Routledge, 2000).

Léveillé, Pauline, "L'Image des femmes dans les proces-verbaux du Comité d'Instruction Publique," in Marie-France Brive (ed.), *Les Femmes et la Révolution française: Actes du colloque international, 12-13-14 avril 1989, Université de Toulouse-le Mirail*, vol. 1, *Modes d'action et d'expression nouveaux droits – nouveaux devoirs* (Toulouse: Presses universitaires du Mirail, 1989), 461–471.

Linton, Marisa, *The Politics of Virtue in Enlightenment France* (New York, NY: Palgrave MacMillan, 2001).

Livesey, James, *Making Democracy in the French Revolution* (Cambridge, MA: Harvard University Press, 2001).
Loft, Leonore, *Passion, Politics, and Philosophie: Rediscovering J.-P. Brissot* (Westport, CT: Greenwood Press, 2002).
Lucas, Colin, "The Crowd and Politics," in Colin Lucas (ed.), *The French Revolution and the Creation of Modern Political Culture*, vol. 2: *The Political Culture of the French Revolution* (Oxford: Pergamon Press, 1988): 259-285.
Manson, Michel, *Les Livres pour l'enfance et la jeunesse sous la Révolution* (Paris: INRP, 1989).
Marchand, Philippe, "Recrutement et formation des regents des collèges du Nord au 18e siècle: réalité et projets," in Donald N. Baker and Patrick J. Harrigan (eds), *The Making of Frenchmen: Current Directions in the History of Education in France, 1679-1979* (Waterloo, Ontario: Historical Reflections Press, 1980): 483-492.
Martin, Xavier, *Human Nature and the French Revolution: From the Enlightenment to the Napoleonic Code*, trans. Patrick Corcoran (New York, NY: Berghahn Books, 2001).
Marx, Karl, *The Eighteenth Brumaire of Louis Bonaparte* (New York, NY: International Publishers, 2004).
Maslan, Susan, *Revolutionary Acts: Theater, Democracy, and the French Revolution* (Baltimore, MD: Johns Hopkins University Press, 2005).
Maslan, Susan, "The dream of the feeling citizen: law and emotion in Corneille and Montesquieu," *SubStance*, 35:1 (2006): 69-84.
McManners, John, *Church and Society in Eighteenth-Century France*, vol. 2: *The Religion of the People and the Politics of Religion* (New York, NY: Clarendon Press, 1998).
McManners, John, *The French Revolution and the Church* (New York, NY: Harper & Row, 1969).
Melton, James Van Horn, *The Rise of the Public Sphere in Enlightenment Europe* (Cambridge: Cambridge University Press, 2001).
Ménissier, Thierry, "République et fraternité. Une approche de théorie politique," in Gilles Bertrand, Catherine Brice and Gilles Montègre (eds), *Fraternité: Pour une histoire du concept* (Grenoble: Les Cahiers de CRHIPA, 2012): 35-52.
Michelet, Jules, *History of the French Revolution*, ed. Gordon Wright (Chicago, IL: University of Chicago Press, 1967).
Morange, Jean and Jean-François Chassaing, *Mouvement de réforme de l'enseignement en France, 1760-1798* (Paris: Presses universitaires de France, 1974).
Mornet, Daniel, *Les Origines intellectuelles de la Révolution française, 1715-1787* (Lyon: La Manufacture, 1989).
Mortier, Roland, "The 'philosophes' and public education," *Yale French Studies*, 40 (1968): 62-76.
Narrett, David, *Adventurism and Empire: The Struggle for Mastery in the*

Louisiana-Florida Borderlands, 1762–1803 (Chapel Hill, NC: University of North Carolina Press, 2015).

Ong, Walter J., *Orality and Literacy: The Technologization of the Word* (London: Methuen, 1982).

Ozouf, Mona, *Festivals and the French Revolution*, trans. Alan Sheridan (Cambridge, MA: Harvard University Press, 1988).

Ozouf, Mona, *L'École de la France: Essais sur la Révolution, l'utopie et l'enseignement* (Paris: Gallimard, 1984).

Ozouf, Mona, *L'Homme régénéré: Essais sur la Révolution française* (Paris: Gallimard, 1989).

Ozouf, Mona, "Regeneration," in François Furet and Mona Ozouf (eds), *A Critical Dictionary of the French Revolution*, trans. Arthur Goldhammer (Cambridge, MA: Harvard University Press, 1989): 781–791.

O'Connor, Adrian, "From the classroom out: educational reform and the state in France, 1762–1771," *French Historical Studies*, 39:3 (2016): 509–534.

O'Connor, Adrian, "Nature, nurture, and the social order: imagining lessons and lives for women in ancien régime France," *French Politics, Culture & Society*, 30:1 (2012): 1–22.

O'Connor, Adrian, "'Source de lumières & de vertus': rethinking *éducation*, *instruction*, and the political pedagogy of the French Revolution," *Historical Reflections/Réflexions Historiques*, 40:3 (2014): 20–43.

O'Neal, John C., *The Authority of Experience: Sensationist Theory in the French Enlightenment* (University Park, PA: The Pennsylvania State University Press, 1996).

Palmer, R. R., "How five centuries of educational philanthropy disappeared in the French Revolution," *History of Education Quarterly*, 26:2 (1986): 181–197.

Palmer, R. R., *The Improvement of Humanity: Education and the French Revolution* (Princeton, NJ: Princeton University Press, 1985).

Palmer, R. R., *The School of the French Revolution: A Documentary History of The College of Louis-le-Grand and its Director, Jean-François Champagne, 1762–1814* (Princeton, NJ: Princeton University Press, 1975).

Pancera, Carlo, "La Tendre mère," in Marie-France Brive (ed.), *Les Femmes et la Révolution française: Actes du colloque international, 12–13–14 avril 1989, Université de Toulouse-le Mirail*, vol. 1, *Modes d'action et d'expression nouveaux droits – nouveaux devoirs* (Toulouse: Presses universitaires du Mirail, 1989): 473–479.

Poirrier, Philippe, *Les Politiques culturelles en France* (Paris: La Documentation française, 2013).

Popiel, Jennifer, *Rousseau's Daughters: Domesticity, Education, and Autonomy in Modern France* (Durham, NH: University of New Hampshire Press, 2008).

Popkin, Jeremy D., *Revolutionary News: The Press in France, 1789–1799* (Durham, NC: Duke University Press, 1990).

Rasmussen, Dennis C., *The Problems and Promise of Commercial Society: Adam*

Smith's Response to Rousseau (University Park, PA: The Pennsylvania State University Press, 2008).

Rideau, Gaël, "Un corps séparé: L'Université et les pouvoirs urbains à Orléans aux XVIIe et XVIIIe siècles," in Thierry Amalou and Boris Noguès (eds), *Les Universités dans la ville: XVIe-XVIIIe siècle* (Rennes: Presses universitaires de Rennes, 2013): 81–99.

Riley, James, *The Seven Years War and the Old Regime in France: The Economic and Financial Toll* (Princeton, NJ: Princeton University Press, 1986).

Rosanvallon, Pierre, *The Demands of Liberty: Civil Society in France since the Revolution*, trans. Arthur Goldhammer (Cambridge, MA: Harvard University Press, 2007).

Rosenfeld, Sophia A., *A Revolution in Language: The Problem of Signs in Late Eighteenth-century France* (Stanford, CA: Stanford University Press, 2001).

Rosenfeld, Sophia, *Common Sense: A Political History* (Cambridge, MA: Harvard University Press, 2011).

Rosenfeld, Sophia, "On being heard: a case for paying attention to the historical ear," *American Historical Review*, 116:2 (2011): 316–334.

Rothschild, Emma, "Condorcet and Adam Smith on Education and Instruction," in Amélie Oksenberg Rorty (ed.), *Philosophers on Education: New Historical Perspectives* (London: Routledge, 1998): 208–225.

Rothschild, Emma, *Economic Sentiments: Adam Smith, Condorcet, and the Enlightenment* (Cambridge, MA: Harvard University Press, 2001).

Schechter, Ronald, "The terror of their enemies: reflections on a trope in eighteenth-century historiography," *Historical Reflections/Réflexions Historiques*, 36:1 (2010): 53–75.

Sepinwall, Alyssa Goldstein, *The Abbé Grégoire and the French Revolution: The Making of Modern Universalism* (Berkeley and Los Angeles, CA: University of California Press, 2005).

Sewell, Jr., W. H., "Le Citoyen/La Citoyenne: Activity, Passivity and the Revolutionary Conception of Citizenship," in Colin Lucas (ed.), *The French Revolution and the Creation of Modern Political Culture*, vol. 2: *The Political Culture of the French Revolution* (Oxford: Pergamon Press, 1988): 113–117.

Shapiro, Gilbert, and John Markoff, *Revolutionary Demands: A Content Analysis of the Cahiers de Doléances of 1789* (Stanford, CA: Stanford University Press, 1998).

Shovlin, John, *Political Economy of Virtue: Luxury, Patriotism, and the Origins of the French Revolution* (Ithaca, NY: Cornell University Press, 2006).

Sledziewski, Elisabeth G., *Révolutions du sujet* (Paris: Méridiens Klincksieck, 1989).

Smart, Annie K., *Citoyennes: Women and the Ideal of Citizenship in Eighteenth-Century France* (Newark, DE: University of Delaware Press, 2011).

Smith, David, *Bibliography of the Writings of Helvétius* (Ferney-Voltaire, France: Centre International d'Étude du XVIIIe siècle, 2001).

Spang, Rebecca L., *Stuff and Money in the Time of the French Revolution* (Cambridge, MA: Harvard University Press, 2015).
Spencer, Samia (ed.), *French Women and the Age of Enlightenment* (Bloomington, IN: Indiana University Press, 1984).
Staum, Martin S., *Minerva's Message: Stabilizing the French Revolution* (Quebec City: McGill-Queen's University Press, 1996).
Steinbrügge, Lieselotte, *The Moral Sex*, trans. Pamela E. Selwyn (New York, NY: Oxford University Press, 1995).
Swann, Julian, "Politics: Louis XV" in William Doyle (ed.), *Old Regime France, 1648-1788* (New York, NY: Oxford University Press, 2001): 195-222.
Sydenham, M. J., *Léonard Bourdon: The Career of a Revolutionary, 1754-1807* (Waterloo, Ontario: Wilfrid Laurier University Press, 1999).
Tackett, Timothy, *Becoming a Revolutionary: The Deputies of the French National Assembly and the Emergence of a Revolutionary Culture (1789-1790)* (Princeton, NJ: Princeton University Press, 1996).
Tackett, Timothy, *Religion, Revolution and Regional Culture in Eighteenth-Century France: The Ecclesiastical Oath of 1791* (Princeton, NJ: Princeton University Press, 1986).
Tackett, Timothy, *The Coming of the Terror in the French Revolution* (Cambridge, MA: Harvard University Press, 2015).
Todorov, Nicola Peter, "Le Transfert du canton dans l'Allemagne napoléonienne," in Yann Lagadec, Jean Le Bihan, and Jean-François Tanguy (eds), *Le Canton: Un territoire du quotidien?: Actes du colloque organisé à l'université Rennes 2 Haute Bretagne, 21-23 septembre 2006* (Rennes: Presses universitaires de Rennes, 2009): 61-72.
Trenard, Louis, "L'Enseignement de la langue nationale: une réforme pédagogique, 1750-1790," in Donald N. Baker and Patrick J. Harrigan (eds), *The Making of Frenchmen: Current Directions in the History of Education in France, 1679-1979* (Waterloo, Ontario: Historical Reflections Press, 1980): 95-114.
Trouille, Mary, "La Femme mal mariée: Mme d'Epinay's challenge to *Julie* and *Emile*," *Eighteenth-Century Life*, 20:1 (1996): 42-66.
Van Kley, Dale, *The Religious Origins of the French Revolution: From Calvin to the Civil Constitution, 1560-1791* (New Haven, CT: Yale University Press, 1996).
Velicu, Adrian, *Civic Catechisms and Reason in the French Revolution* (Burlington, VT: Ashgate, 2010).
Vignery, Robert J., *The French Revolution and the Schools: Educational Policies of the Mountain, 1792-1794* (Madison, WI: State Historical Society of Wisconsin, 1965).
Viguerie, Jean de, *L'Institution des enfants: L'Éducation en France XVIe-XVIIIe siècle* (Paris: Calmann-Lévy, 1978).
Vovelle, Michel, *La Chute de la monarchie, 1787-1792* (Paris: Édition du Seuil, 1972).

Walker, Lesley H., *A Mother's Love: Crafting Feminine Virtue in Enlightenment France* (Lewisburg, PA: Bucknell University Press, 2008).

Wick, Daniel L., *A Conspiracy of Well-Intentioned Men: The Society of Thirty and the French Revolution* (New York, NY: Garland Publishers, 1987).

Williams, David, *Condorcet and Modernity* (New York, NY: Cambridge University Press, 2004).

Woloch, Isser, *The New Regime: Transformations of the French Civic Order, 1789-1820s* (New York, NY: W.W. Norton & Co., 1994).

Yolton, John W., *Locke and French Materialism* (New York, NY: Oxford University Press, 1991).

Index

Note: texts can be found under authors' names

Académie française 41
Montyon Prix d'Utilité 41–42, 46n. 64
academies 4, 6, 10, 18, 61, 82–83, 87, 90, 98, 107, 114, 142–145, 160, 190, 214–217
  suppression 215–216
adult education 101–102, 135, 150, 202–204, 207
agrégation 11, 54, 58, 79, 148, 173, 175, 178–179, 184
agricultural education 57, 113, 117, 148, 174
Aix-en-Provence 64, 81, 162, 169, 175, 177, 192n. 22
Antiquity 32, 39, 72, 79, 166, 169, 204, 208
Arbogast, Louis François Antoine (1759–1803) 111, 190, 218
Assembly of Notables 70
Auch 183
Audrein, Yves-Marie (1741–1800) 111, 162
L'Averdy, Clément-Charles-François de (1723–93) 52–54

Barère, Bertrand (1755–1841) 205–206
Beaurien, M. 146–148
Berne, Switzerland 33–34
biens nationaux 87–88, 90, 130, 138, 141, 146, 150, 167, 180, 213
Bienvenue, M. 143, 146–148
binding mandate 72, 92n. 9, 127, 234
Bouquier, Gabriel (1739–1810) 218–221
Bouquier Law 220–222
Bourdon, Léonard (1754–1807) 136–139, 218
bourses 52–53, 104–105, 190, 213–214
  see also scholarships (financial)

cahiers de doléances 126–129, 162
catechisms 76, 115–116, 129, 172, 206–208
Châlons-sur-Marne 27, 184
  Académie des Sciences, Arts et Belles-Lettres 1, 39–40, 63–64
Chalotais, Louis-René de Caradeuc de La (1701–85) 28, 55–58, 63
Champagne, Jean-François (1751–1813) 185, 215

Champion de Cicé, Jérôme Marie
    (1735–1810) 93 n.31, 97, 99
Chapelier, Isaac Le (1754–94) 98
Church 3, 18, 21, 51, 58, 88–90, 111, 143,
    160, 163, 176–177, 180, 219
citizenship 2, 8, 12–13, 15, 20, 42,
    61–62, 72–75, 82, 100–103, 108,
    112–113, 117, 119–120, 134, 166, 171,
    188, 207, 217, 233–234, 237
civic education 76–78, 84, 117, 129,
    135, 235
civic sentiments 9, 72–77, 79, 84–85,
    100, 108, 115–117, 119, 134–135, 145,
    151, 188, 200–202, 207, 234–235
Civil Constitution of the Clergy
    87–90, 105, 111, 146, 180–181, 184,
    211, 236–237
civil society 6, 28–29, 32, 34, 42, 57, 61,
    113, 117, 134, 178, 189, 210, 232, 234
clerical oath 89–90, 111, 117,
    145–146, 180–185, 211, 236
collèges 10–12, 18, 20–22, 27–28, 48,
    50–53, 56–59, 61, 77, 82–83,
    86–88, 90, 105, 136, 138, 141–145,
    160, 167–168, 170, 176–177,
    179–180, 182–183, 190, 202, 208,
    213–214, 216–217, 233
  criticisms 32, 78–80, 86, 143, 145,
    168, 172, 214–216
  post-Jesuit reforms 50–54, 58
  suppression 213, 216–218
Commission of Public Instruction 218
Committee of Public Instruction 11,
    75, 98–99, 111–113, 131, 152, 162,
    186, 190, 200, 202, 206, 208, 210,
    214–215, 221
Condillac, Étienne Bonnot de
    (1714–80) 5, 26
Condorcet, Marie-Jean-Antoine-
    Nicholas de Caritat, marquis de
    (1743–94) 8, 11, 29, 75, 81, 97–99,
    110–120, 186, 190, 199, 203–206,
    213–214, 217

Constitution (1791) 1–2, 71–72, 91,
    97–104, 106–107, 113, 115, 118,
    133–134, 140, 144, 148–151, 162,
    186–190, 233
constitutional committee (National
    Assembly) 2, 76, 78, 91, 97–100,
    109, 131–132, 137, 139
constitutionalism 60, 72, 75, 129, 131,
    137, 139–141, 234, 237
corporations 22, 87–88, 90, 130,
    177–178, 180, 185
  abolition 87–90, 144, 177, 211
  criticisms 89, 144–145, 214–215, 219,
    221
corps enseignants 83, 90, 180, 185
Coupé, Jacques-Michel (1737–1809)
    215
Creuzé, Michel-Pascal (1736–1804) 182

*Declaration of the Rights of Man and
    Citizen* 72, 92, 118, 126, 139, 166,
    170, 207, 210, 214, 217, 219
Degranthe, M. 167, 170–173, 175, 177
Diderot, Denis (1713–84) 29, 32
Dorsch, Antoine-Joseph (1758–1819)
    148–149
Duclos, Charles Pinot (1704–72)
    27–28, 61
Dumouchel, Jean Baptiste (1748–1820)
    164
Dupont de Nemours, Pierre-Samuel
    (1739–1817) 11, 59–62, 86–87, 90,
    98
Mémoire sur les municipalités 11,
    59–62

Ecclesiastical Oath *see* clerical oath
éducation 75, 114–116, 135, 202–203, 234
elementary education *see* primary
    instruction
emulation 36, 77–78, 80, 84–85,
    103, 136, 145, 171, 188–189, 200,
    206–207, 210, 234

INDEX

Enlightenment 3–5, 7, 9–11, 13–14, 18, 22–23, 26, 29–31, 38–40, 43, 48–49, 114, 131, 139, 232
enseignement libre 83, 101, 143–144, 147, 175–176, 211–212, 219
Épinay, Louise Florence Pétronille Tardieu d'Esclavelles d' (1726-83) 40–42
Les Conversations d'Émilie 41–42
equality 33, 62, 71, 78, 101–102, 108, 112, 117–120, 135, 139, 141, 144, 151, 207, 215, 219
Estates-General 2, 56, 70–71, 127–128, 137, 162

February Edict (1763) 51–52, 167
female education 5, 10, 19–20, 24n. 8, 30, 38–43, 73, 82, 101, 103–104, 112–113, 129, 150, 202
Fénelon, François (1651-1715) 4, 27
festivals 12, 22, 76–78, 84–85, 90, 97, 99, 101, 109, 117, 134–135, 151, 166, 188, 199, 203, 206–207, 219–221, 235
Fouché, Joseph (1759-1820) 213–214
fraternity 33, 84, 97, 151
French (language) 19, 105, 165, 204–206
  dialects (patois) 29, 204–205
  instruction 19, 28–29, 49, 55, 79, 102, 112–113, 135, 138, 164, 170, 209, 217

games (as education) 33, 80, 101, 203, 207, 219–220
Garat, Dominique Joseph (1749-1833) 213–214
General Will 32, 75, 110, 126–127
Genlis, Stephanie-Felicité du Crest de Saint-Aubin, comtesse de (1746-1830) 40–41
Gérard, Laurent-Gaspard (17..-18..) 136
Gossin, Pierre François (1754-94) 78–80, 85, 99

Goyon d'Arzac, Guillaume Henri Charles de (1740-1810) 15 n.1, 63–64
Grégoire, Henri Jean-Baptiste (1750-1831) 204–206, 209–210, 215, 218
Guizot, François (1787-1874) 231
Guyton de Morveau, Louis Bernard (1737-1816) 55–58, 111, 218

Habermas, Jürgen (1929 –) 42, 126
Helvétius, Claude Adrien (1715-71) 5, 10, 30–31, 34–38, 64, 178, 232
Hentz, Nicholas (1753-1842) 203, 215
history (instruction) 76–77, 135, 148, 172, 174, 177, 188, 217

instruction 75, 114–116, 135, 202–203, 234
instructors 108, 112, 117, 136, 140, 148, 163, 182–183, 188, 210, 221, 231–233, 235–236
  competition among 82–83, 143–144, 148, 171, 175, 221
  oversight of 3, 51, 82–83, 86, 106, 144, 147, 163, 175–176, 192 n. 22, 212, 220–221
  recruitment and training 3, 54, 56–58, 86, 88, 105–106, 113, 145–149, 151, 163, 169–174, 177–179, 181, 188–189, 209–210, 212, 221, 236
  as role models 36, 57, 140, 145, 170, 174, 234

Jacobins 139–140, 142–143, 156 n. 56, 208, 221, 229n. 100
Jesuits 18, 48, 183
  expulsion 7, 10–11, 13, 18–19, 23, 32, 43, 48–50, 53–55, 89, 173, 231
judicial reform 72, 76, 97, 141, 158n. 89, 160

Lacépède, Bernard-Germain-Étienne de La Ville-sur-Illon, comte de (1756-1825) 111

Laclos, Pierre-Ambroise-François Choderlos de (1741-1803) 39-40
Des Femmes et de leur éducation 39-40
Lafayette, Marie-Joseph-Paul-Yves-Roch-Gilbert du Motier, marquis de (1757-1834) 98
Lakanal, Joseph (1762-1845) 206, 214, 218
Latin 19, 21, 28-29, 49, 55, 79, 105, 135, 138, 164, 170, 204
Lepeletier, Louis-Michel de Saint-Fargeau (1760-93) 199-200
letter-writing 6, 10, 12, 120, 126-127, 129-133, 139, 141-142, 149, 152, 152n. 3, 161-162, 208-209
representative government and 12, 126-132, 149, 151, 152n. 2, 154n. 24, 161, 187
liberty 79, 82-83, 101-102, 108-109, 119, 132, 135, 137, 139, 144, 178, 219
libraries 95n. 69, 155n. 33, 209, 217
Limoges 183
Lisieux, Collège de 50-51, 215
literacy 19, 23n. 4, 64, 73-74, 82, 94n. 53, 102, 118, 139-140, 149, 235
Locke, John (1632-1704) 4-5, 26-27
Louis XIV, King of France (1638-1715) 22
Louis XV, King of France (1710-74) 23, 34, 48, 51-52, 54, 56, 59, 163, 173
Louis XVI, King of France (1754-93) 11, 59-62, 70-71, 81, 91, 97-98, 131, 134, 163
Louis-le-Grand (Collège) 51-55, 167, 170, 185, 215
Lyon 129, 133, 174

Madelaine, Louis Philipon de la (1734-1818) 63
Major, J.-F. (17..-18..) 169, 173-175, 199
Malesherbes, Guillaume-Chrétien de Lamoignon de (1721-94) 35, 74
Marat, Jean-Paul (1743-93) 201, 203
Masuyer, Claude Laurent (1759-94) 214
mathematics (instruction) 28, 49, 55, 105, 113, 135, 138, 142, 170, 172, 174, 177, 188, 209, 217
Maupeou Revolution (1771-74) 54, 59, 63
Michelet, Jules (1798-1874) 126-127, 152
military education 105, 107, 128, 172, 174, 177, 217
Miolan, M. 175-177
Mirabeau, Honoré Gabriel Riqueti, comte de (1749-91) 8, 76-78, 81-85, 98-99, 104, 112, 127, 132, 134, 143, 146, 148, 173, 175, 200, 211, 219-220
Travail sur l'éducation publique 81-85, 94n. 49
Montesquieu, Charles-Louis de Secondat, baron de La Brède et de (1689-1755) 27, 29, 36, 232
morals (instruction) 21, 57, 76-77, 102-103, 108, 112-113, 116-117, 119, 135, 138, 148, 166, 172
music 76, 101, 135, 206-207

National Assembly 2, 10-12, 70-73, 76-79, 81, 86-91, 97-100, 102-103, 106, 108, 110-112, 120, 126-127, 129-135, 137, 139-142, 146, 149-152, 160-162, 164-166, 173, 179-186, 190, 208, 211, 218-219, 232, 237
committees 11, 131-132, 151, 154 n. 26
National Convention 10, 12, 75-76, 114, 120, 191, 199-205, 209-210, 212-222, 231, 237
National Guard 77, 182
nationalism 4-6, 13, 49, 56-57, 61-62, 71-73, 84, 100, 126, 141-142, 163, 204, 207, 222, 231
natural sciences (instruction) 21-22, 28, 40, 49, 55, 79, 113, 119, 133, 148, 150, 177, 187, 213, 220, 235

Necker, Jacques (1732–1804) 63

oaths 178, 180
  civic oath 106, 117
  see also clerical oath
October Days 78, 98, 119
Orléans 179–180, 183, 192n. 18, 193n. 37, 195n. 67

Paris 7, 13, 18, 22, 48, 50, 53, 58, 71, 79, 84, 101, 107, 110, 126, 129, 139–140, 162, 164, 168, 171–173, 184–186, 190, 215–217, 237
Parlement of Paris 35, 48–53, 55
parlements 11, 43, 56, 58, 173, 232
patois *see* French (language), dialects
petites écoles 18–19, 61, 138, 142, 160, 175–176, 216–217, 233
  see also primary instruction
physics (instruction) 24n. 17, 105, 122n.34, 138, 172, 217
Physiocracy 59–62, 112, 134–135, 146
political clubs 10, 12, 130, 142, 216, 234, 237
political participation 6, 8, 60–63, 71–75, 77, 85, 104, 108, 110, 126–127, 130–134, 136, 139–140, 149, 151–152, 200, 202, 204, 206–207, 234–235, 237
Pont-Levoy 182–183
primary instruction 58, 73, 101–103, 106, 108, 112–113, 128, 138, 150, 172, 174, 176, 187–190, 201–204, 208–209, 218, 220, 222
printing press 82, 126
prizes 76, 171, 188, 207, 210
public instruction 2, 8–9, 11–14, 33, 72–86, 91, 97–100, 108–109, 113, 115, 117–120, 132, 135–136, 139, 143, 151, 160–161, 168, 188–189, 200–202, 206–208, 210, 217, 222, 234–237

public opinion 59, 74, 81–82, 167–168
public sphere 6–8, 42, 62, 126, 166

Quatremère de Quincy, Antoine-Chrysostôme (1755–1849) 111

Rabaut Saint-Étienne, Jean-Paul (1743–93) 75, 98, 114, 119–120, 139, 202–203, 206
regeneration 2, 11, 14, 72, 84, 110, 115–116, 137, 145, 148, 160, 162, 169, 184, 188, 190, 199, 201, 203–204, 207, 212, 236–237
religious instruction 19, 21, 49, 102, 107, 129, 148, 163, 172, 176, 188
religious orders 21, 36, 53–54, 57–59, 83, 88–89, 105, 144, 147, 163, 165, 176–178, 180–181, 211
Rennes 135, 142–143
representative government 1–2, 9–14, 26, 59, 61–62, 70–75, 78, 80, 85, 91, 100, 104, 108–109, 122n. 52, 126–127, 130–131, 134, 140, 149, 151, 161, 164, 202, 233–235, 237
republicanism 12, 199, 202, 204, 206–208, 214–215, 217, 219, 222
revolutionary wars 8, 13, 120, 186, 190, 200–201
Rivière, Lambert (1753–1828) 145
Robespierre, Maximilien (1758–94) 199, 218
Rolland d'Erceville, Barthélemy-Gabriel (1734–94) 52, 55–56, 58–59, 77, 141, 162–163
Romme, Gilbert (1750–95) 75, 111, 200, 212, 218, 220
Rousseau, Jean-Jacques (1712–78) 10, 30–36, 38, 41, 70, 72, 100, 136, 141–142, 205, 232
  Considerations on the Government of Poland 32–34
  "Discourse on Political Economy" 32, 34

Rousseau, Jean-Jacques (1712–78) (*cont.*)
  Émile 7, 31–32, 34, 49
  legislator's dilemma 70, 72, 140–141, 178, 235
  Social Contract 34, 70
  rural education 64, 113, 140, 150, 171, 204

Saint-André, Jean Bon (1749–1813) 216
Saint-Marthe, Collège 181–182
scholarships (financial) 33, 53, 83–84, 104–105, 112, 120n. 3, 141, 146, 172, 217, 220
Scholasticism 4, 28
seminaries 18, 87, 150
sensationist philosophy 5, 26–28, 31, 34–36, 38, 80, 145
Seven Years War 49
1789, Society of 98–99
Sieyès, Emmanuel-Joseph (1748–1836) 77, 98, 178, 200, 204–205
sociability 2, 7–8, 14, 27, 29, 33, 72–76, 79–81, 84–85, 100, 102, 108–110, 115–120, 134, 137, 139, 151, 170–171, 174, 188–190, 202, 204, 206–207, 234–235
social order 73, 102, 109, 112, 118, 131, 137
  hierarchy 85, 109, 136, 144, 173, 234
  mutability 6, 49, 231
socialization *see* sociability
songs *see* music
State 1, 3, 6, 20–22, 32, 36, 43, 49–51, 53, 55, 57–64, 72, 74, 84–85, 89, 102, 104–108, 112, 116, 130–131, 140–147, 160, 163, 170, 172, 174–176, 184, 207, 209, 218–220, 222, 232, 234, 236–237

Talleyrand-Périgord, Charles-Maurice de (1754–1838) 8, 11, 81, 95n. 69, 97–111, 150, 152, 186–189, 199, 202, 213, 219–220
  Rapport sur l'instruction publique 99–111
Target, Guy-Jean-Baptiste (1733–1807) 78, 192n. 22
Terror 13, 183, 214, 237
textbooks 57, 61, 86, 129, 164, 189, 201, 208–210, 212, 219, 225n. 47, 231, 233, 236
theater 76–77, 109, 136, 206, 219
tithes 87–88, 90
Toulouse 22, 132, 167, 211, 217
Turgot, Anne-Robert Jacques (1727–81) 11, 59–62, 99
tutors (private) 18, 20, 37, 151, 170, 201, 219

universities 10, 18, 21–22, 28, 51, 54, 56, 61, 88, 90, 106–107, 110, 128, 142–145, 160, 163–164, 167, 190, 202, 213–214, 217, 233
  suppression 213–214, 216–217
University of Paris 50–54, 79, 111, 164–167, 174–175, 214
University of Poitiers 162–164, 181–182

Valognes 179
virtue 8–9, 29, 35–38, 74–76, 80, 91, 108, 110, 115, 117, 137, 143, 168, 170–171, 200, 206–207, 234–235
Voltaire (François-Marie Arouet) (1694–1778) 5, 26, 30, 35, 63

Wouves, Pierre, 127, 140, 149–151, 186
  Appel à l'opinion publique sur l'éducation nationale, 1, 110, 140, 149–152

EU authorised representative for GPSR:
Easy Access System Europe, Mustamäe tee 50,
10621 Tallinn, Estonia
gpsr.requests@easproject.com